STATELESS
IN PARADISE

STATELESS IN PARADISE:
A Stranded Soul's Fight for Freedom

The Journey of a Stateless Person to United States Citizenship

MIKAEL OKUNS

ISBN (eBook): 978-1-968012-05-2
ISBN (softcover): 978-1-968012-06-9
ISBN (hardcover): 978-1-968012-07-6

Library Of Congress Catalog Card Number: 2025912541

All photos not otherwise credited are used by the permission of Mikhail Sebastian Okunuga.

Published in the United States of America by:
Lynx Publishers
15728 Lorain Avenue
Cleveland, Ohio 44111

Behind The Bookstore, Edgartown, Martha's Vineyard

PREFACE

I never planned to become a symbol—or to write a memoir. I only meant to leave Los Angeles for a few days, to ring in the New Year with sunshine and a fresh perspective. But that quick trip turned into a harrowing, year-and-a-half-long exile on a small island, where I was suddenly no one, nowhere, and with no way home.

Stranded in American Samoa, I was forced to confront a reality most people will never imagine: statelessness. Not just a legal term, but a daily sentence—without identity, without protection, and with no embassy to turn to. For over 500 days, I lived in limbo, clinging to Wi-Fi in a local McDonald's to reach the outside world and plead my case. All the while, I bore the invisible scars of a broken immigration system and a bureaucratic misunderstanding that erased my place in the world.

This book is a witness account. A map of what it means to fall between definitions—between countries, identities, rights, and recognition. It traces not only my physical displacement but also the deeper journey through fear, frustration, advocacy, and, ultimately, resilience.

I write not to relive the pain, but to remember—and to ensure that the thousands of others like me are not forgotten. Statelessness is not a remote issue. It is a human crisis that strips away safety and belonging, yet demands you keep moving forward. My hope is that this memoir serves as both a mirror and a megaphone—for those who've felt invisible, and for those willing to see us.

If you are holding this book, I ask that you not only read it, but feel it. Imagine a life where a passport is just a piece of paper, and your existence depends on whether someone else believes it holds meaning. Then ask yourself: what makes someone belong?

This is my story. But it could so easily become someone else's. And perhaps, in reading it, you'll find a part of yourself in the in-between spaces where I was forced to live.

Thank you for listening.

– Mikhail

CONTENTS

My mother and father. My twin brother
Nikolai on the left and myself on the right

A Window Beyond the Wall

I was born on February 26, 1973, in Baku, the capital of the Azerbaijan Soviet Socialist Republic—one of the republics within the vast, iron-clad structure of the Soviet Union. My twin brother and I entered the world fifteen minutes apart. We weren't identical, but we shared a bond shaped by time, place, and the complex realities of growing up behind the Iron Curtain. Our family home was a multigenerational household, full of noise, warmth, and everyday Soviet routine. Alongside our parents and grandmother were my older sister and a half-brother from my mother's first marriage.

My mother had a life before me—one that was marked by both love and deep sorrow. Long before I was born, she was married to a man who served as an officer in the army. From all that I've been told, he was a disciplined, kind-hearted man, deeply devoted to both his duty and his family. Together, they had two children: my older brother and my sister.

When he eventually retired from military service, he didn't slow down. He transitioned into civilian life and began working for a construction company. It was honest work, physically demanding and far removed from the regimented world of the army, but it was work that allowed him to continue providing for his young family. My brother was only about five years old at the time, full of questions and energy, already starting to resemble his father in little ways. My sister, still a baby, had only just begun to recognize the faces around her. Her memories of him would later be drawn mostly from photographs and the stories others would tell.

Then, everything changed in an instant.

One day, while on the job at a construction site, tragedy struck. A section of the building they were working on—specifically the roof—collapsed without warning. It happened so suddenly, no one had time to react. My mother's husband, the father of her two small children, was

17

killed instantly. There was no final goodbye, no moment to prepare. Just a phone call, and the world as she knew it was shattered.

The loss devastated her. She had loved him with her whole heart, and in the space of a single moment, that future they had been building together—brick by brick, day by day—was gone. Her grief ran deep, but she did not allow it to consume her. Instead, she made a decision, one that would shape the next decade of her life: she promised herself she would never marry again.

My mother, father, brother Nikolai, my half-sister Tamara with her daughter Yekaterina, my half-brother Karen, his wife, Karina. My grandmother Miriam in the center and myself

It wasn't that she had closed herself off to love, but the pain was too much, too raw. She couldn't imagine giving her heart to another or asking her children to adapt to a new father figure. So, she turned inward, gathering her strength and focusing all of it on her children. For the next ten years, she lived quietly, almost entirely for them.

She moved back in with her own mother—my grandmother— seeking comfort in the familiar walls of her childhood home. Together, the two women raised my brother and sister with fierce devotion. They built a world of warmth and safety, where the children were surrounded by love, even though a piece of their foundation was missing. My mother worked hard to be both mother and father, guiding them through their early years, trying to give them the best life she possibly could. There were no men in her life during that time. No dates. No flirtation. Just family, healing, and the slow passing of time.

And then, life surprised her.

After a decade of quiet perseverance, of solitude and sacrifice, something changed. She met my father.

Life in the USSR was a strange mix of security and restriction. On one hand, we were granted certain comforts: education and healthcare were free; housing was provided by the state; and public transportation, though crowded, was affordable and reliable. Neighbors were like extended family, and community meant something tangible. Celebrations—New Year's, birthdays, weddings—were collective efforts. Family members and neighbors would gather in the kitchen, preparing dishes for hours, exchanging stories, laughter, and sometimes quiet frustration at what we couldn't say aloud.

But underneath this communal life was a rigid system that controlled nearly every aspect of our existence. The government dictated what we studied, what we read, even what we were allowed to dream. Freedom of speech didn't exist. Travel outside the Soviet bloc was a privilege rarely granted—almost always to those with high-ranking party ties. While most countries issued a single passport primarily for international travel, we had two: a domestic passport and a separate international one, the latter notoriously difficult to obtain. The process involved intrusive applications and party approval. Most citizens never stood a chance.

Even as a child, I felt the weight of that suppression. I craved something more. I consumed international news and studied maps as if they held the key to another life. While many of my classmates were content with the small freedoms we had, I was hungry for the world. I dreamed of France—the culture, the elegance, the language. It seemed like a world untouched by censorship or grey concrete apartment blocks.

At school, we had a pen pal program. Most students wrote to peers in fellow Soviet republics—Ukraine, Moldova, Georgia. But I waited, eyes scanning the pile of letters for those rare envelopes postmarked from outside our borders. I found a way to connect with pen pals from Brazil, Germany, and the Netherlands. One of them was a Brazilian hairdresser. Another, a girl from Holland. Each letter was a treasure, a symbol of life beyond the Soviet reach. I'd rush to our mailbox daily, heart pounding with hope. When one arrived, it was like oxygen. I'd read and reread it, then carefully craft a reply, often walking miles to the post office to send it. In those days before cell phones or the internet, handwritten letters were lifelines to a different world—and mine became a way to escape, at least in spirit.

Academically, I wasn't the best student, but I had a deep love for certain subjects: history—especially world history—geography, literature, and languages. When the time came to choose a second language at school, I selected German. I loved the sound of it, and our principal, who also taught the language, was an inspiring figure: punctual, strong, and deeply respected. But my mother had other plans. She insisted I take English, reasoning that my older sister, who had studied it, could help. She couldn't, really—her knowledge was limited—but I reluctantly switched.

The English teacher we had didn't make things easy. She was more interested in pop songs and gossiping about her latest finds on the black market than in actually teaching us grammar or vocabulary. But I was determined. I began studying English on my own using whatever books I could find, and eventually took private lessons to strengthen my skills.

Looking back now, it was one of the best decisions I made. English is the most widely spoken international language—a key to understanding the world and being understood by it. Wherever life has taken me, the ability to communicate in English has opened doors, created connections, and expanded possibilities.

I didn't know it then, but those moments—of studying late into the night, of waiting by the mailbox, of dreaming of France—were shaping me. They were carving out the path that would one day lead me beyond the limits of the life I knew, into a world I had once only imagined through the eyes of others.

Lessons Beyond the Classroom

My school years were spent alongside my twin brother—we were in the same class, sharing not only textbooks but also a fair share of mischief. I've already mentioned that I wasn't the perfect student. While I had a deep passion for subjects like history, literature, geography, and languages, others, particularly physics, chemistry, algebra, and geometry, were simply not for me. Those classes often felt like an eternity. To break the monotony, I would sometimes burst into song in the middle of lessons, disrupting the class and much to the frustration of my teachers. More than once, I was kicked out of the classroom and told I couldn't return until my parents had been summoned to school.

This kind of behavior wasn't constant, but it was frequent enough. My twin brother and I seemed to take turns in stirring up trouble. One day it was me; the next, he'd pick up the baton, pulling some prank or causing a distraction. Our parents were regular visitors at the school, often called in to address our antics. Of course, I knew it wasn't the right thing to do—but I was a restless child.

My twin brother Nikolai and myself

When you're young and bored, sitting still for long stretches can feel like a punishment. Acting out was, in part, my way of entertaining myself—and sometimes, gaining the attention of my classmates. Looking back, it was equal parts comedy and chaos. Like a circus show, it had its moments of humor, but when your parents are humiliated in front of your class, it stops being funny.

In the Soviet Union, discipline was harsh and often public. Corporal punishment was not only common, it was entirely legal. Teachers could hit students in front of the class, and even pressure parents—especially fathers—to do the same. It was seen as a legitimate method of teaching respect and obedience. Those were very different times.

Despite my occasional troublemaking, I was deeply engaged with the subjects that truly fascinated me. I was captivated by figures like Peter the Great, Nicholas II, Napoleon Bonaparte, Winston Churchill, and Russia's great literary minds—Mikhail Lomonosov, Alexander Pushkin, and others. I would study hard to do well in those classes, aiming for the best grades in history and languages.

The Soviet education system was structured rigidly. Children typically begin school at the age of seven. After eight years, around age fifteen, we had to sit for a series of state exams covering all subjects. If a student passed, they had two options: continue for two more years to complete secondary school and become eligible for university entrance, or branch off into vocational education. I chose to continue. I wanted to finish all ten years—some records refer to it as eleven—because my ambition was to pursue higher education. At one point, I dreamed of becoming a history teacher.

My aspirations shifted frequently during those years. I wanted to be a biologist. Then a veterinarian—I've always had a love for animals and plants. On another day, I imagined myself a historian, and occasionally, in the ambitious way children dream, even the President of the Soviet Union. At one point, I set my sights on attending the prestigious Moscow State Institute of International Relations, the gateway to becoming a diplomat. But getting into that school required more than good grades. It required connections—often political ones—or the right family background, preferably a child of a high-ranking Communist Party official. For most, including myself, that path was blocked.

My older sister was exceptionally gifted in technical subjects. Physics, chemistry, and math—all came naturally to her. She dreamed of becoming a doctor, but admission to medical universities was fiercely competitive and often corrupt. Many bright, deserving students were denied entry simply because their families couldn't afford to bribe admissions officials. My mother, recognizing this harsh reality, persuaded my sister to pursue another path. With her skills in science and math, she was guided toward engineering and went on to study at the Azerbaijan State Oil Academy, specializing in oil refining.

My older half-brother followed a different path altogether. He left school after eight years and trained as a carpenter, though he eventually became a waiter at the International Hotel "Intourist" in Baku, serving foreign guests—a rare position that offered a glimpse into a world beyond the Soviet borders. My twin brother also chose not to complete the full ten years of schooling. After eighth grade, he transitioned into vocational training and worked in a technical field—perhaps as an electrician or plumber, though I don't recall the specifics clearly.

As for me, I was determined to pursue higher education. I believed—and still believe—that education is the key to independence, progress, and personal fulfilment. In a society where so much was restricted, knowledge felt like the one true path toward freedom.

A Curious Child in a Restrictive World

As a child, I was intensely curious, restless, hungry to understand the world beyond the grey walls of the Soviet life I was born into. School was just one small piece of my education. What truly lit a fire in me was reading. Books were my escape, my portal to other worlds, my way of knowing more, so I could answer questions, participate in conversations, and make sense of things that didn't always make sense around me.

Not far from our apartment building, hidden in what felt like a forest or an overgrown park, was a small library. It was quiet, almost secret, and I loved that. I went there often, borrowing books about birds, plants, and biology. I was fascinated by the natural world—what types of birds lived around us, how different plants grew, what made living things thrive. I would spend hours in the woods, collecting flowers, observing nature, sometimes bringing plants home to replant them, hoping they'd grow in our little apartment.

My love for animals also started early. My father used to take me to the aquarium store, and together we'd bring fish home, setting up small underwater worlds in glass tanks. But it didn't stop there. I'd bring home stray kittens, puppies—any little creature that looked like it needed love. My mother, however, wasn't thrilled. In her view, animals belonged outside, in yards or fenced areas—not inside a Soviet apartment. She'd warn me, sometimes dramatically threatening to throw them off the balcony if I didn't get rid of them. I never quite believed she would, but the message was clear: my heart for animals didn't match the practicality of my parents' world.

I wasn't always easy to handle. I had a mischievous streak. I remember standing on our balcony and tossing eggs or potatoes at people passing below—not out of malice, but more from a wild, impulsive sense of fun. I didn't always think things through; I just wanted to stir the stillness, to make something happen. Sometimes I was demanding, especially when it came to things I knew we couldn't afford. If I wanted ice cream, I wanted ice cream—and I didn't hide my disappointment if it wasn't possible. Looking back, I understand the pressure that must have been placed on my parents, especially my mother. I don't think I realized then just how much they were already sacrificing.

Still, in spite of all that noise and emotional chaos, I spent a lot of quiet time at home, especially during the long summers. My father would sometimes take us to the Caspian coast, and I'd swim and play at the beach, but the rest of the time I was in my own world—reading, studying English, diving into biographies of noble, distinguished people. I wanted to know what made them who they were. How did someone become great? What kind of life did it take to be remembered?

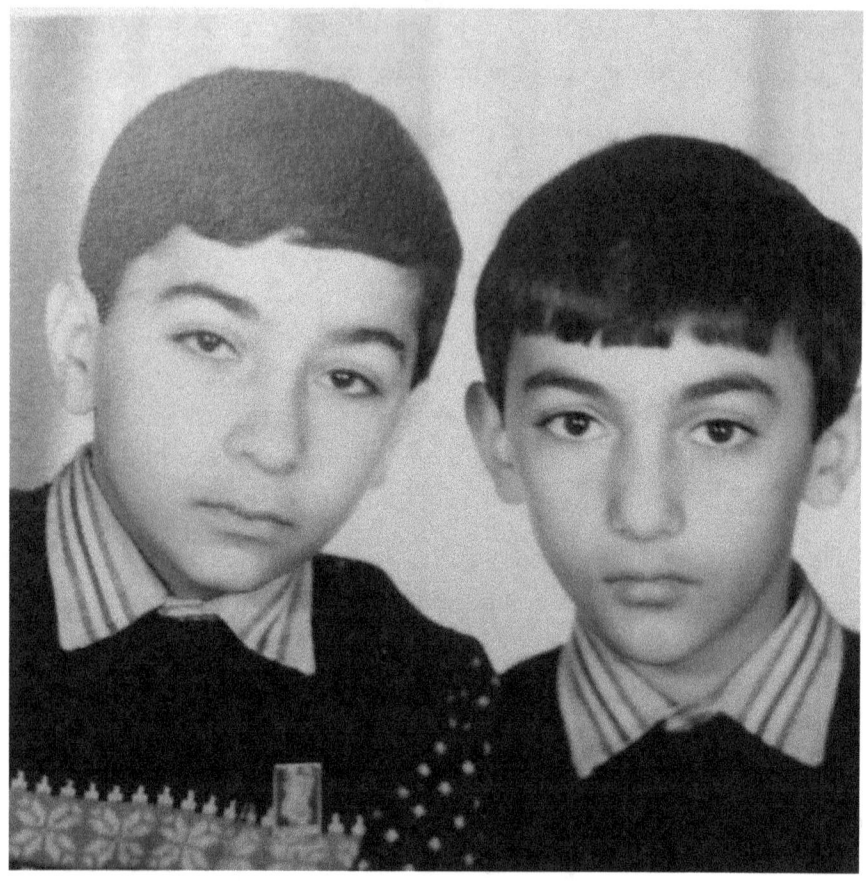

Me and my twin brother, Nikolai

Growing Up Different

Since I spent most of my time at home, in the forest, or in the quiet corners of the park, my circle of friends growing up consisted almost entirely of girls.

Unlike my twin brother Nikolai, who was always outdoors with boys—playing football, laughing loudly, testing the boundaries of childhood freedom—I gravitated toward quieter, more thoughtful companionship. He started smoking at an early age, which worried my mother terribly. She would often send me on little "missions" to talk him out of it, hoping that I could persuade him. I tried, but of course, it didn't work.

Even at school, while Nikolai's world was all boys and sports, mine was filled with girls—my closest friends, confidantes, companions. I remember my aunts joking with my mother that I'd probably be the first to get married, since all the girls were always coming to see me and spending time with me. But little did they know what all of that really meant. No one spoke about it—homosexuality simply didn't exist in the public vocabulary of the Soviet Union. It was invisible, denied, erased. Even words like "gay," "lesbian," or "transgender" were completely foreign. They were never mentioned on television, never discussed in school, never acknowledged even in the medical field. My mother, who worked as a nurse in a clinic, never once heard any open conversation about it—not at work, not at home, not in society.

In the Soviet mentality, especially among Armenians, Azerbaijanis, Georgians, and other families of the Caucasus region, having a son was paramount. Boys carried on the family name. They were expected to grow into men, into providers, protectors. If a child acted differently— say, a boy who was more gentle, more emotional, more artistic—it was just considered a phase, nothing to worry about. "He'll grow out of it," they said. "It's just childhood curiosity."

But I didn't grow out of it. I grew deeper into it.

I didn't understand what was happening to me at first. I just knew I was different. I liked playing with dolls and soft toys. I liked dressing up in my mother's clothes, slipping on her high heels, experimenting with her makeup. Sometimes, when no one was home, I'd put on a little fashion show in our apartment—my grandmother would be my audience as I walked the "runway" from room to room. On some evenings, I'd sneak out wearing her heels and walk carefully through the quiet streets, hiding in the shadows, afraid but also thrilled. I knew it was strange that people wouldn't understand, but to me, it felt natural. Joyful. Creative.

That was the beginning of discovering my inner world—a world not just of femininity, but of art, expression, beauty, and identity. I became obsessed with fashion. My sister subscribed to a Soviet magazine called Moda (Fashion), and I devoured each issue. I'd study the photos from Europe, admiring the styles, dreaming about clothes, and design. I wanted to know everything about this glamorous, colorful world that felt so far away from our grey Soviet apartment blocks.

At school, the division was clear: boys learned carpentry, plumbing, and mechanics. Girls learned sewing, knitting, and cooking. I wanted to be with the girls. I wanted to sew. I wanted to create. So, I would run away from the boys' class and join the girls instead. The teachers didn't approve. They complained to my parents that I wasn't behaving properly, that I was neglecting my assigned "male" classes. But I didn't care. I didn't feel comfortable with the boys. With the girls, I felt free, safe, and understood.

My mother used to call me, half-jokingly, a man-girl. She didn't mean it cruelly—it was more teasing than anything. She thought I was just being silly, doing what children do. She never suspected anything deeper. And truthfully, neither did I. I didn't yet have the words to understand myself. But I knew I wasn't like the other boys. I didn't want to be like them.

The only close male friend I had in school was another boy, Samvel, who, looking back now, I realize was probably gay too. He also had soft mannerisms, a gentle voice, and a curious spirit. We formed a quiet, unspoken bond. We never talked about it—not because we were hiding something, but because we didn't have the language. We didn't know what to say. But we understood each other, and that was enough.

Samvel was born to a unique blend of cultures that shaped both his character and his art. His mother was a Ukrainian woman from the city of Donetsk, known for her sharp wit and strong will. His father, Armenian by heritage, carried with him a deep pride in his roots—resilient, passionate, and steeped in tradition. It was a household where two distinct worlds met: the soft-spoken warmth of Ukrainian soul and the fiery expressiveness of Armenian spirit.

Early in life, Samvel experienced the tremors of political unrest. The conflict between Armenia and Azerbaijan left many displaced, and families—like his—had to make impossible choices. Seeking safety and a chance at stability, they relocated to Donetsk, where his mother had family ties. This move, though born from hardship, would become the soil where Samvel's creative roots would flourish.

From a young age, he was different.

While other children played with toy cars or chased each other around courtyards, Samvel would stage little shows in his living room, using a hairbrush as a microphone and bath towels as makeshift curtains. He had an innate sense of performance, a spark that refused to be dimmed. Laughter, mimicry, music—it all came naturally to him, as though he had been born with a stage in his heart.

That spark eventually turned into something much greater.

In his late years, Samvel will create what would become a local cultural phenomenon: *The Nazarov Show* in Donetsk, Ukraine. It began as a humble parody act, a one-man comedy show, that poked fun at politics, television personalities, and the absurdities of everyday life. But it quickly grew into something bigger. With flamboyant costumes, satirical sketches, and catchy musical numbers, the show drew crowds from all corners of Donetsk and beyond.

He had a gift—one that could make people laugh even when life gave them little reason to smile. And it wasn't just comedy. Samvel infused his performances with emotion, with song, with a kind of theatrical depth that spoke to both the ridiculousness and the beauty of being human.

He wasn't afraid to be bold, to be extravagant. Whether draped in feathers and sequins or delivering a haunting ballad from behind stage lights, Samvel owned every moment. His show became a kind of refuge for many—a place where people could forget their troubles, even if just for an hour, and feel something real.

In parts of Ukraine, especially in Donetsk, his name became synonymous with laughter, with artistry, and with unapologetic authenticity. Fame, in his case, wasn't the product of flashy endorsements or viral trends—it was earned, slowly and honestly, one standing ovation at a time.

But what made Samvel truly extraordinary wasn't just his talent. It was his ability to transform pain into performance, conflict into comedy, and uncertainty into something meaningful. In a region marked by political division and social unrest, he offered something rare: joy.

That friendship lasted through much of my childhood, until the war between Armenia and Azerbaijan forced us to flee our homeland. Everything changed after that. But before the war, before the fear and loss, I was simply a boy trying to understand himself in a world that refused to acknowledge he even existed.

I often wondered, "Is there something wrong with me?" I asked myself, but I never asked my parents. I knew the answer they'd give—or rather, the answer they wouldn't. So I kept my questions quiet. But inside, my curiosity only grew wider, deeper, more persistent.

Discovering Myself: A Journey of Identity and Family

Growing up, my family consisted of two boys—my twin brother Nikolai and my older half-brother Karen—and my sister, Tamara. While my relationship with my twin brother Nikolai was typical of many brothers—full of outdoor games, football, and rough-and-tumble play—my bond with my sister was different. I was very close to Tamara. She was always there for me, helping raise me alongside my parents. Every time she went out, whether to meet friends or take a walk, I went with her. She made sure I was part of her life in a way that felt natural and comforting.

Tamara was a wonderful person. She was studying to become an engineer, but her heart was also in music. She attended music school and played the piano beautifully. I remember her playing classical pieces for me—Beethoven, Mozart, Chopin, Strauss—each note drawing me deeper into a world of sound that felt elegant, refined, and far removed from the daily routines of our Soviet life. Classical music became my gateway to the arts and to Western culture in a time and place where such things were both rare and censored. I would often imagine myself in Vienna, in the 18th century, listening to a waltz in a grand ballroom, or in Mozart's time, just to experience the world that music transported me to. These experiences shaped my understanding of the world in ways I couldn't yet fully comprehend.

At home, we had a gramophone, an old device where you would place a large disc to play music. It was one of the few ways we could access music beyond what Soviet television or radio played. Of course, even that was censored—many foreign films and songs were simply not allowed. But that didn't stop Tamara and me from creating a bond that transcended any restrictions. She was my confidante, my guide, and the one person who could make me feel safe in a world that often felt so limiting.

My mother, on the other hand, was more controlling with Tamara, especially as she got older. In traditional Armenian culture, the expectations for girls were rigid—virginity before marriage, modesty, and strict rules about interactions with men. My mother, perhaps overprotective, would often insist that Tamara take me with her whenever she went out, whether it was for a walk or to the movies. My sister, in her usual kind spirit, did as she was told, even when I made things difficult. I recall one time when we went to the cinema, and I caused a bit of a disaster. I had this ridiculous habit—right in the middle of a quiet movie theatre, while everyone was lost in the film, I'd slip off my shoes and hurl them at unsuspecting strangers in the dark. I have no idea why I did it, but I thought it was absolutely hilarious, forcing

Tamara to crawl around the theatre looking for them while trying to save face. It was chaotic, but it was also a reflection of how deeply she cared for me, how deeply we cared for each other.

Despite our closeness, there were limits to how much Tamara could help me with my schoolwork. She would try to tutor me in algebra, geometry, and physics, but I just couldn't grasp it. It was a struggle. I knew I wasn't meant to be an engineer or a scientist. I didn't want to force myself into subjects that didn't speak to my soul. I wanted to understand the world in other ways—through history, through literature, through the beauty of art and music.

Education in the Soviet Union was not only a privilege—it was a requirement. To get into university, you had to pass a rigorous entrance exam. This meant cramming through subjects that I had no interest in—algebra, geometry, physics, history—subjects that felt like they were designed to turn you into something you weren't. I would spend hours studying, trying to force knowledge into my mind that didn't fit, while my peers, many of whom had parents who could bribe their way into the system, seemed to find a shortcut. It was disheartening, to say the least, and it made me question the value of a system that didn't care for individuality. It was all about conformity. If you failed in one of those subjects, you were out of the running for higher education and had to wait another year. But even those who succeeded had to follow a prescribed path, a set of rules that didn't leave much room for deviation. I knew, deep down, that this wasn't the path for me. I didn't want to be a part of this structured system that didn't align with who I was.

My older brother, Karen, was largely absent from my childhood. He worked a lot and wasn't home much, so I didn't feel the same kind of bond with him that I did with Tamara. I only saw him occasionally, and we never developed that close relationship that many brothers share. But Tamara was always there. Even when she was studying at the Oil Refinery Institute, she'd take me with her to her final exams, where I would sit outside the room and wait quietly, sometimes fidgeting with my shoes, while she took her tests. We'd then go out together, to the movies or on walks, and I'd feel like her little sidekick. She was my world.

But in the quiet spaces of my life, between my sister's piano melodies and my mother's strict expectations, I was also beginning to discover something else about myself. I was beginning to understand that I wasn't just different from the other boys. I was starting to feel that I didn't quite fit into the mold of what was expected of a boy. But this discovery was still in its infancy. I didn't know yet what it meant or how it would change my life. All I knew was that the world I was growing up in didn't have a place for someone like me—not fully. Not yet.

Growing up in the Soviet Union, we were all citizens of a vast and proud nation, a country that, in its propaganda, promised to protect every human being, regardless of skin color, ethnicity, or background. The Soviet Union was a place where racial discrimination was unheard of. We didn't know what it meant to be judged based on the color of our skin or our religious beliefs. In the world I grew up in, no one was ever taught to disrespect someone because of their appearance or heritage. As a child, I had no concept of racism, and I am proud to say that it was never something I experienced or even heard about.

The Soviet government claimed that all people were equal, and in many ways, this was true. We had students from Africa, Asia, and Latin America who came to the Soviet Union to study for free. In fact, education in the USSR was highly esteemed, and I would argue that it was far stronger than the system in places like the United States. Unlike in the West, where tests are often multiple choice, in the Soviet educational system, the emphasis was on deep understanding. Teachers could call on you at any time during class to stand before the blackboard and explain your knowledge of a subject. It wasn't just about filling in the correct answer on a piece of paper. You had to argue your point, defend your ideas, and demonstrate your intellectual depth.

This was something I admired about the Soviet system. It pushed students to think critically and sharpen their minds, rather than just memorizing facts.

Students from countries like Cuba, many of whom came to the Soviet Union to study medicine, received an education that allowed them to become some of the most respected doctors in the world. The Soviet system, while flawed in many ways, certainly had its strengths, and education was one of its most notable features.

The USSR was made up of 15 republics, each with its own distinct nationalities, languages, and cultures. Despite these differences, there was never any overt division or discrimination based on ethnicity or background. Growing up in Azerbaijan, I was surrounded by people from all corners of the Soviet Union. Armenians, Georgians, Russians, Ukrainians, and others lived together, and we never saw each other as different or "other." In the Soviet Union, we were all just Soviet citizens.

Yet, as I reflect on the world today, I realize that this sense of unity is something that has been lost. The divisions and prejudices that now exist, especially around race and ethnicity, were simply not a part of our daily lives. There was no "white supremacy" movement. No one was ever taught to consider themselves superior because of their skin color or national origin. It's something I now see in stark contrast to the world I live in today, where people often call each other names, attack each other for perceived differences, and elevate themselves over others. It's a sad reflection of how things have changed.

As I grew older and learned more about my family's past, I also discovered how my parents came together. My mother, a widow for ten years after the death of her first husband, had two children from that marriage. She had never planned to marry again. She was content with her life, raising her children with the support of my grandmother. But fate had other plans. My father, who had been married to a woman from Siberia and had a son, returned to Azerbaijan after his first marriage ended. His sisters encouraged him to find another wife, and that's when he met my mother.

My mom and my dad

My mother had been hesitant at first, not wanting more children, but my father's sisters convinced her that it would be the right thing to do. After some time, she agreed, and they married. My mother, who was 35 when we were born, hadn't expected to have another child, let alone twins. On February 26th, I was born along with my twin brother. At the time, my twin brother was born with a murmur, which complicated things somewhat. Later in life, I would learn that this was the moment my life took an unexpected turn, though at the time, I had no idea what would unfold.

Mikhail and Nikolai

What my mother didn't realize, however, was that one of her children, one of the twins she had never expected to have, would grow up to be someone who didn't quite fit the mold of what society expected. As I continued my journey of self-discovery, it would become clear that I was different—not just from my twin, but from many of the boys around me. The realization would come slowly, but it would be part of who I was, part of my identity, whether the world was ready for it or not.

Exploring Identity and Silence

As a young boy trying to understand who I was, there was always a nagging curiosity in my mind, a drive to understand what made me different. I knew there was something about me that set me apart from the other boys, but I didn't know what it was. At the time, it was a kind of psychological conflict, trying to make sense of feelings that I couldn't even name, let alone speak about. I asked myself questions that, in the Soviet Union, I couldn't ask out loud. There was no one to talk to about these things, and to even bring them up felt wrong.

One day, I had a very confusing experience that would be a significant moment in my transition into adolescence. I woke up in the morning and noticed that I was wet. At first, I thought it was just an accident, maybe I had wet the bed, but when I touched myself, it felt sticky, almost like glue. I didn't understand what was happening. I felt a surge of fear and confusion. I didn't know what to call my mother or how to explain it. I gathered what little courage I had and went to find her.

When she came to check on me, she simply went to my father and told him that I had "become a man." There was no real explanation, no understanding of what was going on, just the excited confirmation that I had reached some kind of milestone. I recall how, even in the cold winter months, my parents would always remind me to keep my legs warm, believing it was important for the continuation of the family, though they never explained why or how. The talk about sexuality, about growing up, was always vague, almost as if they were too uncomfortable to address it directly.

This lack of open discussion left us to navigate these experiences on our own. My mother never sat down with me, or even my sister, to explain what was happening to our bodies. When I was younger, I asked my mother where children came from, and she told me that birds brought them. I was told that storks were the ones who delivered babies. I imagined them soaring through the clouds with tiny bundles hanging from their beaks, gently dropping them off at front doors like some kind of magical postal service. It wasn't until later that I began to realize just how little I knew about the biology of life, about reproduction, about the complexities of sexuality. These were topics that were never touched upon at home.

Yet, as I continued to grow, my curiosity did not subside. I tried to figure things out on my own, and this led to an unexpected and awkward moment. I remember one day, at school, a classmate, Marseille, came up to me and asked if I had ever "come." When I said yes, he explained to me that I should try rubbing a pillow against myself, like he had seen in a video, and that it would give me a great feeling of "release." At first, I didn't fully grasp what he meant, but I was intrigued.

So, one day, I went home and, as my grandmother sat reading the newspaper, I decided to try what he had suggested. I placed a pillow on the couch next to her and began to mimic what I had been told. Of course, my grandmother noticed, and when she asked me what I was doing, I lied, telling her I was just "exercising." She wasn't convinced, and eventually, she told my mother about it. I overheard their conversation in the kitchen, and while my mother's reaction was to brush it off as a part of growing up, the discomfort in her voice was clear. There was no real explanation or conversation, just a sense of awkwardness.

And then there was my father. I vividly remember the times when I would sit at the kitchen table and cross my legs, something I did out of habit and comfort.

He would scold me, telling me that only "prostitutes" crossed their legs. In his mind, a real man should sit straight, should avoid any behavior that could be seen as effeminate. I didn't understand it at the time, but those comments planted a seed of shame in me, a belief that certain behaviors were not acceptable for a boy, for a man. This was the gendered world of the Soviet Union—one where masculinity was often defined by a rigid set of expectations.

Eventually, as I continued to grapple with my identity, I found myself in a situation that would mark the beginning of my understanding of sexuality in a more intimate way. Back in those days, it was the mariners—the sailors and merchant seamen—who had the rare opportunity to glimpse life beyond the Iron Curtain. As their ships sailed across oceans, carrying goods between the Western world and the Soviet Union, they were among the very few who had direct contact with foreign soil. They saw things most people behind the curtain could only dream of—bright neon signs, colorful packaging, fashion, music, and, of course, certain more private indulgences.

One of the more whispered-about treasures they brought back was pornographic videotapes—grainy, illicit, and passed hand-to-hand like sacred contraband. For men spending weeks or months at sea with no women on board, these tapes became a form of release, a crude yet deeply human attempt to satisfy desire through what was politely referred to as "manual exercise." It was taboo, it was underground, but it was real. And for many, it was their only connection to a world of sensuality that was otherwise entirely censored and out of reach.

A boy from my neighborhood, Arnold, had somehow gotten his hands on a gay porn video from one of those sailors. He watched it, and it sparked something in him. He approached me one day, asking if I was interested in having sex with him. At the time, I didn't fully understand what he meant, but something inside me felt drawn to the idea, even though I couldn't articulate why. I agreed, and that moment began a sexual relationship with him that would continue, leaving me with feelings I had never anticipated—feelings that were far beyond what I had imagined.

The experiences that followed were both confusing and exhilarating. I felt excitement and pleasure, but also a sense of isolation. I had never been taught what these feelings meant or how to process them. They were my own, and they had no place in the world around me. Yet, the joy and satisfaction I found in these encounters were undeniable, even as I struggled to understand them.

The Secret World of Desire

My relationship with Arnold didn't happen daily, but it was consistent—sometimes five or six times a week. Every time we met, the pleasure I experienced overwhelmed everything else in my mind. This secret part of my life was hidden from the world, wrapped in guilt and silence, but it was also a space where I finally felt alive. It felt like stepping into another world, one where my body spoke its own language, where pleasure and excitement met and whispered that I belonged there.

We mostly met at Arnold's place when his parents were away. Occasionally, I would bring him to our apartment, locking my grandmother in her room to keep our secret safe. Looking back, I'm stunned by the lengths I went to protect that secret—but at the time, it felt like the only way. I didn't fully understand what we were doing, but I knew it wasn't something I could talk about. It was too dangerous.

I remember walking past my parents' room once and seeing my father asleep, his legs splayed open, his genitals exposed. I stopped for a moment, not with any inappropriate intent, but with a deep sense of wonder and confusion. How could that part of the body, designed by nature or by God, be something capable of giving such pleasure? At that time, I wasn't thinking of women. My mind was fully preoccupied with Arnold, and with the sensations I felt when I was with him.

The apartment we lived in was small and overcrowded—seven of us in a two-bedroom space. Privacy was a luxury. In winter, when it was cold, my older brother would fold out the sofa bed in the living room, and he once invited me and my twin brother Nikolai to sleep with him "like family." That night, when my brother wrapped his arm around me and pulled me close, I felt his warmth and the touch of his body against mine. I couldn't control what I felt. A spark ignited deep inside me—an arousal so intense I thought I might explode. I didn't act on it, of course, but I also didn't know what to do with the feelings it brought up. They scared me, yet they fascinated me. I couldn't talk to anyone, not my brothers, not my friends, not even myself—not really. So I kept it all inside, asking myself silent questions, too afraid to speak them aloud.

Arnold became my escape and my comfort. Our secret meetings gave me something to look forward to, something that made me feel good about myself, even if I couldn't explain why. All the shame, fear, and questions I had would disappear in those moments of pleasure. That feeling was powerful. It silenced everything else.

Then came summer. School was out, and Arnold went to Ukraine to visit family. When he returned, he asked me if I had ever been with a girl. I said no. I wasn't interested—I never had been. He told me that he had tried sex with a girl in Ukraine and that it felt good. He said he now liked both boys and girls. That word—bisexuality—didn't exist for us back then, but looking back, that's what he had discovered. I, on the other hand, still had no desire to be with girls.

Women, to me, were beautiful—but in a different way. I saw them the way one admires art. A nude woman was like a Michelangelo sculpture, or a painting from ancient Greece—majestic, divine, mesmerizing. But not sexually arousing. I appreciated women as beauty, not as desire.

For me, it was always men. The softness of their touch, the strength of their bodies, the shape, the scent—everything about them stirred something deep inside. A vagina never held curiosity for me. Sausages, however, were always welcome.

Nikolai, my twin, turned out to be straight. He dated girls, though he never married or had children. Our paths, once so parallel, began to diverge in the realm of sexuality. Meanwhile, I kept exploring this hidden side of myself with Arnold.

One day, we decided to be adventurous. There was an unfinished apartment complex being built nearby, meant for military families. Some of the buildings were already occupied, but others were still under construction. Around the site, thick bushes provided perfect cover. That's where we went. That's where we had sex—outside, under the bush. It was risky and wild, but it also felt thrilling.

What I didn't know was that one of my classmates had seen us from her balcony.

She didn't say anything at the time. No shout, no call, just silence. But she watched. And she remembered.

Later at school, when I tried to pull one of my usual pranks on her—dropping a frog into her backpack or teasing her—she stopped me. With a quiet, almost amused warning, she said, "If you don't want me to tell everyone what I saw yesterday, then you're going to become my toy. From now on, you'll do what I say."

Family Tides and Fading Ground

My relationship with Arnold continued until everything was shattered by war, the brutal conflict between Armenia and Azerbaijan in 1989. Families scattered, people fled in all directions, and contact was lost with many of those we once saw daily. Life began to unravel.

Growing up in the Soviet Union meant living modestly. We weren't poor, but certainly not wealthy. We were a working-class family. My father drove buses for the city, my mother worked as a nurse in a clinic, and my grandmother, retired by then, held everything together at home. She cooked, cleaned, and looked after us while our parents worked. But more than that, she loved to read newspapers, staying current with world affairs—a curiosity I inherited. That's how my interest in politics began, sitting beside her as she unfolded those big, crinkly Soviet papers, reading about places I dreamed of seeing.

In 1982, my sister, the one I was so close to, got married. I've spoken about our bond before. She was like a second mother to me, my confidante, my protector. Her marriage to her university classmate, also named Karen, was a turning point for me. The wedding, like all weddings in our culture, was massive—Armenian and Azerbaijani traditions blended into a celebration of food, music, and dancing. There must have been 200 guests. A rented hall, a giant kitchen where relatives cooked for days—it was both joyous and heartbreaking.

Because it meant saying goodbye.

She would leave our crowded apartment to move in with her husband's family. I cried that night. I didn't want her to go. I begged my mother to let him move in with us instead, though our apartment was already bursting with seven people.

But tradition said that the bride moves in with the groom, and so she left. In time, they had two daughters—Yekaterina and Alina. Though they'd hoped for sons, the girls were beautiful, bright, and full of life.

After my sister married, my mother turned her attention to my older brother. She insisted it was his turn to settle down. But he wasn't interested. He was a womanizer—always chasing women, never interested in commitment. Still, my mother, determined as ever, teamed up with a neighbor to find him a wife.

They found Karina, who lived across the street. She was educated, polite, and elegant. She reminded people of a French singer, Mireille Mathieu, recognizable for her iconic hairstyle—a look that has remained almost unchanged throughout her decades-long career.

Her hairstyle is a precisely cut, jet-black bob with straight, full bangs that sit neatly across her forehead. The bob is typically chin-length, sleek, and symmetrical, framing her face with sharp, clean lines. The bangs are blunt and thick, giving her a doll-like, timeless appearance that feels both retro and strikingly polished.

The overall look is very structured, with not a strand out of place—giving off a sense of old-school glamour mixed with discipline, almost like a signature or a uniform. It's elegant, bold, and unmistakably hers—just like her voice.

She (Karina) seemed like the perfect match on paper. They married, and she moved into our apartment.

That's when the trouble began.

Karina wasn't interested in the domestic chores that my mother and grandmother expected from a daughter-in-law. She wouldn't clean, wouldn't cook, and preferred to have breakfast at her mother's apartment rather than with us. She buried herself in books and newspapers, ignoring the routines of our home. Tension grew quickly. My grandmother and mother were furious.

Eventually, they asked my brother to move out and find his own place.

Despite the rocky start, they had two children—a son and later a daughter. I met the boy when he was small, but never got to know the girl. The boy, sadly, was spoiled and difficult, always misbehaving, and my brother wasn't much of a father. He kept cheating on Karina, and the marriage collapsed into arguments, neglect, and even violence. One day, in a rage because she wouldn't cook dinner, he slammed her head into a wall. That was the breaking point.

They separated. She moved to Russia. For a brief time, they reunited, she became pregnant again, but it didn't last. They finally divorced, leaving a trail of pain behind.

As all this unfolded, no one in the family questioned why I wasn't marrying. My parents didn't know my truth—my hidden self. My twin brother, Nikolai, didn't show interest in marriage either. He was focused on money, and we had very little of it. Marriage, in our world, came with financial responsibilities—gifts, housing, and celebrations. It just wasn't in the cards.

Meanwhile, I poured my heart into being the best uncle I could be. When Yekaterina was born, and later Alina, I became their favorite playmate. I sang them songs, tucked them into bed, and took them outside to play. Even though I didn't know how to play the piano, I made up little melodies for them, just like my sister had done for me. Those were warm years, filled with laughter and tiny joys.

And then everything changed.

The Soviet Union, which had seemed like a monolith—unchangeable, eternal—began to collapse. No one expected it, and no one could have predicted the chaos it would unleash. Borders dissolved, systems crumbled, and grief poured into the lives of millions. For those of us caught in the middle—Armenians in Azerbaijan, Azerbaijani families split across ethnic lines—it meant displacement, fear, and the loss of everything familiar.

The ground shifted beneath our feet. And nothing would ever be the same.

Getting into Politics

Before the collapse of the Soviet Union, as I've mentioned before, there were things I disliked about the system—and yet, there were also many things I truly appreciated. One of those things was how much emphasis our schools placed on culture and education. Our teachers constantly encouraged us to visit museums—the Museum of Art, the Museum of History, the circus, the zoo, and architectural landmarks. Sightseeing wasn't just a pastime; it was part of our classwork, a way to educate ourselves beyond textbooks. That exposure helped me develop a deep curiosity about the world, and it's what eventually sparked my love for history. I became more and more passionate about it, eventually dreaming of becoming a historian.

Of course, the Soviet Union had its pros and cons. But what none of us could foresee was just how dramatically things would change, how the very fabric of life would be torn apart for millions. When Gorbachev came to power and introduced Glasnost and Perestroika, it gave the republics within the USSR an opening—a chance to imagine their own futures. And one by one, they began to claim independence.

It was around this time that my curiosity about politics, thanks to my grandmother, turned into something more serious. She loved reading the newspaper every morning, especially world news. I'd sit next to her, soaking in every headline and article. I didn't care much about domestic Soviet affairs; my eyes were on the rest of the world. Foreign politics, international headlines—those were the stories I followed with fascination.

People often say politics is a dirty game. I'd go further—politics is dirty laundry. The more you involve yourself in it, the more you risk: friendships, reputations, even your safety. That truth became real to me when I was just 15.

Back then, Mikhail Gorbachev was still in power. I had a pen pal in Berlin, Germany, and I desperately wanted to visit him. I had no idea how international travel worked, so I did what seemed natural: I wrote a letter to the General Secretary of the Communist Party, Mikhail Gorbachev himself. I asked him how I could travel to Germany.

To my surprise, the letter didn't go unnoticed. It was forwarded to the local Communist Party branch in Azerbaijan. I'll never forget the morning a tall man with long hair knocked on our door. When my mother answered, he asked for me. He introduced himself as a representative of the local Communist Party.

My mother was confused—and then terrified. She had grown up in the Stalin era. For her, writing a letter like that could mean prison—or worse, exile to the Gulag.

He asked us to come to the local Communist Party office that same day. My mother was furious. On the bus ride there, she scolded me.

"You're not going to Germany," she insisted. "I won't let you. We don't have the right to do such things."

At the office, the representative questioned me gently. He asked about my school, my age, and why I wanted to travel to Germany. I explained about my pen pal and my dream of visiting Berlin. He responded with a detailed list of requirements: I had to be 16, apply for an international passport, receive parental consent, and—of course—be approved by the authorities. In other words, it was practically impossible.

We returned home in silence. My mother warned me never to write such letters again. But I wasn't done.

Not long afterward, it was announced that Margaret Thatcher, Prime Minister of the United Kingdom, would be visiting the USSR. I was thrilled. I immediately wrote her a letter, welcoming her to our country and expressing hope that this visit could lead to educational exchanges between our nations. I dreamed of a time when Soviet and British students could learn side by side.

But this letter didn't go where I intended. Like all foreign-bound correspondence, it was intercepted by the KGB. I had no idea this happened—until one day, as I arrived at school, the director and a KGB officer were waiting for me.

They escorted me into the office and showed me my letter. They asked if I had written it. I said yes. They asked if I was seeking political asylum. I said no. I pointed out that not a single word in my letter mentioned asylum. But they didn't believe me.

To them, anyone reaching out to the West was suspicious. They thought I was disloyal, a potential threat. As punishment, they expelled me from school for a day or two. It was terrifying. As young schoolchildren, we were what was called "pioneers"—a Soviet youth organization, something between Boy Scouts and a political grooming program. Every morning, we had to put on our uniforms and tie a bright red scarf around our necks. That red tie wasn't just a piece of fabric; it was a symbol of loyalty to the ideals of the revolution, to communism, to the state. It represented obedience, pride, and unity. We were taught to wear it with honor.

And we had to wear it every single day.

But one day, my tie was taken from me.

Not lost, not forgotten at home. No—I was stripped of it. The KGB themselves said I had *betrayed the dignity of the Pioneer unit*. Those words sounded like thunder when I first heard them. Even as a child, I understood the weight they carried. Betrayal. Dignity. Those were not words they used lightly.

I don't remember all the details—only that something I did (a letter to Margaret Thatcher), or maybe something I said, was seen as disloyal, disrespectful, perhaps even dangerous in the tightly controlled world we were living in. And so they came, not with violence, but with precision. And they took my tie.

Quietly. Officially. As if erasing a part of me.

For a child, that moment was terrifying. Not just because of the punishment itself, but because of what it meant: I had been marked. I was no longer one of them.

That incident caused chaos in my household. My mother was devastated. She feared for all of us. In her eyes, I had brought the shadow of the Gulag into our home. But for me, something had shifted. I'd seen how the system operated, how quickly curiosity and hope could be interpreted as rebellion. And yet, even then, I knew I wouldn't stop seeking truth. No matter the cost.

Sexual Awakening Amidst Political Turmoil

As I mentioned earlier, my sexual relationship with my neighbor, Arnold, continued until the war in Azerbaijan broke out in 1989. I was about 16 years old. At that time, my gay sexuality and growing interest in politics were deeply intertwined, creating an overwhelming mix of emotions and desires.

When Arnold left—where to, I can't even remember—everything changed. After the war began, I didn't have any sexual relationships or physical contact with anyone until I eventually moved to the United States. Looking back, it feels strange to think about how long that period of celibacy was. Those years felt like a void, a time when I was, in a sense, a virgin again.

But before my relationship with Arnold, there was another memory—one I had almost forgotten. It was the first spark of my intriguing desires. It happened when I was quite young, around 9 or 10 years old, during one of our family trips to the Caspian Sea.

My father often took us to the beach, and on this particular day, he was sitting nearby, preparing lunch, while my brother and I swam in the water. Out of nowhere, a man I didn't know approached me and asked if I wanted to learn how to swim. At that age, I didn't think twice about it. I simply agreed, not realizing his intentions were far from innocent.

The man grabbed me from behind, pulling me closer to his body. He began rubbing himself against my back, pretending it was all part of the swimming lesson. At the time, I didn't fully understand what was happening, but I felt a strange, burning excitement—a sensation I had never experienced before. I didn't resist, nor did I say anything. I just let it happen, unsure of what to make of it.

When my father eventually called us over for lunch, the man stopped abruptly and disappeared. I never saw him again. That encounter became my first exposure to sexual feelings, even though I didn't fully comprehend what had occurred.

That experience remained buried deep inside me, a secret I told no one—not my parents, not my sister, not even my brother. The only exception was my twin brother, Nikolai. He knew everything. He tried to convince me to stop exploring these sexual feelings, knowing it wasn't right. But I didn't want to stop. I was captivated by the pleasure, by the fantasy world I had created for myself.

Later, during my teenage years, this secret world of mine expanded. My relationship with Arnold became a significant part of my life. It wasn't just about the physical connection—it was about escaping into a realm of desire where I felt free, even if only temporarily.

Everything came to a halt when the war between Azerbaijan and Armenia erupted in 1989. Life as we knew it was turned upside down. The warm sense of community I had grown up with was suddenly shattered.

Neighbors who used to share tea and conversation with us now turned their faces away. We became enemies in each other's eyes.

Fear consumed everyone. It was dangerous to even step outside to buy bread. News of atrocities spread quickly—Armenians were being expelled from Azerbaijan, and in retaliation, Azerbaijanis were doing the same to Armenians. Stories of violence, rape, and massacres circulated constantly. Pregnant women were killed, their stomachs cut open. Houses were burned to the ground.

For Armenians, these horrors brought back memories of the Armenian Genocide perpetrated by the Ottoman Empire decades earlier, in 1915. The atmosphere was one of terror and uncertainty. We didn't know if violence would reach our street, or if we would survive.

Amidst the chaos, my family began to think about leaving Azerbaijan. Moving within the Soviet Union wasn't easy. Housing was provided by the government, so relocating required a formal apartment exchange. For example, if you wanted to move to Moscow, you had to advertise your apartment in Azerbaijan and find someone in Moscow willing to trade. If they liked your apartment and you liked theirs, you could proceed with the exchange through the management company.

This process was time-consuming and expensive. Travel alone required significant funds, and there was no guarantee anyone would take interest in your apartment. For us, finances were tight. Moving to Russia or the Baltic states, like Latvia, was out of the question.

Eventually, my mother made the decision to move us to Turkmenistan, in Central Asia, which was still part of the Soviet Union at the time. My sister's husband had relatives there, so it seemed like a safer option.

We packed up everything we owned and boarded a ferry across the Caspian Sea. Our destination was Krasnovodsk, a town on Turkmenistan's coast. It was a bittersweet moment—leaving behind the only home we had ever known, but also escaping the violence and uncertainty of war.

That year marked the beginning of a new chapter for my family and for me. It was a time of tremendous upheaval, but also a chance to start over, to rebuild our lives in a foreign land.

This part of my story is shaped by two parallel journeys—one of personal discovery and one of political upheaval. My sexual awakening, though confusing and at times troubling, was a significant part of my identity. At the same time, the war forced me to confront the fragility of the world around me, teaching me about resilience and survival in the face of adversity.

The move to Turkmenistan was a turning point, both an escape and a new beginning, as I left behind not just my homeland but also the secrets and desires that had defined my early years.

The New Land, New Beginnings

When we arrived in Krasnovodsk, Turkmenistan, it felt like stepping into a different world. The air was thick with dust, and the sun blazed down mercilessly on the parched earth. The Caspian Sea, which had once been a symbol of home, now seemed like a distant memory—an ocean I had crossed to escape the violence of war. It felt surreal, yet I couldn't escape the sense of relief. Here, the immediate threat of death, of the violence we had left behind in Azerbaijan, was gone.

Krasnovodsk was a town on the edge of the desert, a small, stark place where Soviet architecture loomed like ghosts of an older time. The apartment we moved into was a modest three-bedroom but clean, with small rooms that smelled faintly of mildew. The walls were thin, and I could hear the sounds of our neighbors through the cracks—every argument, every laugh, every whisper seemed to slip through. It was a new beginning, but the isolation I felt from the rest of the world was suffocating.

For the first time in years, there was a sense of anonymity in the air. I didn't have to worry about the secrets I had kept buried for so long. No one knew me here—not my family, not my neighbors, and most importantly, no one knew the boy I had been in Azerbaijan. I was free to reinvent myself, or at least, that's what I told myself.

But the truth was, the past didn't fade as easily as the memories of war. The internal battle was far from over. I was still struggling with my identity—my sexuality, my memories of Arnold, the confusing, dark fantasies that haunted me—and now, there was a new weight. A weight of shame. I didn't know anyone here, but I couldn't stop feeling like I was still trapped inside the secrets I had carried with me across the Caspian Sea.

The days in Krasnovodsk were quiet. The city had a languid pace—nothing like the constant buzz of Baku or the chaotic energy of war-torn Azerbaijan. Life here moved slowly. My family tried to make do with what we had, adjusting to a new life in a strange land. My mother got herself a job in the clinic, while my sister's husband tried to find work as well. I wasn't sure what to do with myself. I had nothing to occupy my mind except the memories of what we had left behind.

The days blurred into one another. I spent most of my time indoors, reading whatever books I could find in the small local library or listening to the distant sounds of the sea. It was a strange time of reflection—this was supposed to be a fresh start, yet all I felt was a sense of dislocation, like I was still somewhere else. Still in Azerbaijan. Still running.

One afternoon, as I wandered through the narrow streets of Krasnovodsk, I met a man who would change the trajectory of my life once again. His name was "Aleksei." He was 16 or 17 with sharp eyes that seemed to pierce through the world around him. He wasn't like the others. He didn't seem to care about the dust or the heat or the fact that we were all strangers in a strange land. He had a quiet confidence, a kind of world-weariness that resonated with me.

We met by chance—he was sitting on a bench near a street where I often went to walk around. Our conversation started casually, but soon we were talking about everything—the war, the uncertainty of the times, and, oddly enough, my experiences in Azerbaijan. I wasn't sure why, but I felt a connection with him. I told him things I had never told anyone— about Arnold, about the war, about the confusion I had felt growing up.

Aleksei listened quietly, his expression never changing, but I felt like he understood. And for the first time in a long time, I felt like I wasn't completely alone in this world.

He told me about his own struggles—how he had been born into a world of contradictions and had spent years trying to escape it. His father had been a high-ranking official in the Soviet army, but Aleksei had always felt like an outsider. He had left Russia in search of something more, something meaningful, but still hadn't found it. He seemed like someone who was also searching for answers, much like me.

From that day on, Aleksei and I spent more time together. We talked about history, about our countries, and about the things that bound us—the secrets we held and the identities we struggled to define. He became a kind of mentor to me, but also a friend, someone who could see past the facade I had put up to protect myself from the world. We began to explore Krasnovodsk together, walking along the beach, visiting library, and discussing everything from philosophy to the intricacies of Soviet politics. It was during these walks that I began to realize something important—that I wasn't defined by the mistakes of my past, nor by the secrets I carried with me. I was more than just a product of my experiences. I could change, I could grow, and I could find my own way.

But the past wasn't finished with me yet. Aleksei's presence gave me comfort, but it also stirred something in me—a desire to confront the past, to understand my own sexuality and how it fit into the new world I was beginning to build for myself. I knew that I couldn't outrun it forever.

In Krasnovodsk, I found a new sense of purpose. But I also found that the road to self-acceptance and peace would not be easy. Every step I took toward understanding myself seemed to bring up more questions, more contradictions. But with Aleksei by my side, I felt a little less afraid to face them.

As the months went by, the heat of the Turkmen summer began to fade, and with it, something inside of me shifted. I was no longer running from my past. I was beginning to understand it—slowly, painfully, but surely. And I realized that, despite the fear and uncertainty, I was finally starting to take control of my own story.

Exile Within Borders

Coming to Krasnovodsk, Turkmenistan, was never really our choice. It wasn't that we wanted to move or relocate. Compared to the capital of Azerbaijan, Baku—the city I grew up in—it felt like a punishment. Baku was a beautiful, vibrant place, a city of contrasts and history. Its architecture was a unique blend of European elegance and Ottoman tradition. You could walk through one part of the city and feel like you were stepping into a European past; another corner would carry the echoes of Ottoman influence. And then, turn a few streets, and you'd find yourself in a purely Soviet reality.

Baku was diverse, alive. I loved walking along the boulevard, looking out over the Caspian Sea, strolling the streets, stopping by cafés. There was life in the air, color in the buildings, a pulse that matched my curiosity and desire for something more.

In contrast, Krasnovodsk felt lifeless—just a desert town, hot, dry, and suffocating. Sand covered everything. During summer, it was like living inside an open oven. Most people didn't have air conditioning—it was a luxury in the Soviet era. Opening the windows made things worse: hot air rushed in, and with it, gusts of sand that coated the floors and furniture. I wouldn't even call it a city—to me, it was more like a village.

Turkmenistan is different now, I imagine, since it gained independence. But back then, I knew one thing for certain: I had to escape. I had to leave the Soviet Union, that oppressive system, that life of silence and fear. I couldn't be myself there—not fully, not truthfully. I carried secrets with me, especially about my sexuality, and I had to guard them constantly. Exposure meant danger. Exposure meant ruin.

Back in Azerbaijan, before we left, the war between Armenians and Azerbaijanis was escalating. The situation grew hostile, even between neighbors who once lived peacefully side by side. Suddenly, they became enemies. My mother was deeply worried. School was no longer safe for me—the walls were covered with anti-Armenian graffiti: messages telling Armenians to leave, saying Azerbaijan wasn't for them.

So, she made a decision. She sent me to Armenia, to live with her sister, my aunt, and continue my education there. It felt like the only option at the time.

When I arrived in Yerevan, I had that gut feeling—the one that tells you whether a place is going to welcome you or reject you. My gut told me I didn't belong. I could understand Armenian, but I couldn't speak it. And the Armenian spoken in Armenia was different from what we spoke in Baku—back home, it was a mix of Armenian, Azeri, and Russian. In Armenia, it was purer, stricter, more formal.

In school, most subjects were taught in Russian, as we were still part of the Soviet Union. But one day, a teacher of Armenian language came in and announced that all refugee students from Azerbaijan would now take intensive Armenian lessons. I didn't want that. I didn't even like the sound of the language—maybe it was strange of me, but it just didn't resonate. I told her I wasn't interested.

She was furious. She dragged me into her classroom, stood me in front of the other students, and humiliated me. "Look at this boy from Azerbaijan," she said. "He's supposed to be Armenian, but he doesn't speak Armenian. He doesn't even want to learn." The class jeered. They shoved desks at me, threw papers in my face. But I stood my ground. I wasn't going to be bullied into submission, especially not by someone who used shame as a teaching method.

Then came the earthquake—the massive one that struck outside of Yerevan. Buildings collapsed. People died. I wanted to help. I volunteered to go to the epicenter to assist however I could. But the school director refused. "Your education comes first," she told me. She acknowledged my desire to help, but ordered me to stay.

Life in Armenia was not easy. I didn't like the city. I didn't like the environment. I felt out of place. One day, I tried to run away—to leave my aunt's apartment, go to the train station, and return to Baku. At the time, the trains still ran between the two countries. I thought I could make it.

But they found out I hadn't gone to school. Someone told them they saw me heading toward the station. They stopped me. My aunt gave me a long lecture about what kind of image I was creating—that I would make it seem like I was mistreated, that I wasn't welcome. "You're here to finish school," she said, "and you will stay."

And so I stayed. I finished my year in Armenia. But as soon as I graduated, I packed my things and left Yerevan. I returned to Baku, where my parents were still living at the time

Tongues of Identity

Growing up in Baku, Azerbaijan, I didn't speak Armenian. As I mentioned before, Russian was the official language of education and government across the entire Soviet Union. Local languages like Azerbaijani or Armenian were present and used on some governmental levels, but never to the extent of Russian. There weren't many—if any—schools where all subjects were taught in the local languages. Everything was in Russian.

There were international schools too, where instruction was in English, but those were for elite families. That world was not for us. So, for me, Russian naturally became my native tongue. It was the language I spoke in school, in public, in writing. My parents spoke Russian as well, even though both they and my grandmother used Armenian at home when speaking to each other.

My grandmother tried to speak Armenian with me, but I always answered in Russian. I understood what she was saying—I just couldn't speak it fluently. I remember her saying to me, "You have to speak Armenian. It's your language. You're Armenian." But something deep inside told me I couldn't be just Armenian—not if I didn't speak the language. And beyond that, I didn't even like how Armenian sounded.

There was something else, something unexplainable. I felt I couldn't be 100% Armenian, no matter what my grandmother said. She insisted on that purity—"You are one hundred percent Armenian," she would say. But I didn't believe such a thing existed. I remember once asking her:

"Grandma, do you really think that during the genocide, back in 1915, maybe some Armenian girl was raped by an Ottoman soldier? And maybe she gave birth to a child, because abortion wasn't an option, and maybe that child's blood got mixed. So, today, someone like me might carry that legacy?"

She was furious. She didn't want to hear it. "No," she said, "I am one hundred percent Armenian." But to me, that kind of certainty didn't make sense.

The languages I was drawn to were Western European—French, German, and English. I liked how they sounded. I liked studying them, practicing, and listening. Armenian wasn't one of them. Azerbaijani wasn't either. I didn't enjoy the sound or the structure of those languages. But Russian—Russian felt natural. It was my native tongue.

I loved the sound of it, the literature, the culture. I devoured Russian books.

At the same time, I was deeply invested in learning English. I spent hours expanding my vocabulary, practicing phrases, and trying to reach a level where I wouldn't need a translator.

That was my childhood—shaped by identity, shaped by language. And then came exile.

At sixteen, I found myself in Krasnovodsk, Turkmenistan—across the Caspian Sea from Baku—in a new school, surrounded by new students, in a completely different environment. I had to finish my final year of school there to graduate. Most people in that town were Russian or Turkmen. In my new class, the majority were Russian.

At first, I wasn't accepted. I was the outsider. But by the end of the year, things had settled. I adapted. I made friends. I finished school.

My dream then was to become a historian. History wasn't just a subject for me—it was something I lived, something that lived in me. I wanted to study it seriously, at the university level. So, I decided to try entering a Pedagogical Institute in Yerevan, Armenia, where I had relatives and a bit of support. It was still the Soviet Union at that time, and it seemed like a logical choice.

But things didn't go as planned. To get accepted, I had to pass several entrance exams—including Russian composition, grammar, and, of course, history. I passed the history exam, but I made some grammatical errors on the Russian composition, which disqualified me.

I was devastated. I returned to our relatives' house in tears. My sister was visiting Armenia at the time, and I remember crying to her about how much I wanted to enter university—how crushed I was that I couldn't.

So, I returned to Turkmenistan, heartbroken, unsure of whether I would try again next year. That failure haunted me.

At that time, my sister was still living in Baku. When our family fled Azerbaijan for Turkmenistan, she stayed behind with her two young daughters and her blind mother-in-law, caring for them. Her husband had already gone to Krasnovodsk to look for work. But what we didn't know was that he was also cheating on her.

Whenever she asked him if she and the children could join him in Turkmenistan, he made excuses. He kept saying the time wasn't right. She didn't feel safe in Baku—the war was escalating, the neighborhood was becoming dangerous—but he kept stalling.

Eventually, she traveled to Armenia, hoping to find a safer environment and figure out her next steps. That's where she was when I failed my exams.

In the end, we were the first ones in our family to move to Krasnovodsk, but my sister and her daughters were still in Baku, still in danger, still trying to escape.

The Cost of Curiosity

After my failed attempt to enter the Pedagogical Institute in Yerevan, I returned to Turkmenistan feeling lost and uncertain about my next steps. I didn't know what to do with myself, so I began working at the very same school I had attended as a student. My role there focused on organizing artistic performances and staging plays based on Russian literature. I worked closely with the students, making sure everyone had a part to play and felt involved. I enjoyed it more than I expected. There was something deeply fulfilling in nurturing creativity and bringing stories to life.

My father continued working as a bus driver after we relocated to Turkmenistan, and my mother found work at a local clinic. Life moved forward, and soon enough, the time came for my compulsory military service. In the Soviet Union, every young man was required to serve in the army at the age of 18. My mother did everything she could to keep me from being drafted, citing medical reasons, but I was determined.

Perhaps it was a kind of youthful defiance—or maybe curiosity—but I wanted to see the Soviet Army with my own eyes. I had heard many troubling rumors, and I wanted to know the truth for myself.

We were gathered by military recruiters and put on a train headed from Turkmenistan to Moscow. I had no idea what division I would be assigned to or what life in the army would look like. I already sensed that I wasn't cut out for military life, but I was committed to experiencing it firsthand. Upon arrival, we were taken to a quarantine facility outside Moscow, where we were housed in cold barracks for a couple of weeks. The hierarchy was clear: soldiers who had already served nearly two years were considered the "elders," while new recruits like me were easy targets.

The atmosphere was hostile and confusing, full of unspoken rules and quiet threats. Every morning began with mandatory runs and physical exercises. The stronger, more athletic recruits were sent to elite divisions. The rest were assigned to various duties on base. But there was something darker lurking beneath the surface.

In the absence of women, some men became predatory. I noticed that certain older soldiers would target the more vulnerable or effeminate recruits. One night, while I was asleep in my bunk, I was woken by two men—one Russian, the other from Dagestan. They led me to a small, dimly lit room where several other soldiers were using drugs. Their eyes were glassy, their energy erratic. They told me, quite plainly, that they had brought me there to rape me.

My heart sank. I was surrounded, terrified, and powerless. I tried to talk them out of it, to plead with them. One of them asked me coldly, "If I rape you, what are you going to do—stab me in my sleep?" His words hit me like ice. I knew they didn't see me as a person. I was just prey.

By some miracle, the drugs began to take effect, and they started to drift into a stupor. I tried to run, but they caught me and dragged me back. Somehow, after more talk, they decided to let me go. I returned to my bed shaking, unable to sleep, too scared to think clearly.

The next morning, I called my father and begged him to get me out of the army. My older brother, who had always been fiercely protective of us, took the first flight to Moscow. When he arrived at the base, he demanded to know who had tried to assault me. I pointed them out but begged him not to retaliate. I didn't want to be labeled a snitch—I feared what they might do if my brother left and I was alone again.

Still, my brother confronted one of the perpetrators, a fellow Azerbaijani. He spoke to him in their native language, warning him in no uncertain terms that if anything happened to me, he would pay dearly. After that, everything changed. The men who had once threatened me now treated me with an odd kind of reverence. They called me their "friend" and assured me that if anyone bothered me, I could come to them.

I survived that chapter of my life, but it left a deep mark. The army didn't break me, but it showed me the cruelty people are capable of— and the importance of having someone willing to stand up for you when you're most vulnerable.

After my brother left and I remained in the army, I knew for certain that military life was not for me. I had entered the army with the hope of gaining some insight into what life there was like, but it was clear I was wasting my time. My real dream was to attend university, and I felt like I was being robbed of that opportunity.

One day, a fellow soldier, whose name I don't recall, took me to a medical clinic that was stationed right next to our base. He revealed something to me that shook me to the core: the clinic was a place where elderly soldiers would go to select young recruits for sexual services. If they wanted someone for sexual pleasure, they would simply walk into the clinic, pick a boy, and that was it. It was a grim, disturbing revelation, and I felt completely powerless. I didn't know who to turn to, and I was all alone in this foreign environment.

When my father visited me and I explained how badly I wanted to leave the army, he knew the situation was dire. But leaving the army wasn't simple. It required a legitimate reason, a compelling case. So, we decided to fabricate one. My father bribed a doctor (though I never asked how he did it), and I was admitted to a hospital outside Moscow for what was supposed to be a medical condition.

At the time, food was in scarce supply across the Soviet Union, and we knew that bribing officials often involved offering goods, perhaps food or something else valuable, as the government-controlled "talons" rationed food. Lines would form for basic goods, and the black market was where people could buy necessities, but it required both cash and connections. It was a tough time to be alive in the Soviet Union, especially during the final years before its collapse.

Once I was in the hospital, I used the opportunity to further distance myself from army life. The nurses were suspicious of my presence and seemed to suspect that I wasn't there for treatment, but for escape. When my sister visited, she joked that the letter I had sent to the Ministry of Defence—demanding the resignation of the Soviet leader - had worked, because soon after, he did resign. It was a bittersweet moment, but it gave me some sense of accomplishment. **P.S.** It was the 1980s, and the Soviet Union was deeply entrenched in a brutal and senseless war in Afghanistan. Young conscripts, barely eighteen, were being drafted from every corner of the republics and sent off to fight Mujahideen fighters in unfamiliar, mountainous terrain. Thousands never came back. Their bodies were mutilated or lost, their families receiving only sealed coffins—often without any certainty that their sons lay inside.

The government deceived its own people. When young men were drafted, they were told they'd be serving in East Germany or within the Soviet borders. But many were quietly loaded onto military planes and dropped into the heart of a violent conflict in Afghanistan, without warning or explanation.

I was a teenager in Krasnovodsk, Turkmenistan, and even then, I felt the deep wrongness of it all. I was angry—furious, even—not just at the war, but at the lies. I wrote a letter to the Soviet Minister of Defense, demanding his resignation. I accused him of betraying the youth of the country, of sacrificing innocent lives for a meaningless war. I called out the deceit and brutality. I signed my name.

That act of protest triggered an official response. The Ministry sent a directive straight to the military office in my town. Soon after, officials appeared at my parents 'workplaces. My mother was terrified. My father, a quiet man, said little, but I saw the worry in his eyes. Another letter. Another summons. Another threat.

They dragged us to the military office. The officer who spoke to us held my letter in his hand and demanded to know why I wrote it. Did I reject the Soviet system? Did I know what consequences such defiance could bring? I told him simply that I didn't't want to be sent to Afghanistan to die in a war I didn't't believe in.

He tried to scare me. "Behind this office is a prison," he said. "Would you like a tour?" I didn't't flinch. "Yes, absolutely," I replied.

My mother begged me to stop. She was panicked, on the verge of tears. Maybe the officer saw our fear. Or maybe he saw my conviction. He said he would report back to Moscow that I was just a young, misguided boy—that I didn't't understand the gravity of what I'd done. He said, out of respect for my parents, he would close the case.

But he warned me not to write another letter like that again.

Eventually, I was sent back to the base, and I was told to wait for a few weeks before being formally discharged. But I couldn't bear the thought of staying any longer. One night, I quietly made my escape. I knew the routine of the guards and waited for the right moment when they would be changing shifts. I made my move, climbed over the protective fence, and ran. I managed to take a train to the Moscow airport, despite not having a ticket. At that time, security wasn't as tight as it is now, and I was able to slip past the boarding gate and board a plane to Turkmenistan, bound for Ashgabat.

On the flight, I took a seat, but when the flight attendants began their final count of passengers, they noticed two extra seats. When they asked for my ticket, I had to make up a story about it being with my friend on the other side of the plane. They told me I had to leave, but the girl sitting next to me, who had her own plans, managed to lock herself in the restroom and stay on the flight. She made it home, while I was forced to disembark, but the whole experience felt like a wild adventure.

I had made it out of the army, but my journey was far from over.

Escape and Reinvention

The Soviet army was never my goal, nor was it my path. For some, the army was a way to secure benefits, to gain a sense of purpose, or to follow in the footsteps of their families. My father and older brother both served in the army—my brother stationed in East Germany for two years, and my father, mostly aboard a submarine, also in East Germany. They both had their reasons, but for me, it was different. The army wasn't for me, and deep down, I knew it. I was a different person, one who didn't fit into that world.

Looking back, I should have listened to my mother when she tried to help me avoid military service. She saw it coming, but I was too stubborn, too eager to prove myself. It became an experience I would never forget—one that would shape me in ways I couldn't anticipate. But escaping the army, even though I had to wait to be formally discharged, felt like an act of liberation.

Afterward, when they realized I had escaped, a warrant was issued for my arrest. Escaping from the army wasn't taken lightly—those caught faced severe penalties, including prison time. But just months later, when the Soviet Union collapsed and I was in Turkmenistan, that warrant became irrelevant. It no longer mattered, and I was free. No one came after me.

In the army, I had to hide so much of who I was. I couldn't share my truth, not about my sexuality, nor about anything from my past. In a setting where masculinity was defined by certain behaviors—how you walked, talked, and acted—I felt like an outsider. Maybe it was the way I moved, the gestures I used, or even the way I spoke, but people could sense that I didn't fit the mold. I found myself questioning my every action—was my voice too soft? Was my walk too different? It was a constant internal battle, trying to hide who I really was, so no one would find out.

Growing up, my family never confronted me about my differences, even though they must have noticed. I never had the conversation with them—no one ever asked if something was wrong, or if I was hiding something. It was as though they chose to ignore what didn't fit into their understanding of what a "real man" should be.

But after leaving the army and returning to Turkmenistan, I was determined to start over. My goal was to enter university. While preparing for that, I worked at the local library, though it was a job considered more appropriate for women. At 18, I was the only male employee surrounded by female librarians, but it didn't bother me. I loved to read, and I wanted something to do with my time. I became friends with one of the librarians, Violetta. We talked a lot, and I shared with her my disappointment about failing to get into university in Armenia. She gave me great advice: after the collapse of the Soviet Union, the rules had changed for university entrance exams. If you wanted to study medicine, you only needed to take the biology exam. If you wanted to be a historian, you took the history exam. No more unnecessary subjects.

That's when I decided to study English. I loved the language, and I knew it would give me more opportunities than pursuing a history degree. I started taking private English lessons, determined to prepare myself for the entrance exams at Turkmen State University in Ashgabat.

The day of the exam arrived. I had prepared thoroughly, studying everything I could about the United States. The night before, I had watched a film about Abraham Lincoln and the Emancipation Proclamation. I even dressed the part, wearing a T-shirt with the American flag on it, along with a baseball cap that had the same design. When I arrived for the exam, the panel of professors asked me to pick a ticket. I opened the envelope and saw that I had to write about New York City—exactly what I had been studying. I sat down and wrote everything I knew.

The verbal exam was next. They asked me questions about New York City and London, and then came the question that made everything click: "Who was the president of the United States who abolished slavery?" I had just watched a film about Lincoln the day before, so I confidently answered, "Abraham Lincoln." I was proud of myself, knowing that the question had come up at the perfect time.

In the end, I passed the entrance exam, and I was accepted into Turkmen State University to study English in the Department of Foreign Languages. It was a new beginning, and I was ready to embrace the future.

The Path to Language and Self-Discovery

Before I got the job at the library in Krasnovodsk, Turkmenistan, I worked at the local oil refinery. I wasn't particularly interested in the work there, but I took the job to support my family financially and help my parents. The refinery hired me at an entry-level position, where I was trained by a tutor to learn how to use machines to shape metal into various forms. It was fascinating at first—I was curious and even tried creating objects like metal candles. However, the job was dangerous. The machines had sharp blades, and one wrong move could cost you a finger or worse. Despite the risks, my real motivation wasn't the job itself but simply earning money to help out at home.

Later, I learned that two Dutch visitors, possibly from the government or private investors, were coming to visit the refinery. They were accompanied by an Armenian translator, who was translating from

English to Russian and vice versa. I saw this as a rare opportunity to practice my English, so I asked my supervisor if I could leave work early to join them and listen to their conversations. It was very rare to encounter foreigners in Krasnovodsk, and I couldn't pass up the chance. The translator agreed, and I was able to sit with them, absorbing as much of the English conversation as I could. I was nervous at first, unsure of how to express myself in English, but the translator encouraged me to try speaking on my own. She told me that if I didn't start speaking for myself and making mistakes, I would never improve. That advice stuck with me, and it ignited my passion for learning English and eventually becoming a translator.

After passing my entrance exams, I moved from Krasnovodsk to the capital, Ashgabat, to continue my studies. My parents helped me with the transition, and I stayed with a distant relative who had an apartment in the same building where his elderly mother lived, instead of staying in a university dormitory.

Before leaving for Ashgabat, I had my first real encounter with Americans. The Peace Corps had arrived in Turkmenistan, bringing teachers to our town to teach English. I became determined to meet them and improve my language skills. One of the teachers, a woman from the U.S., invited me to speak to her students. She knew my English was better than theirs, and she wanted me to help them practice. It was a unique experience, speaking to a class of Russian- speaking students in English. I also spent time with the teacher, showing her around town, taking her to local clubs, and just trying to get to know her. I tried my best to dress well, even though I wasn't sure what "proper" meant at the time. My mother was a bit worried because I was spending time with a foreign woman, and they weren't sure if I was interested in her romantically. But for me, the purpose of our meetings was purely to improve my English, not to pursue anything personal. Looking back, I realize she may have expected something more, maybe a romantic gesture, but that wasn't my interest at the time.

Before moving to Ashgabat, I also took private English classes with a group of other students. My tutor was a kind woman who told me that

67

I was the only one in the class who was improving so much. I shared with her my aspirations to move abroad, initially hoping to go to France because I was fascinated by its culture, food, and fashion. However, as I studied English, I started considering London as a potential destination. My tutor, in a moment I now think of as a kind of prophecy, told me, "You won't go to England. You will end up in the United States. Your future is in the United States, not in Europe." At the time, I didn't give it much thought, but eventually, that "curse" turned out to be true—my life led me to the United States, just as she predicted.

After continuing my studies in Ashgabat, I felt like I was stepping into a new chapter of my life, one that was more aligned with who I was becoming. My English skills were improving every day, and with each lesson, I felt a sense of accomplishment. But my dreams weren't just about learning a language—they were about reaching for something bigger. I wanted to travel, to experience the world beyond the borders of Turkmenistan. I had always dreamed of living abroad, of seeing the places I had only read about in books.

My experiences in Ashgabat—whether it was through private classes or talking to the few foreign visitors who crossed my path—continued to shape my understanding of the world. I was no longer just a boy from a small Soviet town. I was someone who was reaching beyond the confines of my past, trying to carve out a future that reflected the person I had always dreamed of becoming.

And then, just like that, everything changed. The Soviet Union collapsed. The world I had known was unraveling, and along with it, my plans, my dreams, and the path I had laid out for myself seemed to be shifting. But in that chaos, there was also opportunity—new doors were opening, new possibilities were emerging.

As I stood at the crossroads of my life, unsure of what the future would bring, I held on to one thing: the belief that I was meant for more. That belief was the driving force that pushed me to pursue my dreams, even when the path ahead was uncertain.

In hindsight, that "curse" my English teacher had spoken about—that I would end up in the United States—didn't feel like a curse at all. It was a prophecy, one that had been planted in my mind long before I even understood what it meant. And as I embarked on the next chapter of my life, I could feel it pulling me forward, toward a future I had yet to fully imagine.

Shifting Landscapes: Education, Independence, and New Horizons

Turkmen State University. Ashgabat, Turkmenistan

Studying at the university in Ashgabat, Turkmenistan, was a transformative experience for me. I was incredibly proud to have made it to university, as it felt like a turning point in my life. My mother always emphasized how important education was, saying that without it, you could end up doing odd jobs for the rest of your life. So, I focused on my studies, majoring in English, but also taking courses in Latin,

German, literature, history, philosophy, and a variety of other subjects. It was a real shift from the Soviet-era educational system, and I found it fascinating to be studying at this level.

At the university, we were fortunate enough to have teachers from the United States and Canada, many of them members of the Peace Corps who had come to teach English. Up until then, English in the Soviet Union was mostly based on British English, but the arrival of American teachers was a revelation. I had always loved British English for its sophistication, clarity, and elegance. It seemed refined and perfect—after all, English was the language of the Queen. But when I started hearing American English, it felt like an explosion of energy. The American pronunciation was harsher, rougher, and simpler, which appealed to me in a different way. I liked how the Americans made the language more accessible, breaking it down and simplifying it. While I still admired British English, I became increasingly drawn to American English, its straightforwardness, and its unique expressions.

This preference for American English didn't sit well with my teacher, who was firmly rooted in the British method. She would often correct me or subtly criticize me when I used American terms or expressions, but I didn't let it discourage me. I was focused on my goal of mastering English, and I was determined to embrace both its British and American forms.

In the background, the world around me was changing. I began university just about as the Soviet Union was collapsing, if I recall correctly. The Baltic States—Latvia, Lithuania, and Estonia—had already declared their independence, having always felt somewhat more aligned with the West than the rest of the Soviet republics. These countries had been a kind of window to the outside world for the Soviets, a glimpse of what Western Europe might be like. I had never visited the Baltic States during Soviet times, but I would later end up living in Latvia, in the capital, Riga. It's strange to think how life would unfold in ways I couldn't have imagined back then, as Latvia would eventually join the European Union and NATO, and I would visit every winter.

Meanwhile, Turkmenistan was adapting to its newfound independence. Ashgabat, the capital, was a beautiful city, with new monuments and hotels springing up thanks to the oil and gas revenue. The country's new ruler, a former Communist Party member, Saparmurat Niyazov, took to calling himself the "Father of All Turkmen People" and had monuments of himself erected all over the country. Italians and Turks were brought in to help build and manage the new hotels, and the streets were renovated. Despite these changes, Turkmenistan was still lagging behind in some areas. For instance, it took the country until 1996 to establish its own passport. Until then, Turkmenistan continued to issue Soviet-era passports, even though it had become an independent nation in 1991-1992. I recall that Turkmenistan had worked closely with Switzerland to design a new national passport, which felt like a step into the modern world.

As the country moved forward, I was faced with a new reality. My Turkmen language teacher informed me that the government planned to make Turkmen the primary language of instruction at all educational levels. Russian was being phased out, and soon, all courses would be taught in Turkmen. This created a difficult situation for Russian-speaking students like me, and many chose to transfer to universities in Russia. I wasn't in a position to make such a move.

Financially, it would have been impossible for me to afford studying in Russia without my parents' help, so I stayed in Ashgabat and continued my studies.

During the summer break, I found a job that would change everything. I was hired by an Austrian company, IP Consulting, as an interpreter. This job opened my eyes to new opportunities and set me on a path that would eventually lead me out of Turkmenistan. The experience changed my perspective on the world and made me realize that there were possibilities beyond the borders of my so called "home country", possibilities that I would soon pursue.

Crossroads of Desire and Identity

Working at IP Consulting in Turkmenistan was a pivotal and transformative experience in my life. It was unlike any job I had held before. As an interpreter, I found myself immersed in a dynamic mix of office work, field assignments, and frequent interaction with new people. I was excited by the challenges this role presented, but my journey to that point was marked by a series of unexpected events.

IP Consulting was an Austrian-based company, managed by a Turkish businessman from Vienna. The company primarily operated in Turkmenistan due to the influx of foreign enterprises, especially in the oil and gas industries. However, there was a shortage of young professionals who spoke multiple languages, which made me a valuable asset. As most locals were proficient in English, I was hired as a translator and interpreter, a position that would allow me to work closely with foreign companies that had entered Turkmenistan to establish business ties.

My first assignment with IP Consulting was working with an American company, John Deere, which was exporting cotton pickers and combines to Turkmenistan. My role involved translating for the local workers, helping them understand how to operate the machinery. Alongside me, engineers from the United Kingdom oversaw the technical aspects of the project. This was the perfect opportunity for me to improve my English skills, especially in technical language, as I had to quickly learn complex vocabulary to describe the parts and functions of the machines.

Though I found the work intellectually stimulating, I never disclosed my past or my sexuality to anyone at the office or university. I kept my personal life a secret, as I did not feel comfortable discussing it with others. However, there was something in my work environment that began to stir emotions I had long suppressed.

One of my colleagues, a British engineer named Tom, sparked a complex internal conflict within me. Tom was charismatic, attractive, and easy to talk to.

But it wasn't purely a sexual attraction; it was more about the connection I felt toward him, a desire to be close to him, to help him in any way I could. This feeling, one I had buried for years, began to resurface. I found myself going out of my way to assist him, even offering to do his laundry during a work trip to a town outside of Ashgabat. His reaction, however, was not what I expected. He seemed uncomfortable with my gestures, and I sensed that he noticed something in my behavior that I had not yet fully understood about myself.

Things escalated when I made the impulsive decision to call Tom's girlfriend in England. He had been speaking to her regularly, and as his contract neared its end, I foolishly inquired whether she would consider letting him extend his stay in Turkmenistan. This was a mistake. Tom's girlfriend became upset, expressing how much she loved him and couldn't bear a long-distance relationship. I now realize that my actions were not only inappropriate but also revealing of a side of myself I had not yet come to terms with.

Tom's discomfort with my behavior became evident, and it soon became the subject of conversation between the IP Consulting management and the British engineers. Tom confronted me, accusing me of overstepping boundaries and behaving in ways that were, in his words, "typical of a gay person." I was taken aback by his comment. I had no concept of what being gay meant in the context of my behavior. Growing up in the Soviet Union, I had never encountered any meaningful discussions about sexuality or identity. I didn't understand that my actions were signaling something to Tom that I had yet to fully understand myself.

As a result of this misunderstanding, I was removed from the John Deere project and reassigned to a new project with Mercedes-Benz, a German company. Although the shift was disheartening, I recognized that I had made a mistake. I had let my emotions influence my behavior in ways that had unintended consequences. It was a tough lesson, but it gave me the chance to reflect on my actions and how they were shaped by deeper, unresolved feelings about my identity.

While working with Mercedes-Benz, I was also studying German, hoping that fluency in the language would provide an opportunity to move to Austria, a country I admired. I had long dreamed of living there, but this shift in my professional trajectory reminded me that life often takes unexpected turns. What began as a plan to improve my skills in German became a step toward rethinking my future in ways I hadn't anticipated.

In retrospect, my time with IP Consulting and the complex dynamics I experienced with Tom were formative moments in my life. They forced me to confront parts of myself that had been buried for years. Yet, it was also an opportunity to grow, learn, and move forward in ways that would ultimately shape my path toward self-acceptance and a future I hadn't yet fully imagined.

The Road I Never Meant to Take

As my university studies continued and I worked as an interpreter for an IP Consulting company, my life took a surprising turn. Looking back, I don't know if it was fate or simply a consequence of the times, but that job ended up changing everything for me.

During the summer break—perhaps in September of 1993, though I can't remember the exact date—I found myself more immersed in work than in school. I was learning far more from British and American professionals and other foreigners I interacted with than I ever did sitting in a classroom with non- native English teachers. The work was exciting, intellectually stimulating, and rewarding. I began to question the point of returning to university when I was already improving my English daily and making money—money that I gave to my mother, who had done so much for us growing up.

Despite knowing I had only about a year and a half left to get my diploma as an interpreter, I just… let it go. I ignored the messages from classmates and the concerns from teachers. I don't know what I was thinking. Maybe I wasn't thinking at all. My job consumed me—it felt real, immediate, alive. In contrast, the university started to feel like a distant obligation.

Then came an unexpected twist.

I was assigned to work with the Mercedes-Benz company. One day, a secretary called and told me I needed to travel to Krasnovodsk. A ferry was arriving from Baku, Azerbaijan, carrying Mercedes-Benz representatives. My task was to meet them, greet them, and accompany them back to Ashgabat.

I followed instructions. I arrived in Krasnovodsk in the evening and met two people from the company. I brought them home, where my mother cooked dinner. We sat around the table talking, and I translated our conversation. My mother was beaming with pride. She couldn't hide how impressed she was that I spoke English so fluently and could understand everything being said. That moment reminded me that my time at university hadn't been wasted after all—I had built something meaningful from it. And it felt good. I felt proud, not just for myself but for being able to contribute to my family. My education had been free, thanks to the Soviet system, and now it was finally paying off in a real way.

Not long after that, I received a phone call from Ashgabat. They asked if I had an international passport. I didn't. At the time, it was extremely difficult to get one, especially in Turkmenistan, which had become independent after the collapse of the Soviet Union. The transition to independence was slow and clumsy in some former republics, particularly in Central Asia. Unlike the Baltic states or parts of the Caucasus that adapted quickly, countries like Turkmenistan lagged behind.

A passport wasn't just a document—it was a privilege. Citizens couldn't leave the country freely. In fact, as the new regime grew more authoritarian, getting permission to travel abroad became nearly impossible. It reminded me of North Korea, where the government tightly controls movement and information. To leave, you needed to provide solid justification and go through layers of bureaucracy.

I explained to the secretary that I didn't have a passport. She told me I needed to get one as soon as possible—I was being sent abroad. I didn't even know where.

At the time, I had my own secret plans. My hope was to get a passport, go to the Austrian embassy in Moscow, apply for a visa, and travel to Austria as a tourist—with no intention of coming back. I dreamed of starting a new life in Europe. Austria felt closer to the culture and lifestyle I had always admired.

But then everything changed.

They told me I was being sent to the United States.

That was never part of my plan. I had never even dreamed of going to the U.S. In fact, I didn't want to go. Growing up in the Soviet Union, we were bombarded with propaganda painting the United States as a broken society—jobless people, homeless on the streets, no access to education or healthcare. Capitalism was the enemy. The U.S. was a cold, unforgiving place where the rich thrived, and the rest were left behind. We were told that Americans were out to destroy us. During the Cold War, that narrative was relentless.

So the U.S. never held much appeal for me.

I pleaded not to be sent there. I tried to explain that I had other plans, that I wanted to pursue different opportunities. But they insisted. Later, I realized it might have been a convenient way to get rid of me for a while—maybe to let things cool down after everything that had happened with Tom, the British engineer. There were other translators who could have gone. But for some reason, they said they needed them in Ashgabat, and that I was more "free" to travel.

I didn't know anything about the United States. I knew Washington, D.C. was the capital. I'd heard of New York City, maybe Florida. But when they told me I was being sent to Houston, Texas, I was completely clueless. I didn't know where Texas was. I didn't know anything about Houston.

When people asked me, "Where are you going in the U.S.?" I answered honestly: "Houston, Texas." And when they asked, "Where is that?" I just shrugged. "I don't know."

Even though I tried so hard to avoid this path, it didn't matter. The decision was made for me.

So, as expected, they prepared an official invitation letter for me to present at the U.S. Embassy in Ashgabat. I was told I would be traveling to the United States on a government-level assignment, accompanying the Vice Minister of Agriculture. He was scheduled to undergo heart surgery at the Houston Medical Center in Texas and needed someone to interpret for him during his treatment and recovery. Since he didn't speak English, I was selected to go with him as his translator. I knew he would be traveling with his girlfriend and his son, so I figured my role would be strictly professional.

But deep down, I didn't want to go.

I tried everything I could to avoid getting the visa. When the day came for our interview at the U.S. Embassy in Ashgabat, I went with the Vice Minister. They had assigned an embassy translator to assist us, but I immediately refused to speak Russian. I insisted on speaking English directly to the consular officer. I was at the U.S. Embassy, after all— why shouldn't I speak the language, I had worked so hard to learn?

The interview began with the usual questions: Why are you going to the United States? How old are you? What do you do?

I answered confidently. "I'm 22 years old. I'm studying at the university and working at an IP consulting firm as a translator. I've been asked to accompany the Vice Minister to the United States for his heart surgery, to help him communicate before and after the procedure."

But the consular officer looked skeptical. He turned to the Vice Minister and asked, "Why are you taking this young man with you when you could find someone in the United States who speaks Russian?"

The Vice Minister responded honestly. "It would be much more economical to take a translator from here, rather than pay high hourly rates for one in the United States."

Then the officer looked back at me and said something that gave me hope: "I don't know if I'll grant you a visa. People your age often go to the U.S. and don't return."

I seized the moment. "Well, to be honest," I said, "I don't even want to go to the United States. I've never planned to. But if you think I'll stay there, do you think I'd call your embassy and say thank you, I'm not coming back? I'd just stay and not return."

It was a calculated risk—I hoped this bold response would make him deny my visa.

The translator relayed everything I said, and the Vice Minister was furious. "Why did you say that?" he snapped at me. "They won't give you a visa now!"

But I didn't care. I was determined not to go.

The officer kept a straight face and simply said, "Leave your passport here and return tomorrow at 12 noon for the decision."

The next day, I returned, hoping I'd succeeded in sabotaging my trip. I approached the reception window, and the staff told me to wait. A few moments later, someone—I think it was a consular officer, maybe even the ambassador—came out and handed me my passport.

I opened it with anticipation, praying for a denial.

But there it was: a tourist visa. Thirty days to enter the United States.

I was devastated. I tried to hide the news from my company, thinking maybe I could say I didn't get the visa. But I was too afraid. They had connections, and I knew they could easily verify with the embassy. If I lied, I might get in trouble. So I admitted the truth: my visa had been approved.

The company quickly began preparing for my departure. They booked my flight—Ashgabat to Istanbul, where I would spend the night, then from Istanbul to Frankfurt, and finally to Houston, via Dallas, on German Airlines, Lufthansa. I was scheduled to leave on December 15, 1995. The plan was to stay in the U.S. for only two weeks.

I told my mother I was going for a short business trip. I'd be back in two weeks. At that point, I still had no intention of staying. America wasn't part of my dream. I just wanted to see it with my own eyes, work, and come back. I was curious—curious to know whether the Soviet propaganda had been telling the truth. Was the U.S. really a land of poverty, homelessness, and inequality?

At the time, I was living in a rented apartment in Ashgabat. I had recently moved out of a relative's apartment after she passed away and her son and daughter-in-law made it clear they didn't want me there. I told my new landlady I'd be back soon. It was just a two-week trip, after all.

But I didn't know then that those two weeks would change the course of my entire life.

Leaving Turkmenistan wasn't easy. I had mentioned before how difficult it was for people to travel abroad, especially if you weren't ethnically Turkmen. If you were from another nationality—Russian, Armenian, Azeri, Ukrainian—your chances were close to zero. You needed government-level approval or strong connections.

In my case, the company I worked for had to step in and vouch for me. They had a close working relationship with the Turkmen government and basically told them they had no choice—I was the only qualified person for the job. They promised I would return, and that seemed to convince the authorities. That promise was the only thing standing between me and the U.S.

And here's another complication: I wasn't even considered a Turkmen citizen. I still held a Soviet passport.

After the collapse of the Soviet Union, all the former republics began implementing new rules for citizenship and immigration. Russia, for instance, had a policy that you could only become a Russian citizen if you had been officially registered in Russia before 1991. I wasn't. Turkmenistan's rules were more vague, but still strict—you had to be registered in Turkmenistan after the collapse in order to eventually become a citizen.

But I wasn't registered anywhere. Not in Ashgabat. Not even in Krasnovodsk. When I left my hometown to study in Ashgabat, I had officially unregistered myself and never re-registered at the dormitory or anywhere else. So, according to their law, I didn't exist as a Turkmen citizen.

The passport I held was a relic of a country that no longer existed— the USSR. Yet, oddly enough, even five years after the Soviet Union collapsed, international airlines were still accepting Soviet passports for travel.

And so, I flew to the United States with a Soviet passport in hand.

I had maybe $2,000 with me, though I can't remember exactly. My plan was simple: buy a few things for my mom, things she needed for the household, do my job as a translator, and return. I didn't even say a proper goodbye to my parents. I was so sure I'd be back in a couple of weeks. I thought I'd return to my job, keep looking for opportunities, and eventually find a way to go to Europe. Maybe continue my studies and finally get my diploma.

But even that plan had its own doubts. Diplomas from the Soviet Union weren't exactly respected anywhere in Western countries. Everyone knew the system was corrupt—bribes for grades, degrees given out like favors. But for people like me, people who really wanted to learn and succeed, it was frustrating. The Soviet education system, despite its flaws, was incredibly rigorous. For those who took it seriously, it provided a strong foundation.

Still, even with a diploma from Turkmenistan or any other former Soviet republic, it was hard to get a proper job in the West. Most countries require re-qualification—additional courses, credential evaluations, or certifications that meet their standards. So, I was already asking myself, "Even if I finish my degree, what's it really worth in the West?"

I began thinking: maybe I could find a university in Europe that offered free education. Maybe I could enroll, study, and work there. But back then, I didn't know how the system worked. I thought, naïvely, that if a country allowed you in, you could just go, study, and build a life. I had no idea about visas, permits, and immigration bureaucracy. It was a confusing, complicated world I wasn't prepared for.

Still, one thing gave me hope—I finally had an international passport. I could physically leave Turkmenistan. I could travel. And that meant something.

So, I boarded that airplane, a big, beautiful aircraft of Turkish Airlines, and took off from Turkmenistan for the first time.

What I didn't realize, as the plane lifted off the runway, was that something my English tutor once told me about America would come back to me—but only after I arrived there.

The Price of Silence

Back in Krasnovodsk—this small, quiet town on the Caspian Sea in Turkmenistan—we tried to start over after fleeing Azerbaijan. As I've mentioned before, we became refugees, escaping the violence and ethnic cleansing triggered by the conflict between Armenia and Azerbaijan over Nagorno-Karabakh territory. That disputed region, with its majority-Armenian population, wanted independence or unification with Armenia after the collapse of the Soviet Union, but Azerbaijan claimed it as part of its own territory. The fighting escalated quickly. What started as a territorial dispute became a human tragedy.

We left behind our home in Baku, fleeing for our lives. Like so many others, we ended up in Turkmenistan, in a town none of us had ever heard of—Krasnovodsk—because my sister's husband had a distant relative there. He went ahead to find work, and my mother decided we would follow, so we could be close to my sister.

At that time, my sister stayed behind in Baku with her two young daughters and her blind mother-in-law. Her husband was already in Krasnovodsk, looking for a job. Eventually, he found work—some kind of engineering job, I don't remember exactly where. But even though he had settled, something felt off. He wasn't trying to bring his wife, children, or mother to Turkmenistan. My sister was doing everything she could to survive, to keep the children safe. The neighborhood was turning dangerous. Being Armenian in Baku had become a death sentence.

Despite the fear, the isolation, and the collapse of normal life, her husband kept delaying their reunion. At first, it seemed like excuses. Then I started noticing strange behavior—he'd come home from work, drop off laundry at our house for my mother to wash, and then disappear again. Always "working late." Always busy. But something wasn't right.

One evening, I decided to follow him. He drove to an apartment building and parked. I watched from a distance. After a while, he came out, arm in arm with a woman I didn't recognize. That's when I realized the truth: he was cheating on my sister. The woman turned out to be the daughter of the director of the school where I later worked. She was Russian-Tatar, and they were clearly more than just friends.

It was heartbreaking. He wasn't just delaying his family's return—he was avoiding it entirely. And all this time, my sister was still in Baku, desperately trying to get out.

Eventually, she couldn't take it anymore. The violence, the fear—it was too much. She bought a ticket and flew to Krasnovodsk with her children and mother-in-law. When her husband met them at the airport, he didn't even hug her. He went straight to the children, ignoring his wife completely. My sister told me he looked at her with cold detachment, like she was a stranger.

Soon after, she discovered the truth for herself. She followed him one night in a taxi and saw him with the other woman. It shattered her. My parents tried to talk to him, to understand what was happening, but his response was blunt: he didn't love his wife anymore. He wanted a divorce. He had someone else. And as for his children, he said they would grow up just fine without him.

The pain this caused my sister was unbearable. She still tried to fix things. One week, he'd spend time with her and the kids. Next, he'd be back with the other woman. It was a yo-yo of false hope and betrayal.

Then came the breaking point.

One night, he came home late again, the usual excuse—"working late." His mother opened the door, but she had had enough. She told him, "You no longer have a wife or children. Go back to that woman." And she slammed the door shut in his face.

He didn't come back that night.

Hours passed. My sister began to worry. She left the house in the middle of the night and went to his garage, where he kept his car. The light was on. The door was locked. She knocked, then banged, then screamed for help. Neighbors woke up and came to assist. When they broke the door down, they found the engine running. He was inside, lifeless—suffocated by carbon monoxide.

He had taken his own life.

My sister ran home, shaking, pale, in shock. She collapsed at the front door. My mother opened it, and all my sister could do was cry out, "Karen is dead." She fell to the floor, inconsolable. It was a nightmare none of us could have imagined.

Everything spiralled after that.

The Wolf Ointment and the Wound That Never Healed

Before Karen's death, as I mentioned, my sister tried everything in her power to keep her family strong, united, and from falling apart. The woman he was seeing worked at the library of one of the schools in Krasnovodsk. Desperate for a solution, my sister once visited a woman in town known to be a shaman and fortune teller. After listening to her story, the woman offered a supposed remedy: a so-called "wolf ointment." The instructions were clear—this ointment needed to be rubbed onto the body of the girl Karen was involved with. But it had to be done with gloves. The shaman warned that if the ointment touched the person applying it, they would be cursed and never get married.

I didn't believe in such things, but my sister was desperate. She was ready to try anything. She believed this ritual might help stop the affair and bring her husband back. One day, she turned to me and asked me to carry out the mission. She would disguise me to make sure the girl wouldn't recognize me. It was summer, hot and sweltering, but my sister dressed me in winter clothes to conceal my identity. I wore heavy gloves, thick layers, and even removed my glasses so I wouldn't be recognized.

We took a taxi to the school. I was nervous and unsure how I would manage to get close enough to apply the ointment. Everything would have to be improvised. When I arrived at the library, I asked for the girl by name. She sat behind a desk, her hands hidden, her blouse buttoned high to her neck. There was no easy access to her skin, so I waited, trying to make conversation, hoping she would move.

I made up a story—I told her I was the ex-boyfriend of her sister, a medical student, and that I had come back to see her. She looked puzzled. She told me her sister had never mentioned anyone like me. Then she noticed my hands, wrapped in bandages. I claimed I had burned them in an accident. I was lying, nervously improvising, waiting for my chance.

Then, just as I had hoped, someone entered the library to return a book. The girl lifted her hands from beneath the desk and began signing paperwork. I seized the moment. I reached out and grabbed her hand, rubbing the ointment into her skin while thanking her, as if our interaction had been entirely normal. I rubbed quickly and firmly, repeating my thanks, and then I ran out of the library where my sister was waiting in a taxi.

We went home immediately. I took off the disguise, washed my hands, and changed back into my normal clothes. Later that day, Karen came to our apartment. He asked my sister if she had sent me to the library. She denied it. He questioned my mother, my twin brother— everyone gave the same answer: I had been home all day, wearing my usual clothes.

It almost felt like something out of a comedy. For a short while after that, Karen stayed away from the girl. He spent more time at home, coming straight from work. My sister thought maybe the ritual had worked. But it didn't last. Before long, he was back to his old behavior, disappearing after work, seeing the girl again.

What this whole situation showed me was how desperate my sister had become. She believed in anything, tried everything people told her, clung to every possibility, no matter how irrational, just to save her marriage. She was deeply in love with her husband and simply couldn't accept losing him. But as time passed, it became clear: if someone no longer wants to be part of a relationship, there's nothing you can do to stop them. No ritual, no spell, no reasoning will change their heart.

Today, as a married person myself, I take relationships seriously. Marriage is sacred to me. When you get married, you make vows to stay together through good times and bad, in sickness and in health, in poverty and wealth. Those vows should mean something. Life throws challenges at us. We may argue, disagree, and hurt each other. But none of that, in my view, should ever justify breaking those sacred promises.

Because love isn't just about feelings—it's about commitment, endurance, and choosing each other, every day.

...So, the whole situation was going out of control, and then my sister was left to face not just betrayal and abandonment, but also the looming shadows of uncertainty—how to raise two daughters alone, how to deal with the shame that often follows a broken marriage in traditional society, and how to rebuild her sense of self after someone she trusted shattered it completely.

Karen's death brought even more chaos into our lives. While his actions had hurt my sister deeply, none of us wished for his life to end like that. His suicide was like a bomb that went off in the center of our already fragile family. My sister blamed herself for a long time. She questioned whether her confrontation pushed him to that decision, or if perhaps the shame of being exposed, or the pressure from both families, became too much for him to bear. But no matter how many times we tried to tell her it wasn't her fault, the guilt never truly left her.

The aftermath was heavy. People in Krasnovodsk started talking, and whispers passed from balcony to balcony like wind through the desert air. Some blamed my sister, others blamed the girl, and some blamed his weak character. My mother tried to keep everything together, both for my sister and for the grandchildren who were too young to understand what had happened to their father. My mom aged almost overnight, and my sister, once strong, proud, and radiant, became quiet and withdrawn.

At night, I would hear her cry. Quiet, muffled sobs. And I, being young but old enough to understand pain, would just lie there in silence, knowing I couldn't fix anything. I think that was the first time in my life when I fully realized that sometimes love is not enough. Sometimes, no matter how much you want something or someone to stay, they simply won't. Or can't.

But what I admired most was how, eventually, my sister pulled herself out of that darkness. Slowly. Gently. She started working again. She moved out of Turkmenistan to Armenia first. She took care of her daughters with fierce dedication. She became stronger, not in a loud or defiant way, but in a quiet, dignified one. She never remarried, and I think a part of her heart remained broken forever. But she found her own peace, her own meaning, and I believe she transformed her pain into something sacred—a strength that only those who have suffered deeply can ever carry.

That period in Krasnovodsk taught me many things—not just about love and betrayal, but about the strength of women, the complexity of relationships, and the limits of tradition and belief. It also taught me that no matter how dark things get, if you're surrounded by people who truly love you, you can begin again.

Even during the funeral, when neighbors, friends, and relatives filled the house to pay their last respects to Karen, the air thick with sorrow and whispered memories, my sister sat alone in the kitchen, motionless.

In the living room, people gathered tightly around the coffin, heads bowed, some quietly sobbing, others murmuring to one another about the life Karen had lived. The chairs were all taken, some stood in corners, tissues in hand, wiping away tears as they shared stories of his generosity, his strength, his laughter.

But my sister couldn't bring herself to enter.

I found her standing by the stove, staring into nothing, her hands still, her face pale. When I asked what was wrong, she looked at me with empty eyes and said, almost in a whisper, *"I'm afraid to go in there. I don't have any tears left to cry. And if I don't cry, people will say I didn't love him."*

She wasn't cold. She wasn't heartless. She was simply... *empty.* All cried out. Grief had taken everything, even the tears. But in our culture, that wasn't enough. People measured love by outward expressions—by wailing, weeping, and visible devastation. And if a widow didn't cry, tongues would wag. Whispers would grow. Judgments would be made.

So, I did what I could to protect her.

I went to the counter, took an onion, and sliced it open right in front of her face. The sting hit almost immediately. Her eyes began to burn, water welled up, and soon enough, tears began to fall, not from sorrow, but from survival.

I gently turned her toward the living room and nudged her forward, back into the room packed with mourners, now with tears streaking down her cheeks. She stepped inside, the picture of a grieving, heartbroken wife.

No one questioned. No one whispered. The performance had been preserved.

Sometimes, in the face of unbearable loss, all we can do is carry each other through, even if it means crying with the help of an onion.

The Flight to the Unknown

It was December 15, 1995—well, technically, it was December 14th, but I was already checked in at the airport, sitting in the plane as it prepared for takeoff. I had just left Turkmenistan, bound for the United States, and as I looked out the window, the familiar landscape of Ashgabat began to fade into the distance.

The thoughts swirling in my head mirrored the feeling of the plane lifting off the ground: uncertain, but also thrilling. Did I make the right decision?

For months, I had debated whether I should leave everything behind. I had chosen to accept this trip to the United States, but was it the right choice? What about my education? Should I have pursued it further? I had stepped away from the traditional path of academia to follow my passions, to be involved in my job, and immerse myself in what I loved doing. Was that a mistake? Should I have kept going to school? Was there something more I could have done, a path I missed?

As the plane soared over Turkmenistan, bound for Istanbul, my mind continued to circle with questions. Yet, as much as I pondered, I realized there was no turning back now. This was the beginning of something new—a new chapter in my life. It wasn't just about the destination; it was about the journey. It was about stepping out into a world that, for years, I had only heard of, dreamed of, and hoped to one day experience. The communist regime that had shaped my youth had kept me in a bubble, limiting my opportunities. But now, that bubble had burst, and I was about to see the world I had always imagined.

The flight was long, but my excitement was palpable. I couldn't help but wonder what awaited me on the other side of the world, what new possibilities I would find. There was so much I hadn't yet seen, so much I could learn. The anticipation grew, and I pushed my lingering doubts to the back of my mind.

Istanbul, Turkey

After landing in Istanbul, we spent a day exploring the city. Istanbul—a fascinating blend of European and Ottoman culture—was unlike anything I had ever encountered. It was a city split between two continents, Asia and Europe, with a rich history and vibrant present. The architecture was magnificent, a stunning combination of ancient mosques, modern buildings, and narrow, bustling streets. I marveled at the beauty of it all, my eyes wide in amazement.

Istanbul was a place of freedom—a stark contrast to the environment I had grown up in. As we walked through the streets, I observed something I had never seen before: independent businesses. Cafes and restaurants, not owned or controlled by the government, where people could gather, relax, and converse. People were free to live their lives however they chose—no government oversight, no restrictions on their personal choices. It felt like a breath of fresh air.

During dinner that evening, I was approached by a Turkish man who asked about my experience in Turkmenistan. I shared with him my dissatisfaction with life there, my yearning for something more. He seemed to sense my restlessness and offered me a job in Istanbul, suggesting that I stay there instead of continuing my journey to the United States.

I wasn't sure why he had singled me out—maybe it was the way I carried myself, or perhaps the way I walked. Maybe it was because I seemed different from the others. I had always felt like I didn't quite fit the traditional mold. But regardless of his reasons, I wasn't ready to stay. I had bigger dreams in mind—dreams of seeing the world, of exploring more than just Istanbul. My ultimate goal was to eventually move to Austria, and I couldn't let anything hold me back.

So, after a brief but enriching stay in Istanbul, I boarded the Lufthansa flight to the United States, bound for Houston, Texas.

Our first stop was Frankfurt, Germany, where we were supposed to transfer to another flight for Houston. We had a couple of hours for a layover, but then something unexpected happened: the vice minister of agriculture, traveling with us, suddenly experienced a health crisis—a heart issue that required immediate medical attention. An ambulance arrived to take him to the hospital, and we were left in a state of uncertainty.

At that moment, my mind raced with possibilities. I was stuck in Germany, without a German visa. My Soviet passport only allowed me to stay in the airport, and the border patrol made sure of that. But part of me wondered if I could somehow escape, if I could leave the airport and stay in Germany, maybe even make my way to Austria. After all, what was the point of going to the United States if it didn't feel like the right place for me?

I briefly considered making a run for it, pretending to leave the airport just to catch a breath of fresh air. But as I stepped out, I was confronted by two border patrol agents who asked for my passport. When they saw my U.S. visa, they questioned my intentions. I explained that I was waiting for my flight, but they insisted that I could not leave the airport without a German visa. So, reluctantly, I returned to the waiting area to board the flight to Houston.

The flight to Houston was uneventful at first, though I couldn't help but reflect on the strange turn of events in Frankfurt. I had been so close to abandoning my flight, to taking a different path altogether, but fate had other plans.

During the flight, I helped the vice minister of agriculture with translating for the flight attendants during meal service. I never imagined I would find myself in such a role—translating between languages on a plane headed to a new land. But then, something even more unexpected happened. A tragedy struck. An elderly woman on our flight, who was returning home, suddenly passed away.

The German flight attendants immediately sprang into action, attempting to revive her, calling for doctors, and doing everything they could to help. But despite their best efforts, the woman didn't survive. The flight attendants, in a thoughtful gesture, placed flowers on her seat in tribute to her. When we landed in Dallas, her body was taken away, and we were transferred to another plane, Continental Airlines, to complete the journey to Houston.

As I passed through immigration in Dallas, an African American officer asked me about my visa and how long I planned to stay in the United States. I explained that I was here to assist the vice minister, who was scheduled for heart surgery at a medical center in Houston. I told her that I wasn't sure how long I would stay, as the recovery time depended on the surgery.

Understanding my situation, the officer extended my stay for another two months, allowing me more time to stay in the country and assist as needed. And just like that, I was officially in the United States, unsure of what the future would bring but eager to face it head-on.

A Glimpse of America—Confusion and Curiosity

As we landed in Houston, Texas, the long, stretched limousine that awaited us was a testament to the official nature of the trip. It was an odd experience—driving through the city in a car so much more luxurious than anything I had encountered in my life. But as I gazed out the window, expecting to see the towering skyscrapers I had always associated with the United States, I was taken aback. The sprawling city was filled with smaller, more modest buildings—three, four, maybe five stories at most. Where were the iconic high-rises?

I remember asking the person who had picked us up, "Is this the United States? Where are all those high-rises we saw on Soviet TV?" The response I received was as surprising as it was humbling. "High-rises are only in the big cities like New York. Houston is considered more like a village in America," he explained. It was a stark realization that the image of the United States I had formed over the years was not entirely accurate. In fact, it felt quite different from the grandiose picture I had imagined.

But eventually, as we drove through downtown Houston, I did see a few high-rises, and there it was—the glimpse of what I had envisioned. It was the America I had known about. But even then, there was something unsatisfactory in the realization. The grand cities were there, but not in the way I had pictured. I had imagined every city in the U.S. to be a sprawling metropolis of concrete towers. It was a bit jarring to realize that reality didn't match the expectations my mind had built over the years.

We arrived at the Marriott Hotel at the Houston Medical Center, and the work of translating and assisting the vice minister with his medical visits began. Most of my time was spent at the hospital, helping the doctors, translating medical terms, and ensuring that everything went smoothly in preparation for the surgery. But despite being immersed in the day-to-day work, there was something gnawing at me—a growing urge to see the outside world. I had come to America, and though I was here for a specific purpose, I didn't want to leave without seeing at least a little of what the country had to offer.

As the vice minister went through his medical process and had some downtime before his surgery, I took the opportunity to explore. I ventured out of the hospital and into the streets of Houston. It was unlike anything I had ever seen. The streets were teeming with cars, something that had always seemed so foreign to me. I saw bridges that seemed to stretch endlessly into the distance, and the buildings loomed large, but it was still a strange mix of modernity and simplicity.

At one point, I found myself walking on what I later learned was a freeway, completely unaware that it was not intended for pedestrians. When a police officer stopped me, asking for my identification, I was taken aback. I explained that my passport was back at the hotel and that I was just a tourist trying to see the city. The officer kindly explained that the freeway was for cars, not people, and that I shouldn't walk there. It was a humbling moment, and it made me realize just how much I still had to learn about the culture and geography of this new world.

Houston, it seemed, was not a pedestrian-friendly city. Everywhere I looked, people were in their cars. The streets were made for vehicles, not people on foot. It was an overwhelming contrast to the communal way of life I had grown up with in the Soviet Union, where walking was the norm and public transportation was readily available. I found myself wondering where, then, people walked. It was a new puzzle to solve in a place so different from everything I had known.

During my stay, I met a variety of people at the hotel. One of them was a Jewish-American woman who owned a jewelry store. I can't remember her name, but she was warm, welcoming, and very helpful. She took it upon herself to introduce me to some of the local slang, which was a bit of a culture shock. I had been taught British English— polite, formal, and structured. But here, people greeted each other with a casual, "What's up?" It sounded so strange to me. I could never quite get the rhythm of it right. "What's up?" I would say, unsure of the correct tone, while everyone laughed and corrected me.

Another person who helped me navigate this new world was Arlene, a woman who worked at the medical center, though I wasn't sure of her role—she might have been a medical assistant or worked in reception. Arlene was charming and took the time to explain how life worked in the United States. From how to hail a cab to which restaurants were the best for newcomers, she seemed to know everything. I was grateful for her insights as she helped me adjust to this new, foreign environment.

However, there was one person I didn't quite expect to clash with: the vice minister. While I had spent hours translating for him and assisting him in his medical procedures, I began to feel a growing frustration. The vice minister, though appreciative of my work, was not entirely pleased with my tendency to venture out and explore the city. After all, my primary purpose in the United States was to assist him, and he was growing impatient with my absences.

When I returned after visiting the zoo and botanical garden, he lectured me for disappearing without his permission.

"I need you here with me, translating, not wandering around," he scolded. I understood his point, but at the same time, I felt I couldn't just be confined to the hospital for the entire two weeks. I had come to America, after all, and I wanted to experience it for myself. Still, I acknowledged his frustrations and promised to stay close to him during his recovery.

As the days passed, the vice minister's surgery came and went, and he began his recovery. I found myself reflecting on my time in Houston, unsure of what to make of it all. The initial excitement of being in the United States had started to wane, replaced by a deep sense of doubt. I had come here with a clear plan: help the vice minister, return to Turkmenistan, and continue with my life. But now, with the surgery behind us and the trip nearing its end, I was torn.

I had begun to wonder if I could make a life here. Was Houston truly representative of what America had to offer? And if it wasn't, what other parts of America could be different? Could I find a place where I felt more at home? The more I thought about it, the more confused I became.

I had no real desire to stay in the United States permanently, but something kept pulling at me, something I couldn't quite name. The way people lived, the freedom they seemed to have, was intriguing. It was so different from the life I had known. But at the same time, I didn't feel completely drawn to it.

As the days passed, I continued to buy household items for my mother and even bought an iron for my landlady, but deep down, I couldn't shake the feeling of being at a crossroads. I wasn't sure if I wanted to stay or go. I was struggling to reconcile my love for the new experiences with the deep sense of disconnection I felt. Houston, Texas, was not the place I imagined myself living, but perhaps there was another part of America that would speak to me more. Yet, I didn't know where to start.

The Point of No Return

The departure day had arrived, and the time for making a choice was quickly slipping away. The limousine, which was meant to take us to the airport, waited outside the hotel, signaling the end of my stay in the United States. But as I sat there in my room, staring out of the window at the unfamiliar landscape of Houston, I was consumed by a whirlwind of conflicting thoughts. What was the right decision? Should I return to Turkmenistan, continue with my plans to go to Austria, or should I simply stay here and try to build a life in America? The decision weighed heavily on me, and the pressure to make the right choice was immense.

On the one hand, returning to Turkmenistan felt like stepping back into a suffocating life. The country, in the aftermath of the Soviet Union's collapse, was turning into a dictatorship, with increasing government control over every aspect of life. I had already seen enough of what the system had to offer. The idea of returning to a place where the government held power over everyone's lives, where freedom was limited, and where the possibility of leaving again seemed so unlikely, made the thought of returning unbearable. The reality of Turkmenistan after the fall of the USSR was a far cry from the imagined freedom I once hoped for.

Turkmenistan—a country where homosexuality is not just taboo but criminalized, punishable by a prison sentence of up to five years. A place where personal identity can become a legal liability. It is also a land marked by deep religious conservatism, where tensions have flared between the predominantly Muslim population and the small Christian minority. In such an environment, difference—whether in faith, orientation, or thought—is often met not with curiosity, but with suspicion, silence, or even open hostility.

Yet, on the other hand, the idea of staying in America, a country that felt both foreign and intoxicating, was terrifying. I had no idea how the immigration system worked, no understanding of how to navigate life here. I had come to this country as a translator for a medical mission, not with the intention of staying. My visa was about to expire, and I was unsure how I could remain legally. The naivety of my 22-year-old self, facing such a monumental decision with little understanding of the consequences, was striking. But something inside me told me I couldn't go back—not to Turkmenistan, not to that life.

I spent hours contemplating, looking out at the busy streets, watching the cars and people moving in a rhythm I couldn't yet comprehend. I thought about the friends I had made during my time in the hotel, about the friendly American woman from the jewelry store, and Arlene, who had been so helpful in showing me the ropes of navigating this strange new world. But none of that seemed enough to sway my decision to go back. My heart told me I couldn't return to the place that felt like a prison. The idea of staying here in America, though uncertain, felt like a chance to breathe, to finally find a place where I could explore who I was and what I wanted from life.

As the final moments of the decision loomed closer, I knew I couldn't go back. I couldn't step back into a life where I felt so trapped, so restricted. It wasn't just about the physical freedom—it was about the emotional and psychological freedom I had been craving for so long. So, with a heavy heart, I made the decision. I would stay in the United States. I didn't know what would happen or where I would end up, but I couldn't return to Turkmenistan.

I picked up the phone and called my mother, the person I loved most in the world, the person I knew would be devastated by my decision. She cried, asking me how I could do this to her and our family. She didn't understand, and I couldn't find the words to make her see why I had to do this. But I tried to explain that I couldn't live the rest of my life in Turkmenistan, that I needed to find my own path, even if it meant taking a huge risk. The emotional weight of leaving my family behind, of making them feel betrayed, was unbearable, but I had no other choice.

The limousine arrived to take us to the airport, and I told the vice minister of agriculture that my luggage was already in the car, ready for the flight. But inside, my heart raced. As we approached the airport, I knew the moment had come to act. I had planned everything. I would defect. I would not board the plane. I would stay behind.

As the airport loomed closer, my decision felt both final and terrifying. I was about to break from everything I had known, to leave behind a life that, for better or worse, had defined me. But I was also stepping into an unknown future, a future full of uncertainty. I had no idea how I would survive in this new world, how I would make a living, how I would even manage to stay legally. All I knew was that I couldn't go back, that I needed to make this leap. And so, as the limousine pulled up to the airport, I made my decision—I would stay.

I left the safety of the vehicle, my heart pounding in my chest, and walked away from everything I had known, choosing the uncertain freedom of a new life over the stifling predictability of my old one.

As I mentioned, I hid my luggage at the hotel where we were staying and told the minister that it was in the trunk of the car, ready to go. Of course, he still had my passport. When we arrived at Houston Intercontinental Airport, the driver began unloading the luggage from the trunk. That's when he noticed I didn't have mine. He looked at me, puzzled, and asked, "What's going on? Where's your luggage?" I calmly told him that I had decided not to return to Turkmenistan. He froze, his eyes widening in shock. After a long, tense silence, he finally asked, "Do you realize what you're doing? Do you have anyone here? Do you know the trouble you're causing? I made a promise to the government to bring you back."

I looked him in the eye and replied, "First of all, I'm old enough to make my own decisions. I didn't ask you to make any promises to the government on my behalf. I'm a free individual, and I'm making my choice." He was furious, clearly upset. He kept trying to convince me to reconsider. He asked if I had any friends in the U.S. – I didn't. "What are you going to do here?" he asked. I simply responded that I would figure it out, that I was going to stay and see what happened. If I didn't like it, I could always go somewhere else – but that wasn't my plan.

Earlier, during the drive from the Houston Marriott Hotel to the airport, there was a British man in the limousine. I didn't know his exact connection to the minister, but it was clear he was well-dressed and older, possibly involved in some business with Turkmenistan. Since the rest of the group didn't speak English, I started talking to him. I explained my decision to stay, and he immediately advised against it. "If they find out you're staying here illegally, you'll be deported. You should just board the plane and go back to Turkmenistan," he said. I told him I couldn't go back to that place. It was a country that persecuted people, restricted freedom, and held no opportunities for someone like me, especially since I didn't speak the local language. I felt trapped there.

I then asked the British man if he could lend me some money. I had already spent most of what I had on things I bought for the trip. He took me to an ATM, and the only thing he could give me was $30. It wasn't much, but it would have to do.

When we got to the check-in counter, I asked the minister to give me back my passport. He reluctantly handed it over. I followed him and the others all the way to the gate. In 1995, airport security wasn't as strict as it is now, so non-ticketed passengers were allowed to go through the security check and say goodbye at the gate. When the boarding process began, I told the minister I was not boarding the flight. I thanked him for everything and explained that I couldn't go back to Turkmenistan. He seemed confused and asked how he would explain to his superiors what had happened. I told him I'd just tell them that I had fallen ill and needed to stay in Houston for treatment.

When I later tried calling the company to explain, I was told that they had been instructed not to speak to me anymore. If I called, they were told to hang up.

My decision to stay had been seen as a betrayal.

Standing there at the airport, watching the plane take off without me, I felt a wave of panic. What had I done? I was in a foreign country with no friends, no family, and no money. I had only $30 in my pocket. What would I do now?

How would I survive? Where would I sleep? How would I get food or find work? It was a terrifying realization.

At one point, I considered going back to the airline and asking to board the next flight back, but something inside me told me not to. So, I took the shuttle back to the Marriott Hotel, where I still had my luggage. I hoped the staff wouldn't notice anything strange, since I'd been staying there for a while. When I arrived, a new shift had taken over at the front desk. They didn't know I had checked out, so I slipped in unnoticed and found a place to sit. I felt disoriented, unsure of what to do next. Hunger started to set in, so I went out to get some fast food to curb my appetite. Then, I came back to the hotel, still unsure of where I would sleep or how I would change clothes. I couldn't keep wearing the same clothes every day. People would notice something was off.

As I sat there, consumed by confusion and uncertainty, a valet guy came over. He was from Syria, and he had seen us coming and going from the hotel. He asked what had happened to my group. I told him they had left, and he asked what I was doing. I told him I had decided to stay and not go back.

A Leap of Faith

I remember my conversation with the valet at the hotel. When I told him that I had made the decision to stay in the United States and not return to Turkmenistan, he looked at me with a mix of shock and concern. He immediately placed his finger on his lips, motioning for me to be quiet, as if he feared someone might overhear.

He explained, softly but firmly, that if U.S. authorities found out I was staying illegally—or had overstayed my visa, even though it was still valid—I would face deportation. I was taken aback. The word "deportation" was foreign to me. I had never even heard of it before, nor did I understand the consequences it entailed.

He then asked me if I had a place to stay, to which I answered no. He also asked if I had a Social Security card, and when I replied that I didn't know what that was, he patiently explained that a Social Security card was required to work legally in the U.S.

Despite my lack of knowledge, he was determined to help. He kindly offered to drive me to the Social Security office to see if I could obtain a card. I agreed, unsure of what to expect. At the Social Security office, I nervously showed my Soviet Union passport and American visa. When the clerk saw my visa, she explained that because it was a tourist visa, I was not eligible for a Social Security card. I couldn't legally stay or work in the U.S.

After the disappointing news, I returned to the valet's car, explaining what had happened. With a steady calm, he asked where I planned to stay next. I told him I didn't know. He seemed to think for a moment and then suggested that I visit the Armenian church in Houston. "You're Armenian, right?" he asked. I nodded. He said the priest there might be able to help me, offering me a chance for some guidance or assistance.

I wasn't a devout Christian, but growing up in the Soviet Union, we weren't encouraged to believe in God. However, I had always been curious about different religions. Back in Turkmenistan, I had visited several churches—Presbyterian, Russian Orthodox, Baptist—trying to understand why different faiths worshiped the same God in such different ways. Though I wasn't sure what the church could do for me, I agreed to visit.

When I arrived at the church, I explained my situation to the priest. I told him I had decided to stay in the U.S., that I had nowhere to go, and that I was seeking help. His first question was about my last name, perhaps to ensure it sounded Armenian. When I told him I didn't speak Armenian, his demeanor shifted. He scolded me, asking how I could call myself Armenian if I didn't speak the language. His words stung, and his attitude felt harsh, even for a priest.

He informed me, rather curtly, that he couldn't offer any assistance. "You should leave," he said. But I wasn't going to leave. I looked at him, standing in the house of God, and reminded him that the Bible teaches us to love and help one another. "You can't turn me away," I said. "I'm here, and I will wait for you to help me."

Hours passed, and still, the priest seemed to ignore my presence. Just as I began to wonder how long I would sit there, a man walked into the church. He had come to make a donation. The priest briefly spoke with him and mentioned me. The man approached me with kindness in his eyes.

His name was Vladimir, and he was from my hometown, Baku. Azerbaijan. And as he listened to my story, he offered help. He invited me to his apartment, where I could meet his family and figure out what to do next. Vladimir's family was warm and welcoming. His wife, son, and daughter offered me a place to stay temporarily while I tried to figure out my next move.

Vladimir and his family fled Azerbaijan during the war, leaving behind everything they had ever known in search of safety and a new beginning. They eventually found refuge in the United States, settling in Houston, Texas—a city foreign in every way, yet filled with the quiet hope of starting over.

Life wasn't easy, but they worked hard to rebuild.

His wife found a job as a housekeeper in a hotel, quietly cleaning rooms with care and dignity, doing whatever she could to help keep the family afloat. Their son, still young but determined, took a job delivering pizzas, driving through the sprawl of Houston day and night to earn what he could. His daughter, newly a mother herself, stayed home most days, focused on caring for her child—a task both exhausting and sacred, especially in a land so far from her own.

They had escaped the war, yes—but survival didn't stop at crossing a border. It continued in small, daily acts of persistence. They were building a life, one shift, one delivery, one lullaby at a time.

At Vladimir's apartment, I met Andrei, a Russian Jew from Siberia who worked as a pizza delivery driver. Although Andrei didn't speak much English, he generously offered me a spot on his couch in his one-bedroom apartment, free of charge. In return, he asked if I could help him improve his English skills.

I agreed, feeling a sense of relief. Andrei took me back to the Marriott to collect my luggage, and I moved into his apartment, not yet understanding that this seemingly small act of kindness would present a whole new set of challenges.

Strangers, Shelter, and Survival

After moving into Andrei's apartment, life felt a little more manageable, even slightly more hopeful. Andrei, a Russian Jew from Siberia, worked long hours as a pizza delivery driver, and while he was out, I often stayed inside, glued to the television. American TV became my unexpected teacher. I was determined to adjust to this new world, and language was my first challenge. The English I had learned back in school was British, proper, and formal. But American English? It was full of slang, speed, and cultural references I'd never heard before. Watching sitcoms, news, and talk shows helped me tune my ear, sharpen my vocabulary, and better grasp American pronunciation.

But while TV taught me the language, it couldn't help with my growing discomfort. I didn't want to be a burden. I was grateful for Andrei's couch, but I needed a way to contribute, to earn money and support myself. The problem was that I had no work permit, no Social Security number, and no legal right to be employed. Andrei was honest with me: I'd have to find work "under the table." I didn't even understand the phrase at first. Only later did I realize it meant getting paid unofficially, off the books, invisible to the system.

My first job was humble but important to me: delivering pizza flyers. I would pedal a bicycle through neighborhoods, leaving flyers on doors, in mailboxes, or under windshield wipers. I was paid twenty cents per flyer, and occasionally more if someone actually placed an order. The bicycle, surprisingly, was a gift from a kind woman I had met at the Marriott Hotel. She was an American Jew, the owner of a jewelry store in the hotel, and one of the first people to truly see me, not just as a foreigner, but as someone in need. When I confided that I had chosen not to return home, that I had nowhere to go and no one to help, she stepped in. She rented a small moving truck, brought furniture—chairs, pans, small household items—everything to help me feel a little more stable. She also had a quiet intuition about me, something unspoken.

She once gently asked if I was gay. I didn't answer. I couldn't. Not yet. But she didn't push. Her kindness remained intact.

Soon after, I heard about a small international grocery store owned by a Lebanese-Armenian man. The store catered to immigrants hungry for the tastes of their homeland. I visited, explained my situation, and was offered a job. It was grueling: twelve-hour days, seven days a week, for $300 a week. But I accepted without hesitation. I had no safety net. No family. Just myself.

Life with Andrei began to shift. I was helping him with English, and we maintained a polite friendship. But something changed during a trip to a department store. He was speaking with a beautiful saleswoman, asking about perfumes. I couldn't tell if he was flirting or just being friendly—American customer service was still a mystery to me. Trying to be lighthearted, I sprayed one of the perfumes on him and asked what he thought. I was cheerful, playful—But to him, it was something else entirely.

His demeanor changed immediately. Defensive. Cold. Accusing. He asked me outright if I was gay, implying that my behavior was inappropriate, even threatening. I was shocked. That wasn't my intention at all. I apologized and pulled away. But the tension didn't fade. When we returned home, it only escalated.

He became distant, resentful. Eventually, he asked me to leave. I had nowhere to go.

Then came the night that changed everything. The confrontation turned physical. He struck me. Kicked me in the face. Blood streamed from my nose. I had never fought anyone in my life, never lifted a hand in violence. I was stunned, terrified, and bleeding.

Someone advised me to call the police. I hesitated, but eventually picked up the phone. When the officers arrived and saw my injuries, they handcuffed Andrei and took him away. At the station, he called his friends. Soon, they were knocking at the door, urging me to drop the charges. If I didn't, they threatened to report me to Immigration. "They'll deport you," they warned. "You'll be gone."

I was trapped. Bruised and battered, both physically and emotionally, I stood at a crossroads. I didn't want to press charges—but I also didn't want to betray myself, to let someone harm me without consequence. I didn't know how the American legal system worked. I didn't know what protections I had, if any. All I knew was that I was alone, in a foreign land, with nowhere left to turn.

From Shelter to Struggle

After the incident with Andrei, I knew I couldn't stay there any longer. I had saved up a bit of money and, unsure of where else to go, rented my own apartment in the same complex. It felt safer to remain in familiar surroundings. With the help of the kind woman from the Marriott Hotel—the one who owned the jewelry store—I managed to furnish the place. She brought me kitchen supplies, a couple of chairs, even some pots and pans. Thanks to her generosity, I made the new apartment feel like a home.

Meanwhile, the pressure from Andrei's friends intensified. They kept urging me to drop the charges, warning me that if I didn't, they would report me to immigration authorities. Eventually, I relented. At the courthouse, the prosecutor asked if I was being coerced, and if I understood that dropping the charges meant my medical expenses wouldn't be covered. I told him yes—I wasn't forced, and I understood the consequences. And just like that, it was over. I never heard from Andrei again. I think he moved out of the complex. Despite everything, I was still grateful he gave me shelter when I had nowhere else to go. I never intended to hurt him or make him uncomfortable. What happened in that department store was never meant to provoke or mislead—it was misunderstood, and tragically so. But his violent reaction, the way he cornered me and beat me... that changed something in me. I had never experienced such cruelty so personally. It opened my eyes to how quickly people could let fear and impulse override reason and compassion.

I continued working at the grocery store, where I spent two more years. I climbed ladders, stocked shelves, packed cheese and fish, and helped with deliveries. It was gruelling—eight in the morning until eight or nine at night, seven days a week. But it paid the bills. I was proud that I could send money to my parents and even help my sister a little. Though I needed help myself, I often sacrificed my own needs to support my family. It was tough. Lonely. But I managed.

Still, I couldn't stop thinking about what I'd left behind—my education, my goals, my dreams. I enrolled in Houston Community College and began taking Spanish classes. Living in Texas, I was surrounded by Spanish speakers, especially among my coworkers and the customers. I wanted to communicate better, and the classes helped me build conversational fluency. In time, Spanish became my third language, after Russian and English. I also signed up for computer classes, wanting to understand the basics of technology.

At that time, I rarely thought about my legal status. I was so consumed by work and survival that I didn't even realize I was becoming what the world calls "stateless." The concept didn't exist in my vocabulary. I couldn't comprehend how someone could lose their citizenship just because their country collapsed. But that's what happened. With no valid passport, I couldn't travel freely or seek protection. I was floating—without a home, without a flag.

While working at the grocery store, I met all sorts of people, especially Russian-speaking immigrants—many of them Jewish—who shared bits of their own stories with me. One woman in particular was especially kind. I had helped her often, and eventually I asked her if she knew anyone who could help me find a better job. I didn't want to stay in retail forever. Back when I was studying in Turkmenistan, I had told a teacher that I wanted to travel the world or maybe one day run my own travel agency. That dream had always lingered in the back of my mind, and little did I know—it was quietly waiting to become reality.

Learning the Road, Losing Illusions

While working at the grocery store and commuting everywhere by bicycle, I realized just how vast and pedestrian-unfriendly Houston really was. Riding to and from work every day became exhausting, and I started thinking seriously about getting a car. Eventually, I bought a used one—I think it was a Mazda or Honda, though I can't quite remember. It sat parked in the grocery store's lot because, truthfully, I had no idea how to drive. Back in the Soviet Union, owning a car was never an option, so I never learned.

One rainy morning, I decided to take a day off work to teach myself how to drive. With the keys in my hand and zero experience, I slid into the driver's seat and started the engine. Slowly, cautiously, I began moving through the streets until, without realizing it, I found myself on the freeway. Cars sped past me like rockets while I crawled along, completely unaware of how fast I was supposed to be going. People honked angrily, and I was terrified.

I didn't even understand how to exit the freeway—I just kept going straight, completely lost. After about an hour and a half, I finally figured out what an "exit" sign meant and pulled off at a gas station. I asked the attendant where I was, and he told me I had driven far outside Houston. I'd need to head back—another hour and a half.

That experience, terrifying as it was, marked the beginning of my journey toward independence. Slowly, I learned how to drive. I figured out how to switch lanes, how to observe signs and signals, and how to find my way. At that time, there were no smartphones, no GPS, and no Google Maps. You had to memorize streets, use paper maps, or ask strangers. But I did it, and driving became a huge part of reclaiming freedom in a place where everything felt so spread out and unreachable.

It was during that time at the grocery store that I met Cristiana. She was Romanian, beautiful, with striking features and a quiet presence. She worked at the register and always made an effort to talk to everyone, to spread warmth and kindness. At first, she didn't speak much about her past. But one day, she confided in me—she had once been a model, walking the runways for names like Yves Saint Laurent and Pierre Cardin in Paris, London, and Rome.

I was stunned. I'd only seen models in Soviet fashion magazines—goddess-like women wearing elegant clothes, living glamorous lives. How could someone like that end up working in a grocery store? Something didn't add up.

Cristiana didn't reveal much at first. But then, one day, she arrived at work with her head completely shaved. People whispered. Some thought she might be ill. But Cristiana carried herself with confidence. She wore no wig, no headscarf.

When we finally sat down to talk, she told me the full story.

She had married a British man who owned his own company. They lived well—a townhouse, beautiful cars, luxurious furniture. But her husband got into legal trouble with taxes. The government seized everything. They lost their home, their possessions, everything. He eventually returned to the UK, and they separated. Cristiana stayed behind in Texas with nothing. From glamorous photo shoots to scanning groceries, her life had flipped upside down.

The loss shattered her. In search of healing, she turned to Buddhism. Shaving her head was part of her spiritual journey. She began attending Buddhist temples and prayer sessions and talked often about kindness, peace, and giving. Her transformation was deep and sincere. Then, just like that, she disappeared. I later heard she had moved to a village in India to devote herself to helping the poor.

Cristiana's story opened my eyes. It made me realize how fragile success can be. One day you have everything, and the next, nothing. I used to hear people say, "Money can't buy happiness." I understood that now. No, money doesn't bring joy—but it does bring security. Without it, you can't buy food, pay rent, dress properly, or travel. Money may not make you happy, but it gives you the basic means to live. And that, in itself, is a kind of freedom.

Becoming Stateless

Days turned to weeks, weeks to months, and eventually years. Still, I couldn't grasp what was quietly unraveling beneath me: I was becoming stateless.

One day, nearing the end of 1996, I decided to visit the Lufthansa office in Houston to see if I could change the return ticket I had bought long ago. I handed them my Soviet passport, only to be told it was no longer valid. The USSR had collapsed. I needed a passport from one of the newly independent republics—Armenia, Azerbaijan, or Turkmenistan. But I had none of those.

I returned home stunned. It hadn't occurred to me before that I no longer belonged to any country. I was unprotected, vulnerable, without a legal identity. It still didn't fully sink in.

Back at the grocery store, a customer and I got to talking. I told her I was searching for something bigger, something more meaningful. She mentioned a friend of hers—a Russian Jewish woman named Nelly— who ran a travel agency and was looking for help.

When she said "travel agency," something inside me lit up. I remembered telling a university professor that I wanted to explore the world, be like Columbus, discovering new places. I didn't hesitate. I told her I'd love to meet Nelly, even though I knew nothing about the travel business.

Soon, she returned with good news: Nelly wanted to see me. At the interview, Nelly hired me and promised to train me from scratch. I quit the grocery store and entered a new world.

I learned the Amadeus reservation system: how to issue and reissue tickets, reserve seats, process refunds, and book car rentals. It was thrilling. Geography became a living subject—no longer just maps in a textbook. I was suddenly part of a global conversation.

Even before the travel agency, while I was still living with Andrei, he had advised me to file for political asylum in the U.S. based on being a refugee from the Armenian-Azerbaijani conflict. He said it might help me legalize my status.

But there was another truth I wasn't ready to tell: that I was gay.

Living in Turkmenistan, a Muslim authoritarian state, homosexuality was illegal, punishable by up to five years in prison. The law was inherited from the Soviet criminal code. Coming out wasn't an option. It meant danger, disgrace, possibly even death. The society I lived in despised people like me. I had hidden my truth for so long, I didn't know how to reveal it—not even in a country like America, which I wasn't sure would accept me either.

So, I decided, if I filed for asylum, it would be based on the war, on being a refugee. But I didn't have money for lawyers. The few I met were cold, greedy, and charged outrageous fees.

I couldn't understand why I even needed a lawyer. I had lived through everything—I was the best person to tell my story. How could a lawyer, who had never been through what I had, represent me better than I could myself?

I didn't yet understand how the American legal system worked. I didn't understand that stories alone weren't enough. You needed the right voice, the right format, the right advocate.

But I would learn just like I learned to drive. Just like I learned to survive.

Filing for political asylum became one of the few viable options I could pursue. So many painful things had happened to us—things I still can't bring myself to fully disclose. I don't want to go into graphic detail or re-traumatize myself or others by recounting the full extent of what Armenians endured during that time. But the truth is, what we went through in Azerbaijan during the late '80s and early '90s was nothing short of ethnic cleansing. The arrests, the interrogations, the constant threats of death—we lived under the shadow of cruelty and terror. Even our family members suffered.

It's too painful to relive, and I don't want to fill this book with images that would make it harder to read. Instead, I've chosen to write it in a more approachable tone, while still honoring the truth. We had to flee, leave behind everything—our apartment, our neighbors, our sense of safety—and run toward an uncertain future in search of refuge.

To begin the asylum process in the United States, I had to fill out numerous forms and write detailed explanations about what had happened to me and my family. I gathered as much evidence as I could: testimony from friends, personal experiences from school where Armenian students were beaten and forced out, and even documents about our time in Turkmenistan, where we still felt unwelcome as refugees. Turkmenistan, though not a war zone, was not a safe haven either. They didn't want to take in more Armenians, and even there we felt like outsiders, constantly facing subtle and not-so-subtle threats.

There were also traumatic experiences at the university that I've chosen not to include in this book, because some wounds are still too raw to share.

After submitting my asylum application, I received a notice that my case had been accepted for processing. I was told that while it was pending, I could apply for a Social Security number and a work permit. So, I did. My employment authorization was approved, and with it, I received my Social Security card. It stated clearly: "Valid for work only with INS authorization." That meant if my work permit wasn't renewed, I couldn't legally work. But at that moment, it felt like a huge step forward. I also used it to get a driver's license. For the first time, I had the documents I needed to begin building a life in America.

Eventually, I was summoned to immigration court for my first hearing. I went alone. When the judge saw me, she seemed surprised— almost amused—and asked where my attorney was. I explained I couldn't afford a lawyer, and I had come to represent myself. She wasn't impressed. She told me I needed legal representation and a translator, since my "official language" was listed as Russian.

That didn't make sense to me. I told her I spoke English and preferred to represent myself in English. After all, I was in an American courtroom—I wanted to use the language of the country. But she didn't accept that. She postponed my case for three months and gave me a list of pro bono lawyers, encouraging me to find representation and bring a translator.

Over the next few months, I contacted the lawyers on her list, but they were all overwhelmed and unable to take on new cases. The time flew by. When the court date came, I had no lawyer, and I went back alone once again. She was visibly upset that I hadn't followed her instructions.

Again, I explained that no pro bono lawyers were available and that I still preferred to speak in English. She insisted on using a translator. A man from NASA—of all places—was brought in to interpret Russian, but I refused. I didn't want to speak Russian in court. I was emotionally detached from that language—it represented too much of the pain and oppression I had endured. I felt strongly that if I was to tell my story, I had to do it in English.

Frustrated, the judge eventually told me I would have to proceed without a lawyer. But even then, I wasn't allowed to refer to my notes during questioning. Every time I tried to collect my thoughts or reference my evidence, she cut me off. I couldn't fully present my case. It was like being asked to prove the most traumatic story of your life, with your hands tied behind your back.

I had the sense that she held something against me—perhaps for not obeying her instructions, or perhaps for my refusal to use Russian. Either way, she concluded the hearing by saying she didn't have enough evidence to grant me asylum. My application was denied.

She told me I had two options: forced deportation or voluntary departure.

The Deportation Dilemma

Back in immigration court, after my asylum was denied, the judge gave me two options: forced deportation or voluntary departure. The difference, I was told, was that with forced deportation, you would be taken directly into custody from the courtroom and held until the government arranged your removal. With voluntary departure, you were given a set period, usually around 60-90 days, to leave the country on your own. You had to pay for your ticket, gather your belongings, and prove you had left the U.S. within that timeframe.

I chose voluntary departure, not fully understanding what that entailed. At that moment, the judge asked me what country I wanted to be deported to. I thought it was an odd question, but answered honestly: I asked to go to an English-speaking country—Canada, the United Kingdom, Australia, or New Zealand.

To my surprise, the judge immediately shut those options down. She said the United States didn't have agreements with those countries to accept individuals deported from the U.S.

That made no sense to me. Why ask where I wanted to go if I couldn't go to any of the countries I named? It felt like a cruel trick question—one that only highlighted how powerless I really was.

Then she told me I would be deported to Russia.

I was stunned. I wasn't a Russian citizen. I never had a Russian passport. I tried to explain that I held a Soviet passport, which, by that time, was no longer valid. The Soviet Union had collapsed years earlier, and each former republic, including Russia, had become independent, with its own citizenship and immigration laws. I wasn't automatically considered a citizen of Russia just because the U.S. court couldn't distinguish between the Soviet Union and the Russian Federation.

To help the judge understand, I offered an analogy: "Imagine if the United States of America ceased to exist, and all 50 states became independent countries—the Republic of California, the Republic of Texas, the Republic of New York. Just because you once had a U.S. passport wouldn't mean you automatically have citizenship in any of those new republics. You'd need a new passport, a new legal identity. That's what happened to me. The Soviet Union disappeared. Russia is now a different country."

But the judge dismissed it. She said, "Russia and the Soviet Union are the same."

They weren't. They aren't.

To make things even more confusing, I knew that my Soviet passport couldn't be used for travel anymore. I had already experienced this when I visited the Lufthansa office to inquire about changing a ticket—they told me point-blank that Soviet passports were no longer accepted. Without a valid passport, how was I supposed to board an international flight? What airline would even let me on?

Still, the court insisted I'd be deported to Russia—a country I had no legal tie to.

And here's what I also didn't understand at the time: voluntary departure isn't just about buying a ticket and leaving. You have to notify immigration authorities of your travel plans. In some cases, you're required to check in at the airport so that officials can confirm you actually left. If you fail to do that, your voluntary departure turns into a deportation order. On top of that, if you leave under forced deportation, you're banned from reentering the U.S. for 10 years.

If you comply with voluntary departure properly, the ban is usually five years.

None of this was clearly explained to me. I didn't know that I had 30 days to appeal the judge's decision. I had no lawyer. No one told me what steps to take. That 30-day window closed without me ever filing anything, and just like that, my case was over. I was officially considered "in removal."

But no one came after me. No one arrested me. No one checked if I had left. I simply continued living my life, working, trying to support myself, and trying to process the chaos of what had just happened. I had no valid travel documents, no citizenship, and nowhere to go. I was stuck in a legal and emotional limbo, struggling to understand how I ended up in this strange, uncertain place—and what would happen to me next.

Discovering America, Discovering Myself

After my deportation hearing, everything felt like a fog. I wasn't panicked, nor was I particularly scared. I was in a strange in-between space—a vacuum.

There was no sense of urgency, no fear that someone was coming to find me. Life, oddly enough, just continued.

Sitka, Alaska

I kept working at the travel agency, built friendships, and tried to find some rhythm. But deep inside, I still carried this weight: the feeling that I belonged nowhere. My brain couldn't fully accept it. I was a man without a country, without legal status, without a future I could clearly imagine.

But then, something unexpected gave me a sense of direction—literally and metaphorically. I had a driver's license, I had a work permit, and most importantly, I had a desire to explore. Since I couldn't leave the United States, I decided: why not discover it? Why not become my own Columbus?

I traveled beyond Texas—Louisiana, Florida, California, Nevada, New York, Alaska, Puerto Rico, and even the remote Aleutian Islands. Each state was like stepping into a different country, as diverse and vibrant as the world I once dreamed of seeing. Hawaii especially stood out with its beauty, its calmness, and its spirit of aloha. In contrast, New York, with all its skyscrapers and endless motion, felt overwhelming and impersonal. People were always rushing, never stopping. I realized I couldn't live in a place like that. I needed space to breathe, reflect, and simply be.

Aleutian Islands, Dutch Harbour

Traveling across the U.S. allowed me to witness the true face of the country, not the caricature we were fed in the Soviet Union. Yes, America was capitalist and fast-paced. But it was also richly diverse, full of contrasts and contradictions. I met people from all over the world. I saw communities thriving, and others forgotten.

I quickly learned that in America, money is everything. Without money, you are invisible. You don't work—you don't get paid. You don't get paid—you can't survive. It was that simple. In the Soviet Union, we might have had limitations, but we also had a safety net. If you were sick or had to care for a family member, your salary didn't disappear. Here, in the U.S., even a simple illness could push someone into a crisis.

The concept of homelessness also hit me hard. Back in the USSR, homelessness was almost unheard of. Here, I learned that it wasn't just about laziness or addiction, as some people claimed. Many people became homeless because of unexpected medical bills, layoffs, or just bad luck. And yet, some chose it as a way to escape the pressures of modern life.

I started to feel that this country was designed for the rich. A regular person, living paycheck to paycheck, would be lucky just to survive, let alone travel or dream big. Education wasn't free. Healthcare certainly wasn't. I was shocked to find out how expensive it was to see a dentist or how a hospital stay could bankrupt someone. In the Soviet Union, these basic human needs were never tied to your income.

I also discovered the harsh reality of credit scores. Your whole life here could be reduced to a number. Fall behind on a hospital bill or default on a loan, and your credit is ruined. And with bad credit, your future is locked out—no car, no home, no second chance.

All of this was overwhelming. I often wondered how people in this country managed to survive, to smile, to find peace. But slowly, I began to understand. Americans are always in survival mode—because they have to be.

Yet, despite all of this, my travels gave me something I didn't expect: perspective. I wasn't just discovering America. I was discovering myself.

Building Myself, Building Bonds

My time as a travel agent in Houston spanned nearly a decade. Over those years, I grew more confident in my role—booking flights, confirming seats, even pulling off some impossible tricks to make things work. The skills I developed were fulfilling and helped me support myself. But despite this newfound competence, one question lingered in the background: my sexuality. It was something I kept hidden, something I wasn't ready to confront.

Living in Houston, my life was fairly solitary. I went to work, came home, and sometimes found comfort in small, quiet moments: buying music CDs at Blockbuster, renting movies, or catching a film alone at the theatre. I was okay being by myself. As a Pisces, I found peace in solitude, using the time to reflect on everything swirling inside me. But I had friends, too. We'd hang out, talk, laugh—anything to push away the quiet discomforts I was holding in.

I didn't have a plan for the future. In fact, I felt like I was living day by day. My situation as someone without proper documentation left me floating in uncertainty. I couldn't plan for what would come next because I didn't know where I stood. I sent most of my money to support my parents, so there wasn't any leftover to save. Yet, I managed to buy things I'd always dreamed of—clothes, especially. Growing up in the Soviet Union, I'd leaf through fashion magazines, yearning for the day I could wear stylish, beautiful clothes. Now, in the United States, I could. This independence—being able to buy what I wanted with my own money—felt empowering. For the first time, I was shaping my own life, standing on my own feet, without anyone's help.

But despite that independence, a part of me remained hidden. My secret about being gay was something I kept locked inside, along with the fear of my statelessness. And when the time came for a change, I found a new opportunity at a larger travel agency, Airfare Busters. The job was familiar, but it had its own rhythm. I settled into my own cubicle, taking calls, making bookings, and printing out tickets. At the time, before the convenience of online booking, everything was done manually, and I found that process fascinating in its own way. It was an era that now feels nostalgic, even though it had its challenges.

Demi and I reunited in Nafpaktos, Greece. 2024

It was at Airfare Busters that I met Demi. She was Greek-American, tough as nails, but with a heart of gold. She had a way of cutting through nonsense and standing her ground that could make her a bit intimidating. But I came to see her differently. Beneath her hard exterior, she was someone I could count on, someone who became like a second sister to me. We'd hang out outside of work, share our highs and lows, and even get mad at each other from time to time. But that's what family is, right? The ups and downs, the forgiveness, and the bond that hold you together.

With Demi, I found a kindred spirit—someone who understood the complexities of life and wasn't afraid to offer advice or lend an ear. For the first time since leaving home, I had someone I could rely on. Someone who knew my secrets, the struggles I faced, and yet accepted me as I was. We were as close as family, and for me, that bond was everything.

I'm not the type to approach people easily. I tend to observe, to let things unfold naturally. But Demi saw something in me, and she took the first step. From there, our friendship blossomed. And in that connection, I found not just a friend, but someone who helped me navigate the uncertainty I carried within me.

There were times when I felt utterly broke and truly needed money. That's when Demi became my lifeline—my "bank," as I called her. I would borrow money from her, promising to pay it back as soon as I got my next paycheck. Demi wasn't someone who easily lent money to others. She had high standards, and if she did lend it, she expected it to be returned promptly. No waiting around for months. It was always a test, a trial for me, but I respected it. It felt like a safety net, knowing that I had someone who had my back when I was in dire straits.

I learned a lot from Demi. She didn't just give without conditions, but when she did, it was genuine support. She also taught me the value of being upfront, of honoring commitments. She wouldn't let me off easy if I couldn't return the money on time, but she was understanding enough to let me extend the repayment if necessary. To me, Demi wasn't just a coworker or a casual friend; she was someone I could call a true friend—a rarity in my world.

The word "friend" in the Soviet Union held much weight. It wasn't something you threw around carelessly. It meant someone who would stand by you, defend you, and support you no matter what. Demi earned that title in my heart. She was my rock in a city that didn't quite feel like home. I learned to appreciate her tough exterior because underneath it, there was kindness and loyalty—something I hadn't experienced often.

Despite all of this, I still struggled with Houston itself. The sweltering heat, the stagnant air that seemed to rise from the asphalt, the frustrating public transport system—it all made me feel trapped. The bus system was nowhere near what I was used to in the Soviet Union, and I often found myself relying on Demi to drive me to work or to get me around. I'd bought a used car once, but I had no idea how to take care of it. I didn't know that I needed to check the oil or water, so one day, while driving on the freeway, I panicked when smoke started billowing out of the car. I thought it was going to explode. Without thinking, I pulled over, abandoned the car, and walked away. It was a stupid move, but I was so scared and didn't know what else to do.

And then, in the midst of all this chaos, I began to feel the stirrings of change. At Airfare Busters, I started to slowly open up about my sexuality. For the first time, I felt the weight of those hidden parts of me becoming a little lighter. I was still in a period of uncertainty, but I was starting to feel more comfortable in my own skin. It wasn't easy, but it was a necessary step in my journey toward self-acceptance.

Letting Go and Embracing Myself

Joey, a Puerto Rican guy at Airfare Busters, was a character who didn't leave me indifferent. He was openly gay, feminine, and effortlessly attractive. I noticed his charm, his confidence in being himself, and it made me realize something—it was time to stop holding back and start embracing who I truly was. Seeing him live so openly gave me the courage to start letting go of the fear I had carried for so long.

Up until then, I'd kept a tight lid on my identity. Demi knew, of course. We never discussed it explicitly, but I think she understood. After all, I hadn't been with anyone in years—not since my last encounter with Arnold back in Baku. In Turkmenistan, I had never even considered acting on my feelings. It wasn't safe. In the U.S., I was still hesitant, unsure of when the "right" time would be. It wasn't until 1998 that I even felt the courage to start facing my sexuality. I knew deep down that I was gay, but it took time to truly accept it.

When Greg, our manager at the travel agency, approached me about going to a gay club, I felt a mix of nerves and excitement. I had never been to one before. The thought of being surrounded by so many people like myself was terrifying, but I knew it was something I had to experience. So, one night, I took a deep breath, dressed up nicely, and agreed to go with Greg.

As we arrived in the Montrose area, the heart of Houston's gay district, my breath caught. It was like stepping into a world I had only imagined but never dared to enter. People were laughing, dancing, and just being themselves. There was no shame, no judgment—just freedom. And for the first time, I felt like I had found my place in the world.

Inside the club, the atmosphere was electric. There were drag queens performing, male strippers dancing, and everyone was just alive with joy. I watched in awe, feeling my fears melt away. This was the world I had dreamed of when I was in the Soviet Union, where I could be free, where I could be myself without hiding.

I turned to Greg, and I could see the smile on his face. He had helped me break down a barrier I had held for so long. The weight of years of fear, of internalized shame, lifted in that moment. I had found my people, my tribe. And I knew that I could go back to that club anytime I wanted—because it felt like home.

I made a promise to myself that night: I would come back to this space where I could be truly free. No more hiding, no more pretending. It wasn't my choice to be born this way, but it was who I was. And that was okay. I was learning to accept myself, to love myself, and to embrace the person I had always been.

For the first time in my life, I didn't feel like I had to apologize for who I was. And in my heart, I knew that God, who created me in His image, loved me just as I was. I had nothing to fear anymore.

Greg was a striking figure at Airfare Busters. He was a man with a blend of charisma and confidence that stood out, especially in contrast to Joey's more openly feminine energy. Greg's appearance and demeanor gave the impression that he was the kind of person who thrived in control and knew exactly how to command attention. His look wasn't flamboyant like Joey's; rather, he exuded a kind of polished masculinity, one that balanced both his private and professional lives with poise.

While Joey was open and overtly expressive about his gay identity, Greg was more guarded, less transparent in his outward expressions. There was an air of protectiveness about him, particularly when it came to his space within the workplace. He wasn't keen on sharing the limelight with other openly gay people, positioning himself as the "only queen" in his domain, which made him both a bit of an enigma and, at times, a figure to be reckoned with.

Physically, Greg wasn't overly muscular, but he carried himself with the confidence of someone who didn't need to flaunt his strength. His clothes were tailored to his tastes, fitting the role of someone who was both professional and sharp, always well-put-together.

Despite his sometimes-prickly exterior, Greg had a side to him that was approachable, especially when he saw potential in someone. It was clear that his invitation to show me the gay scene in Montrose came from a place of wanting to share something important to him, a part of his identity that he felt could help me open up to my own. He was more than just a manager at work—he was a guide in his own right, leading me toward a new chapter in my life.

But Greg's complexity lay in his contradictions: while he was protective of his position and guarded about sharing his world with others, he had a depth of understanding and a willingness to help someone else break through their own barriers. This made him both someone to admire and someone who could sometimes make others feel like they had to prove their worth to him.

Montrose: A Door to Freedom

After that first night out with Greg in Montrose, something shifted inside me. I had never seen anything like it before—the music, the freedom, the confidence, the sea of men who were unapologetically themselves. That night marked the first time in my life I felt free. Truly free. I returned home with a racing heart and a mind full of images and emotions I had long buried.

The very next day, I went back to work like nothing had changed, but everything had. I couldn't stop thinking about what I saw, what I felt. That sense of belonging, of being surrounded by people who didn't judge me, who lived without fear—it was magnetic. I wanted more. So, I made a decision: I would go back to Montrose every night after work. And I did. I don't remember how long it lasted—weeks, maybe months—but I was hooked on the feeling of finally being alive.

I found myself drawn not just to the scene, but to the people. Men of every race, nationality, and background. It didn't matter where they were from or what language they spoke. None of the things that mattered so much in the Soviet Union mattered here. I was finally in a space where I could connect with others, and with myself.

Demi noticed. She was a bit worried about me going out so much, and at first, she seemed uncomfortable that I was spending time with Greg. They had been close friends, too, and maybe there was a bit of tension, but it passed quickly. Nothing could pull me away from the momentum I was building.

This nightly pilgrimage to Montrose was the beginning of my self-acceptance. For the first time, I didn't feel ashamed. I started to believe that being gay wasn't something to hide or fight—it was something to embrace. I began to see myself as someone worthy of love and pleasure. And I believed deeply that if God created me this way, there was no sin in it. God didn't abandon gay people. He loved everyone. I wasn't broken. I was just… me.

At first, I didn't have the courage to approach anyone. But surprisingly, they started approaching me. Compliments, conversations, and flirtations—it gave me a thrill. I started getting attention from men who were confident, attractive, and interested. It was exhilarating. It reminded me of the feelings I had years ago with Arnold back in Baku, that secret but powerful pull toward a man's body, a kiss, a touch.

Soon, I found myself exploring more than just the nightlife—I began exploring my own desires. I had several sexual encounters, most of them one-night stands. Not because I didn't value connection, but because I wasn't ready for commitment. I was just starting to understand who I was. I was reclaiming a part of myself that had been suppressed for so long.

I learned things in Houston that I'd never even imagined in the Soviet Union. Oral sex, the dynamics of giving and receiving pleasure— it was all new to me, but it felt natural. It wasn't just about satisfying myself. It was about seeing the joy and pleasure in my partner, and knowing I was a part of it. That connection, however brief, felt powerful.

In gay culture, I noticed something different from how I grew up: there was less shame around sex. Words like "slut" or "whore" weren't insults—they were playful, even empowering. If someone called me a slut, I didn't get offended.

Maybe I was one. I was having sex with different men, sometimes every day. But it was something I needed. Something I had longed for. And I wasn't ashamed of it.

I was finally exploring a part of my identity I had never been allowed to understand. And in doing so, I was learning to love myself—not just my body, but my spirit, my journey, and the deep, complicated, beautiful truth of who I was.

Discovering oral sex opened up a whole new dimension of pleasure for me—one that surprised and fascinated me in ways I never expected. There was something deeply intimate and erotic about it, something more than physical. The very idea of wrapping your lips, taking in a man's body—his warmth, his scent, his strength—and surrendering myself to the rhythm of that act felt electric. To feel him tense up, to hear the sound of release, to witness that moment of surrender—it was intoxicating. It was a moment of power and connection, where I felt in control, not as a dominator, but as someone who knew how to bring pleasure, how to offer something deeply fulfilling. That explosive release—it stayed with me. It felt volcanic, primal, unforgettable.

It was in America that I truly discovered this kind of intimacy. My encounters here, with men from all walks of life, awakened a deep hunger in me—not just for physical touch, but for self-expression. Oral sex, in particular, became something I craved, sometimes even more than intercourse. But I did both. I explored. I experimented. I wasn't bound by guilt anymore. Everything I had once believed to be forbidden—everything I had hidden away in the shadows of my old life—suddenly began to feel natural, even beautiful.

And let's not forget—this was the 1990s. Gay marriage was still a dream, not yet a conversation in mainstream society. But the United States, even then, felt like a place where gay people could breathe. We weren't being hunted or shamed like we were in places like Turkmenistan. Here, I could begin to see myself differently. I could accept that I was born this way. That I was worthy of love and pleasure and freedom.

For a while, I even forgot about my statelessness. I didn't care about not having a passport or citizenship. I was too busy embracing life, finally living it on my own terms. When friends invited me to travel overseas, I'd make up excuses: I was working, I was too busy. I couldn't bear to admit the truth—that I had no papers, no legal way to leave the country. But within the U.S., I was free to move, to explore, to be who I wanted to be.

And that included exploring the body and soul of another man. The touch of a man's skin against mine brought me back to an early memory—my older brother and I lying side by side in bed when I was a child. I remembered the fire inside me, the forbidden desire that I didn't yet understand. Back then, I couldn't act on it—I was scared, confused. But now, as an adult, I could finally give in to those long-repressed feelings. I could touch, I could kiss, I could lie between someone's legs and feel ecstasy wash over me. I had spent so many years suffocating under shame and silence. Now, every encounter felt like oxygen.

Those nights in Montrose became a ritual. I met new men and had new experiences. I stopped hiding. I started to feel wanted, desired, and seen. That made life easier in a strange way—both at work and outside. I was less anxious. Less afraid. I walked through life with more confidence.

Even how I dressed changed. I started shopping with a purpose—Armani, Zara, Gucci—choosing clothes that weren't overly provocative, but elegant and slightly suggestive. I wanted to be seen. To turn heads. I liked the idea of walking through a mall and catching someone's eye, sharing a glance that said everything without a word. Sometimes, that glance led to something more—a quiet corner, a shared moment of passion. It wasn't always about love or even connection. Sometimes, it was just about being desired, about feeling alive in my own skin.

And I didn't get tired of it. I was discovering myself, piece by piece. I was learning how to be fully, unapologetically me. I was accepting my body, my desires, and my sexuality. I stopped comparing myself to the past or worrying about what was considered "normal." Because here, in this new life, I finally realized—this was normal. This was me.

New Beginnings in Houston

My life in Houston continued to evolve. I was slowly discovering more about myself, about the city, and about the possibilities that life in America could offer. I made new friends, built connections, and eventually moved into a different apartment.

One of the starkest contrasts between life in the United States and life in the Soviet Union was the ease and freedom of movement, both in housing and employment. Back in the USSR, apartment buildings were government-owned and distributed freely to citizens. People typically stayed in the same apartment for decades, sometimes for their entire lives. Moving was rare, usually driven by necessity—relocation to another republic, a family emergency, or some directive from authorities. Jobs were similarly fixed. Once assigned a position, it was considered sacred. You didn't quit, and you didn't look for something "better" because everything—your salary, your future—was under government control.

In contrast, life in the U.S. was fluid. There were so many apartment complexes, all privately owned or managed, and people moved in and out constantly. It amazed me how easy it was to end a lease, pack up, and start fresh somewhere else—closer to work, or just for convenience. Jobs, too, were treated differently. If someone wasn't happy or wanted higher pay, they simply left and searched for another opportunity. It was a system driven by ambition, challenge, and choice—something completely foreign to me at first, but fascinating to witness.

Even in personal relationships, the cultural shift was noticeable. In the Soviet Union, marriages were long-term commitments. Divorce existed, but it was less common. In the U.S., I observed that many marriages didn't last. People sometimes got married out of loneliness or curiosity, and just as easily parted ways when things didn't work out. The vows felt more like temporary promises than lifelong commitments. It was disheartening to see how easily people gave up on one another.

Amid all these cultural revelations, my own life took a sharp turn. I had been working at a travel agency called Airfare Busters, and I truly loved the job. It was exciting, fast-paced, and fulfilling. I enjoyed helping people plan their trips and working alongside a group of dedicated coworkers. It felt like a small family.

But then something shocking happened—something we, the regular employees, never saw coming. Unbeknownst to us, the owner of Airfare Busters had been involved in money laundering. Our agency operated as a wholesaler—we purchased airline tickets at discounted rates and sold them to customers. But instead of issuing the tickets after taking payments, the owners were simply pocketing the money. Customers would show up at the airport only to discover their tickets had never been issued. The backlash was immediate and fierce.

Complaints poured in, eventually reaching the Texas Attorney General's Office. Still unaware of the full scope, we tried to maintain normal operations, but confusion and panic grew with every phone call from angry travelers stranded at airports. Then, almost overnight, the owners disappeared. The wife packed up and moved to Florida, and her husband vanished completely.

One Saturday, we arrived at the office to find it sealed off. Officials blocked our entrance and informed us that the business had been suspended due to criminal investigations. We weren't even allowed to retrieve our personal belongings. It was over.

I was devastated. I had invested so much emotionally and professionally in that job. The team, the energy, the satisfaction of helping people—it was all gone.

One of my coworkers, an Argentinian-American woman, Marta, and I were the last to hold on, hoping it was all a mistake. But eventually, we had to face reality.

With Airfare Busters gone, I was back at square one—searching for a job, unsure of what direction life would take next. It was a difficult time, full of uncertainty. But life has a way of opening new doors when you least expect it.

I eventually found a position at another travel agency called Save On Travels. To my delight, I reunited with my former coworker Demi, who had left Airfare Busters earlier. It felt like a lifeline—a chance to start fresh in familiar company. Shortly before Demi's arrival, another dear friend was part of our team, Holly, an Australian-American, with whom I used to spend time socially. The three of us became a tight-knit team, bringing laughter, energy, and warmth into the small office.

Save On Travels wasn't as large or flashy as Airfare Busters, but it didn't matter. I was once again doing something I loved—working in travel, helping people, and sharing daily life with people I genuinely cared about. It was a joyful, grounding experience after the chaos I had just gone through.

Acting Dreams in Houston

While working at Save On Travels, I found myself drawn to a new passion: acting. I had always been fascinated by movies—not just as entertainment, but as windows into different lives, emotions, and experiences. I wanted to understand what went on behind the scenes, how characters were built, and whether I had it in me to become someone else on screen, not out of escape, but as a way to explore a different part of myself.

I enrolled in an acting school called Next Actor Studio, located in the Rice Village area of Houston. It was run by Trisha and San, and from the very first day, I was hooked. Their encouragement, energy, and belief that anyone could act if they were willing to open up and push their limits gave me the confidence I needed. Acting became more than a hobby—it became a revelation. It allowed me to transform, to express emotions I often suppressed, and to become someone entirely different from the real me.

Trisha, the owner of Next Actor Studio. Houston, Texas

We began working on various independent films, and I even applied for background roles in big productions, including films connected to Quentin Tarantino. It was exciting to be part of the creative world, even if it meant standing in the background or waiting around for hours. The idea of being on a set, watching how a scene unfolded, seeing the camera crews, lighting, and direction—it all felt magical.

What made acting so transformative was the way it let me discover myself by not being myself. I could play emotional scenes, romantic characters, even dabble in comedy. It awakened a part of me I didn't know existed. And like music—where some singers are discovered early and others bloom late—acting, too, can find you at any age. It's not about timing; it's about readiness.

But acting came with a challenge: it demanded time—and a very unpredictable schedule. Most auditions, filming sessions, and rehearsals happened during the day. That created a conflict with my regular 9-to-5 job at the travel agency.

As my involvement in acting deepened, I had to start taking time off from work, sometimes unexpectedly. I would leave during business hours to attend auditions or join a shoot. This didn't sit well with Tony and Sharon, the owners of Save On Travels. Eventually, we had a serious conversation. I understood their frustration. They needed someone dependable during work hours, and I was increasingly unavailable. In the end, I had to leave the agency. Tony helped me find another job at a smaller travel agency, but the pay wasn't great. The same pattern continued: my heart was in acting, but my bills were paid by travel work.

I considered night jobs, like working in a restaurant, to free up my days for acting. But that brought its own set of problems.

The Waiter Experience

When I first arrived in Houston and was still finding my footing, I briefly worked handing out pizza flyers. Around that time, I also tried working as a waiter in a restaurant owned by an Iranian man. Interestingly, the restaurant itself catered to a Russian-speaking clientele and featured live music, making it feel oddly familiar and foreign at the same time.

I gave it a genuine try, learning the ropes of serving tables. But deep down, I knew this wasn't for me. In the United States, waiting tables is a respected and often lucrative job. But back in the Soviet Union, it had been looked down upon—considered something people did only if they had no education or prospects. That stigma was hard to shake.

One night sealed the deal for me. We were supposed to close at midnight, but a single couple—a Russian husband and wife—refused to leave. They kept drinking, requesting songs, and ignoring every cue that it was time to go. Hours passed. By 2 a.m., then 3 a.m., I was exhausted. But the owner insisted we stay until the last customer left. I couldn't believe it. If the restaurant was closed, how could customers just decide to stay as long as they liked?

Eventually, the woman demanded a cappuccino. I had reached my limit. I politely explained that we were supposed to close hours ago and suggested she enjoy her coffee at home instead. She got angry, demanded her $60 tip back, which I returned without hesitation, and I quit on the spot. That was the end of my waiting career.

I realized then that waiting tables wasn't a long-term solution, not just because of the hours, but because of what it demanded emotionally. I wasn't built to serve difficult customers until the middle of the night— and more importantly, it clashed with my creative drive and my need for structure and dignity in my work.

Acting remained a strong passion, even though it didn't pay the bills. I continued working on independent projects and staying connected with the film community in Houston. But the tension between making a living and following a dream kept growing. Eventually, the time came when I had to make a decision—to leave Houston behind and see what awaited me elsewhere.

Arrest

Being stateless was like hanging in the air, suspended between worlds with no ground to stand on. I didn't belong anywhere. The Soviet Union, the country of my birth, no longer existed, and with it, my passport was gone. In the United States, I couldn't obtain legal status or citizenship. On paper, I simply didn't exist. Physically, I was alive, breathing, and working. But legally, I was a ghost.

And that reality was incredibly frustrating. I didn't know what the future held. I didn't know what to do. I was stuck in limbo, confused, disoriented, and scared.

At the time, I was working at another travel agency called Intra-Tours. The owner's wife was from Costa Rica—American—and her husband was from Spain. We mostly sold tickets to South and Central America. I remember the day it happened vividly.

I was wearing all white—white jeans, white shirt. I had just returned from lunch. As I walked back in, I noticed two men standing by the reception window. It was a common setup; people came in to pick up airline tickets or ask questions. I assumed they were customers.

I approached the window and asked if they needed help. That's when they showed me their badges. Immigration and Customs Enforcement—ICE. They said they had a warrant for my arrest, signed by Attorney General John Ashcroft.

My heart dropped. I felt it sink to the floor. I was devastated. I hadn't done anything wrong. I tried to explain—no criminal record, no shady history. I paid my taxes since I started working in the U.S. I had no place to go. No home country to return to. I pleaded with them not to arrest me. I didn't even open the door at first.

My manager got involved. She spoke with them, vouching for me, telling them I was a good, hardworking person. But they wouldn't listen. I didn't know my rights then. I didn't know they legally needed a court order to enter. I just knew they were there, they had power, and I was helpless.

So why did they come after me?

It all went back to 9/11. When the Twin Towers were hit, we were all glued to the office TV, horrified. It felt like the whole country was about to go to war. We were heartbroken. The violence, the tragedy—unimaginable.

In the aftermath, under George W. Bush's administration, immigration authorities received broad orders: apprehend any immigrant with ties to Muslim-majority countries, or those who appeared suspicious based on origin. They were targeting people from Afghanistan, Saudi Arabia, Lebanon, and other countries.

My mistake? When I filed for asylum years earlier, the application asked for my point of departure. I had written "Turkmenistan"—

because that's where I had last lived before arriving in the U.S. Apparently, that was enough. Turkmenistan borders Afghanistan. So, they looked at my file and thought: Muslim country, border state—suspicious.

What they failed to realize—or simply didn't care to know—was that I wasn't Muslim. I was Armenian, from the Soviet Union. Turkmenistan was under Russian control, Russian was the main language, and I had no religious affiliations that aligned with their assumptions.

But ICE doesn't operate with nuance or deep knowledge. Based on my experience, they didn't seem to understand geography, history, or cultural context. It felt like they hired people off the street, handed them badges, and told them to round up "the others."

They tracked me down through my Social Security number. Since I paid taxes, they saw I worked at Intra-Tours. That was enough.

What made it worse was that at the time of the arrest, I had been actively writing letters to various embassies around the world, trying to find a country that would accept me, grant me asylum, and give me a future. I explained this to them. Again, they didn't care.

They handcuffed me in front of everyone. Told me I was being taken to the airport for deportation, though I had no valid passport, so I didn't understand how that was possible.

Instead, they drove me to a detention facility: the Corrections Corporation of America (CCA), a private prison under contract with the federal government.

And just like that, I went from selling plane tickets to being locked away, stateless, voiceless, and powerless. Arrested not because of who I was, but because of where I came from on paper, because of fear, ignorance, and a broken system that didn't care to ask questions.

Stateless: Caught in the Shadow of 9/11

I never, never in my life, imagined that I would be arrested. That was the last thing I ever thought could happen to me.

Growing up in the Soviet Union, my mother was extremely protective. She always told us, "Don't do anything bad. Don't ever get in trouble with the law. An arrest can ruin your life forever." It didn't even have to make sense—her warnings were firm and constant. Your reputation was everything, and one mistake could destroy your future.

I remember how hard my mother's life was. My father, who worked as a bus driver in Baku, Azerbaijan, had a tendency to drink. Sometimes, after a night of vodka, he would go to work with a hangover, and accidents would happen—right in the middle of the road. His driver's license would get suspended, and my mother had to run to the police station, pay bribes, and do whatever it took to get him released. Sometimes, when he wasn't allowed to drive, he would work as a conductor, collecting bus fares just to keep the family going. Her life was chaotic and stressful, but she always made sure we were protected—taught us never to cross the line, never to give the state a reason to touch us.

That's why my arrest shook me to the core.

I had never even been in trouble before. And now, suddenly, I was being handcuffed in front of my coworkers, escorted out of the building like a criminal. I kept thinking: What did I do? Was overstaying my visa really enough to be arrested? Was filing for political asylum that didn't work out—really a crime?

I didn't even know that people could be arrested just for being undocumented. That reality had never entered my mind. I came from the Soviet Union, where you could freely move between the 15 republics—Estonia, Ukraine, Turkmenistan, and Moldova—without being questioned about your legal status. It never occurred to me that being in a country without the right paperwork could be seen as criminal.

So yes, I was devastated. Completely disoriented.

And it all happened in the context of the 9/11 attacks, which had changed everything in the United States. It was a horrifying tragedy—thousands of lives lost in an instant. The whole country was in shock. But then came the backlash. Suddenly, anyone from a Muslim country—or even nearby—became a target.

ICE didn't care about geography or history. They didn't look at me as a human being. They just saw a name on a file, a country on a map, and a reason to act.

What made it worse was knowing how differently others were treated. In detention, I heard that some people from Saudi Arabia—where, ironically, the actual 9/11 hijackers came from—weren't held in immigration jails. Instead, they were put up in hotel rooms, under surveillance, but treated like guests.

Why? Because of politics. Because of oil. Because the U.S. has a long-standing relationship with Saudi Arabia and didn't want to jeopardize it.

It was a double standard—plain and simple. While people from countries like Afghanistan, Iraq, and Iran were rounded up, deported, and treated like enemies, others were handled with kid gloves.

It was heartbreaking to witness the generalizations. People were attacked simply for being Muslim. Their businesses were vandalized. Some were even shot or killed. In a country that prides itself on freedom and human rights, people had to hide who they were just to stay safe.

And I couldn't wrap my head around it. This was the United States—the land of liberty. And yet here we were, detaining and deporting people without regard for due process, human rights, or basic logic. People like me, who asked for asylum because we feared persecution, were being sent right back to the places we fled. How does that make sense?

When ICE arrested me, they told me they were taking me to the airport for deportation. But I didn't even have a valid passport. My Soviet passport was no longer recognized. I had no legal country of citizenship. Where were exactly they planning to send me?

Instead, they brought me to the CCA detention facility—a private prison run under contract with the government. I was stripped of my clothes and told to put on an orange uniform. I was given a number: 810.

I asked how long I would be staying. "We don't know," they said. "It depends on whether you see a judge or not." No timeline. No answers. Just prepare to stay for months.

It felt like I had fallen into a nightmare—a maze with no exit. I was caught in the aftermath of a national tragedy, a victim of fear, ignorance, and a broken immigration system. I didn't do anything wrong. I didn't hurt anyone. I simply asked for safety, for a chance at a life. And somehow, that made me a threat.

The **Corrections Corporation of America (CCA)** was one of the earliest and most prominent private prison companies in the United States. Established in 1983 in Nashville, Tennessee, it became a key player in the expansion of the for-profit prison industry, shaping the privatization of incarceration on a national scale.

CCA was responsible for building and operating prisons, jails, and detention centers across the country, often through contracts with federal, state, and local governments. These facilities housed a broad spectrum of individuals, from those convicted of criminal offences to immigration detainees and individuals awaiting trial.

One notable example is the **Houston Processing Center**, a facility operated by CCA. It is defined by a high-security perimeter, complete with barbed wire fencing and guard towers, embodying the typical layout of a detention site. The main structure is a single-story building with a pragmatic, utilitarian design, constructed to fulfil the core function of containment rather than rehabilitation. With tightly controlled access points and comprehensive surveillance systems, the center is built for maximum security and operational efficiency.

Love In the Time of Secret

Back in Houston, before my arrest, I had a boyfriend, Michael Barbe. He's no longer alive now; he passed away a long time ago. Michael was ten years older than I, a kind-hearted man from East Texas, from a small town called Nacogdoches. We met at a club in Montrose on my birthday. I went out to celebrate, not expecting anything, and there he was. He was staring at me from across the room, sipping his cocktail with a kind of quiet confidence. His eyes didn't wander—he kept them locked on me, unblinking, almost like a challenge. I tried to ignore it at first, pretending to be absorbed in my drink, in the music, in anything else. But his gaze was magnetic. I could feel it, even when I looked away.

And then he made his move.

Smooth, deliberate, and without hesitation, he walked up to me and leaned in just close enough to be heard over the music. *"What are you up to tonight?"* he asked, his voice low and casual, like we'd known each other for years.

I smiled and told him it was my birthday, that I'd come out for a few drinks, nothing wild—just to relax and celebrate in my own way.

He didn't miss a beat.

"Do you want me to be your birthday gift tonight?"

Straightforward. No games. Just those words, dropped like a spark into the air between us.

We spent the night together, and just like that, we became boyfriends.

Despite the two-hour drive between Houston and Nacogdoches, we made it work, seeing each other every weekend. He was a barber, warm and generous. He even bought me a car, a Buick, just so I could visit him more easily. That gesture made me feel cherished. We would switch weekends—sometimes I'd stay at his trailer, sometimes he'd come to my apartment in Houston. His roommate was a lesbian who lived with her girlfriend, and Michael had his own room. We lived as a couple—buying gifts for birthdays and holidays, traveling together, trying to build something that resembled a home, a family.

I had never been with a man before—not even a woman, not in any kind of real relationship. So, when it happened, it was all new to me. I found myself trying to understand what a relationship truly is—what it means to share your life with someone, to open up, to let another person in. It wasn't just about the emotions or the physical closeness—it was about figuring out how two people, often from entirely different worlds, learn to live beside each other, how they bridge their pasts, their cultures, their habits, their fears. I didn't have a blueprint, only questions—and a quiet hope that love, somehow, would teach me the rest.

I met his mother and his family—they were lovely, welcoming. He was the first man I ever dated. I don't know if I was truly in love or if I was simply obsessed, overwhelmed by the idea of being with someone, especially an American, which still felt surreal. There were no cell phones for me back then, so I used payphones to call him, and we'd talk for hours. I was trying so hard to build something real. Something stable.

But over time, things started to change. Michael stopped visiting. He always had excuses—he was going on trips, he was busy, he wasn't around. My instincts told me something wasn't right. As a Pisces, I follow my heart, and it was telling me loud and clear—something was off.

So one day, I drove to Nacogdoches unannounced. I parked near his trailer and waited. He never showed up. I drove around town searching, hoping to catch a glimpse of him—and then I did. He drove past me in his car, with another guy sitting beside him. He saw me standing there, passed me at first, but then reversed and came back. My heart nearly exploded. I knew.

He didn't explain. He didn't apologize. He introduced me to the guy, without saying who I was. Later, he said this guy was going to sleep in his bed, and if I wanted to stay, I could take the couch.

I was shattered. After all we had shared, I didn't deserve that. If something wasn't working, why not talk about it? Try to fix it? Instead, he just moved on, like I was replaceable. It felt so cruel, so careless. A new toy, a new excitement, and just like that, I was discarded. I couldn't understand that kind of love. I still can't.

But even before that heartbreak, there was something else— something darker. One day, while he was out at his salon, I was sitting in his trailer watching a movie. Something—intuition, fear, maybe destiny—told me to open the cabinet in his room. I don't know why. But I did.

There were pills inside. A lot of them. I didn't recognize the names, so I searched them online. They were HIV medications.

I froze. My hands were shaking. He had never told me. Not once.

I stood there, numb. I began to rewind every memory, every intimate moment. The only time we'd had unprotected sex was once, and even then, he hadn't ejaculated. He told me it took him too long to climax. After that, we always used protection. Still, I was terrified. I didn't know what to do, where to go, or how to feel.

He had kept something so important from me. Something that could have changed my life. I was angry. I was scared. And I felt betrayed on every level—not just emotionally, but physically, spiritually.

When I discovered Michael's secret about HIV, the shock and anger were overwhelming. I confronted him about the pills I found in his cabinet, and he admitted that he had been hiding his HIV status from me. He explained that he had contracted it from a previous boyfriend who had also kept the disease a secret. Michael was afraid to tell me, worried I would leave him. But I couldn't understand how he could keep such a life-threatening secret from me. His actions were reckless and irresponsible, and I felt betrayed on a deep level.

145

At first, I tried to stay calm and told him that I would not leave him just because he had HIV, but I needed honesty. I needed to know the truth, to protect myself and make informed decisions. He apologized, but the damage was done. I began getting regular HIV tests every three months, just to be sure, and thankfully, I was always negative. It was a relief, but the emotional impact lingered.

Soon after that, things between us started to unravel. Michael told me he no longer wanted a committed relationship and wanted to see other people. The emotional toll of it all hit me hard, but I convinced myself that I could handle it. I tried to make sense of everything, but when I found out he had been seeing someone else, I felt betrayed again. I was crushed, devastated. I couldn't comprehend how everything we had shared could be so easily discarded.

The pain became unbearable, and in my desperation, I made a tragic decision. One night, I took an overdose of sleeping pills and got into my car, driving recklessly down the freeway. I was in a dark place, and I just wanted the pain to stop. But somehow, fate intervened. I lost control of my car, and it flipped over, crashing down an embankment. Miraculously, I walked away unharmed, saved only by my seatbelt.

An elderly couple who witnessed the crash stopped to help and called the police. When they arrived, I explained what had happened. They took me to the hospital for a psychiatric evaluation, and I felt deep shame for what I had done. I realized then that no matter how bad things got, my life was more valuable than any heartbreak. You can't let someone else's actions define your worth.

One of the nurses, who was especially upset with me, expressed concern for her own son, who drove the same road at night. She made me realize that my actions could have affected someone else's life, and that hit me hard. I felt terrible, and all I could say was, "I'm so sorry. It was a mistake." I knew then that I had to find a way to move forward.

When Michael came to visit me in the hospital, the nurses were hesitant to let him in, knowing he was the cause of my emotional breakdown. But I told them it was fine. He came in with a teddy bear, trying to apologize. He said he wanted the car back and didn't want me driving it anymore. I agreed to give it back, not because I was angry, but because I needed to let go of everything.

He also told me he wasn't ready for a serious relationship and wanted to see other people. I accepted that and told him that I regretted what had happened but that I would move on. I let him go. The relationship ended, and although it hurt deeply, I realized that I had to take care of myself and not let anyone else's actions dictate my happiness.

One Dorm, Eight Eyes

When I was detained and placed in immigration custody, I knew I wouldn't be allowed to return to my apartment, not even to inform management that I wouldn't be able to pay the rent and would likely be evicted. Before being taken away, I handed my apartment key to a co-worker named Anna, who was from El Salvador. I asked her to contact my ex-boyfriend at the time, Michael, and see if he could come to Houston and collect my belongings. I had no idea how long I'd be gone or whether I'd even remain in the U.S., so I wanted my things taken somewhere safe—either to Michael's place or into storage.

Thankfully, Michael came through. He drove to Houston, went to my apartment, and gathered all my belongings. As I expected, an eviction notice was filed against me shortly afterward, since I couldn't pay rent while being detained.

Inside the facility run by Corrections Corporation of America, things quickly became overwhelming. I had never been in prison before and didn't know what to expect. There were eight dorms in total. Dorms 1 through 6 were for immigrants with criminal records—people who had served time for serious offences like murder, robbery, or rape and were now in custody awaiting deportation. Dorms 7 and 8 were for those of us with no criminal background—just immigration violations like overstaying a visa or crossing the border illegally.

I was placed in dorm 8, which held around 40 people. My assigned number was 810, and I was referred to as "810 top" because I had the top bunk. The dorm was diverse—people from Honduras, El Salvador, Iran, India, Pakistan, Nigeria, Georgia, and Russia, all waiting for deportation.

Deportation procedures varied by nationality. For those from Central America or Mexico, ICE typically transported people from Texas to Louisiana, and from there, they'd be flown back on what I was told were military planes. For those from farther away, like Nigeria or Iran, ICE would secure travel documents and purchase commercial airline tickets. An officer would escort them to a major transit point, such as Amsterdam, if flying with KLM, and once they boarded their connecting flight, their passport would be handed to the pilot to ensure safe delivery to the destination.

The living conditions were harsh. We had one TV shared among everyone, usually switching between English and Spanish channels. There was a small library, a medical clinic, and a commissary where we could buy extra items—if we had money. Luckily, Anna helped me by cashing a check I'd written her and depositing money into my commissary account. Without that, it would've been hard to survive. Anna was incredibly reliable—she even visited me often.

Carmen, the owner of Intra-Tours, came a few times as well.

Some detainees worked jobs inside—kitchen duty, laundry, cleaning. Meals were served early: breakfast around 6 a.m., lunch around 10, and dinner by 6 p.m. Showers were communal, and bathrooms had no doors, leaving no privacy. Once a week, we were allowed outside for a brief walk or exercise. Most of the time, we were confined to the dorm. Roll calls happened daily, and we had to stand by our beds to be counted.

Mentally, it was brutal. I was scared, confused, and unprepared. I didn't sleep well. I lost my appetite. I kept overthinking, wondering what would happen next, where I'd be sent, and how long I'd be detained. Everything about that place reminded me of scenes from prison movies or shows like Prison Break. The unknowns were the worst part.

At one point, I even considered whether trying to go to Canada might be a way out. That's how desperate and disoriented I felt.

In Limbo: A Stateless Life Behind Bars

The idea of moving to Canada came after I contacted an organization based in Buffalo, New York, right near the Canadian border. They explained that in order to seek asylum in Canada, I would need to physically reach the border and surrender myself to Canadian authorities. I would be detained while my case was being processed. That became one of the options I seriously considered—if I could ever be released from the U.S. immigration detention center.

While in detention, I spent most of my time writing letters to every embassy I could find in Washington, D.C.—mostly to European countries, as well as Australia, New Zealand, and Canada. I was desperate. These were my SOS messages, explaining that I was a refugee from the war between Armenia and Azerbaijan. I had entered the United States with a Soviet passport, but the Soviet Union no longer existed. I came from Turkmenistan, a Muslim country where LGBTQ people are imprisoned, and I am both gay and Christian.

Most embassies either never replied or responded with rejection letters. The only one that gave me a proper explanation was the Royal Dutch Embassy. They clarified that asylum applications for the European Union could only be made from within EU territory. As far as they were concerned, I was on safe ground in the United States—a country, where legally, I couldn't be persecuted for my religion or sexual orientation. Therefore, they could not consider my case.

But my biggest obstacle wasn't getting help from other countries—it was my situation in the United States. I had a final order of deportation dating back to 1996. Because I had not filed an appeal within 30 days (something I didn't even know I was supposed to do), my case was permanently closed. I couldn't reopen it, no matter what I tried. I was stuck.

Every day in detention was a torment. I lived with the constant anxiety that the guards would call my name next, either to deport me or release me. But days passed, then months, and nothing changed.

U.S. immigration authorities were tasked with securing my travel documents in order to deport me. But I no longer had my Soviet passport—it had been lost during a move. Even if I still had it, the country it belonged to no longer existed. They contacted the Russian embassy, but Russia wouldn't take me; I wasn't a Russian citizen. Armenia refused, saying I had never lived in Armenia after its independence. Azerbaijan, where I was born, denied me because I was ethnically Armenian, and the two countries were at war. Turkmenistan wouldn't accept me either, because I'd never held formal registration there. One by one, every country said no.

I was truly stateless. And apparently, U.S. immigration officials had no idea how to handle someone like me. When I was first brought into the detention center, the officers asked if I spoke Arabic. I explained that I came from the former Soviet Union, I was Armenian, and my official documents listed Russian as my language. But they didn't believe me. It wasn't until they brought in someone who spoke Russian to verify it that they finally took me seriously.

Desperate, I reached out to the United Nations High Commissioner for Refugees (UNHCR), asking to be formally recognized as stateless. They began an investigation, but I didn't hear back for a long time. Meanwhile, I had to find a way to cope inside the prison. The only real escape I found was the library. I buried myself in books, determined to understand U.S. immigration law—especially the rules affecting people like me.

Most other detainees had passports and nationalities. Deporting them was easy. But I was different. I had no citizenship, no valid documents, and nowhere to go. I was the only truly stateless person there.

The Forgotten and the Forsaken

There were so many people in our dorm, all waiting for deportation. Everyone was praying—praying to be released, praying for their lawyers to do something, anything, to get them out. Many of them had built lives in the United States over the years, even decades. They had businesses, families, and homes. They hadn't committed crimes. Their only "violations" were overstaying visas or crossing the border illegally, driven by desperation.

Some were escaping the harsh realities of their home countries— gang violence, economic collapse, persecution. They didn't have time or resources to establish themselves legally. Instead, they threw themselves into work, trying to survive, trying to send money back home. Others, especially those who had only recently entered the U.S. without documents, were quickly apprehended and deported. But for those who had lived here for years, the idea of being ripped away from their families and lives was unbearable.

Most of them were married, many to U.S. citizens. They had children born in the United States who were American citizens. And now, those families were being torn apart. Fathers were removed from the country while mothers stayed behind to raise the children alone. The cruelty of it was overwhelming.

It made me realize just how much people take citizenship for granted. They don't understand the true value of having a passport, a legal identity—something that says you belong somewhere. For people like me and others who are stateless, there's no such sense of belonging. Without documents, we are invisible. We are denied basic rights— healthcare, education, freedom to travel, even the right to work.

It broke my heart to witness these stories—people who had spent years paying taxes, running businesses, contributing to the economy, only to be deported over technicalities or minor infractions. I remember listening to the story of a man who was a permanent resident but had committed a minor legal violation. Now he was being deported. And yet, in the U.S., there are plenty of citizens with serious criminal records who are never at risk of deportation. No one tells them to "go back to where they came from."

How is that fair?

The majority of crimes in the United States are committed by citizens, not by undocumented immigrants. And when people claim that immigrants are "taking American jobs," they ignore reality. Immigrants do the jobs most Americans don't want. They clean dishes in restaurants, scrub toilets, pick vegetables, and do housekeeping. These aren't glamorous jobs. They're backbreaking, thankless, and often paid under the table because immigrants lack documents. Meanwhile, many Americans won't take those jobs because they believe such work is beneath them. They want office jobs, management roles, and white-collar work.

Immigrants aren't taking jobs. They're filling the gaps and keeping the system running. And many of them, despite working so hard, are still targeted and criminalized.

It's important to remember that the United States is a country built by immigrants. No one has the right to claim ownership here except the Native Americans—the original inhabitants whose lands were stolen. Everyone else came from somewhere else: British colonizers, Irish settlers, people from all over Europe, Africa, Asia, and Latin America. If you trace the DNA of any American, chances are it will point back to another country. So, when someone says, "Go back to where you came from," they should take a long, hard look in the mirror. They are immigrants too—just a few generations removed.

I've always loved history, and if you truly understand it, you know how wrong it is to judge others for seeking refuge or a better life. Immigrants contribute to this country. They don't take from it—they give. And yet, I saw countless people in that detention center who had given so much, only to have everything taken from them.

I remember a man from India who owned a gas station. He was married to a U.S. citizen, but was still facing deportation. I never learned the details of his case. Another man from Nigeria rarely spoke. He seemed lost in thought, probably planning what his future would look like if he were forced to return.

There was a man from Iran, also married to a U.S. citizen with children. His green card had been revoked over tax issues, I was told. He had a final order of deportation, but Iran refused to issue travel documents. However, he did have a passport hidden at home. Immigration came looking for it. His little daughter, no older than six, unknowingly gave it away. When the officers asked her if her father had a passport, she pointed under the mattress. And just like that, he was deported.

Then there was a man from Venezuela. He had committed a robbery using a BB gun. He served five years in federal prison, where he said he found Jesus. He was a kind and gentle man. After serving his sentence, he was transferred to immigration detention and eventually deported. Later, I heard he tried to escape to Aruba but was caught and returned to Venezuela.

Each story was its own tragedy, filled with loss, hope, and struggle. And as I sat there, stateless and forgotten, I couldn't help but wonder how many more stories like theirs would go untold.

Diego, Danger, and Detention

There was a guy from Venezuela I met in detention. I don't recall his real name, but I'll call him Diego. He was very attractive—a handsome man. I felt a kind of attraction to him, not in the way most people might assume. It wasn't purely sexual. It was more about his personality, his masculinity, and his energy. He carried himself with dignity, even in that place. I spent a lot of time talking to him, learning his story.

Diego told me that when he was in his twenties, he fell on hard times. He lost his job and needed money to survive. Out of desperation, he committed a crime. He took a BB gun, walked into a bank, and demanded money. He left with about $2,000 and drove off in his car. He rented a room in a small motel, but it didn't take long for the police to catch up with him. The bank had cameras; they got his license plate. Soon, he was arrested, the money confiscated, and he was sentenced to five years in federal prison.

During those five years, Diego found religion. He read the Bible, found God, and seemed genuinely changed. When his sentence ended, he wasn't released into freedom. He was transferred to immigration custody, waiting for deportation. By the time I was released, Diego had already spent about a year there. He wasn't fighting to stay in the United States. He just didn't want to return to Venezuela. He described it as violent, full of gangs, and feared being forced back into a life of crime just to survive.

After I got out and found work again, I tried to help him. I sent him money whenever I could. He eventually flew to Aruba and worked as a bouncer at a nightclub. He had a girlfriend there and tried to build a life, but fixing his documents proved almost impossible. Aruba, being a Dutch territory, had strict immigration policies, and for a Venezuelan, it was a bureaucratic maze. He decided to stay as long as he could, work, save money, and hope for something better. Eventually, he was apprehended again and deported back to Venezuela. After that, I lost contact with him.

Diego's story was just one among many. There were others, and not all were as kind. One man I remember was Cuban. There's a strange, outdated law in the United States: if you're Cuban and make it to U.S. soil, you're granted permanent residency. It's a relic from the Cold War, from the time of the missile crisis, and for decades, it meant Cubans were treated differently than any other immigrants. Even today, the policy remains, punishing Cuba more than helping its people.

This Cuban man had committed a crime. I don't know what kind, but he was brought into our detention center. Dorms 1 through 6 were for people with criminal records, but those dorms were full. So they placed him in our dorm—Dorm 8, for people like me, with no criminal past. That mistake nearly changed my life forever.

One day, I was shaving in the bathroom. He came up behind me, grabbed me, and whispered that he would force me to have sex with him. I was frozen, terrified. I managed to push him away and told him it was never going to happen. He just smirked and said, "Wait until tonight. It will happen."

All the fear I had buried from my time in the Soviet Army came rushing back. I called the guards and reported him. I told them I didn't feel safe in the same dorm. They began an investigation. They pulled him out, questioned him, and then came back to me. Eventually, they removed him from our dorm.

But after that, I never felt truly safe again. I avoided going outside for walks or exercise. Different dorms shared the same yard, and I didn't know who was watching, who was waiting with a sharp object hidden in their pocket. People like me—gay men, or those perceived as different—we were targets. Most of the others were criminals. Many had spent years in federal prison. They were sexually frustrated and aggressive, constantly looking for prey. With no women around, some turned to other men.

I had to protect myself. I confined myself to the dorm as much as possible. I only went out when I felt sure it was safe. That place wasn't just a detention center. It was a pressure cooker of desperation, violence, and fear. And still, in all of that, there were people like Diego—flawed but good-hearted, searching for redemption.

Every day brought uncertainty. I never knew who might come in next or what they might do. But I survived. I held onto hope. And I never stopped believing that we all deserved to be treated with dignity, no matter where we came from or what mistakes we had made.

Rosie, the Guards, and the Law of Zadvydas

Most of the guards working at the Corrections Corporation of America weren't friendly. The environment was cold, mechanical, and for many of them, we weren't humans—just numbers in a system. A few guards stood out. One was an African-American woman, a lesbian. She treated us with dignity. She understood we weren't criminals, that we didn't deserve to be there, and she showed compassion where others refused to.

Another one, an older African-American woman we all called Mama, was just as kind. She was approachable, respectful, and seemed to genuinely care. But beyond those rare few, the rest—especially the white male officers—treated us like dirt. Their faces said it all. They didn't hide their contempt or racism. If you asked for something simple, like a doctor's visit or access to the library, they'd make it as hard as possible just to remind you that they had power over you.

Despite the constant tension, I never told anyone I was gay. I was in prison. Detention center or not, it was still prison—and I didn't know who I could trust. Criminals were around, too. Safety mattered more than honesty.

But then there was Rosie.

Rosie was Vietnamese. Born male, but in the process of transitioning. She was taking hormones, and everything about her was feminine— from her delicate eyebrows to the way she moved and spoke. She worked in the laundry room and had a sharp elegance about her that made her unforgettable.

We started talking, and eventually she confided in me. She told me she had found ways to have sex with other detainees—men who were desperate for touch and connection. I was shocked. I asked how that was even possible. She explained that she had a connection with someone in the medical unit. If there was someone she wanted, she'd ask the nurse to request that inmate for a fake medical check. Once inside, she'd be given privacy in a room. That's where it happened.

Her story was wild. She told me she'd once been arrested after smashing a beer bottle over a man's head at a club. The guy had approached her, thinking she was a woman, and when things went wrong, she reacted. That's how she ended up in the system. Rosie also managed to smuggle cigarettes in—no idea how—and would sneak them to others who wanted a smoke. People would light up in the bathrooms, then spray air freshener like nothing happened.

Visitation was tightly monitored. Anyone who wanted to see you had to be pre-approved and listed. Once called, you've got about 15 minutes. Guards were everywhere, watching every move, making sure nothing was smuggled in—no cash, no cigarettes, no notes. And after visitation? Straight to the wall. You'd be stripped, forced to bend over while they shined a flashlight up your rectum to check for contraband.

It was humiliating. Dehumanizing. But after a while, you got numb to it. Days blurred. You forgot the time, the date, even the month. To stay sane, I escaped into the library—my only refuge. That's where I found purpose again.

I started studying immigration law. Every book I could get my hands on, I devoured. Somewhere inside me, I believed there had to be a way out—some legal loophole, some technicality that would apply to someone like me: no criminal record, no country to go to.

And then I found it.

Zadvydas v. Davis.

It was a Supreme Court case involving a man named Zadvydas—a Lithuanian by birth, raised in East Germany, and later living in the Soviet Union. He had committed a crime in the U.S., and when the government tried to deport him, no country would take him back. Lithuania refused. Germany refused. He was truly stateless.

The case led to a precedent. The ruling declared that if the U.S. government cannot deport someone within six months, and if that person doesn't pose a threat to society, then indefinite detention is unconstitutional. The law became known as the Zadvydas Law.

That was my light at the end of the tunnel.

I didn't have a country. No passport. No crime. Just years of running and trying to survive. So, I made that law my path to freedom. And when my six months approached, I made my move—using Zadvydas as my ticket out.

Statelessness Reflection

While studying immigration law in the detention center, I stumbled upon something that shifted my entire understanding of my own identity: I wasn't the only stateless person. Until that moment, I genuinely believed I was alone in this condition—that there was no one else like me in the United States. But I was wrong. There are many stateless individuals in this country, unable to be deported, yet with no path to legal residency or citizenship.

The United States has no specific legal framework that addresses statelessness. If a person finds themselves stateless while on American soil, there is no straightforward mechanism for them to apply for permanent residency or eventual citizenship. This absence of recognition contrasts sharply with how certain groups, like Cubans, are treated. Under the Cuban Adjustment Act, Cubans who arrive in the U.S. are automatically placed on a path to permanent residency and, eventually, citizenship. That policy, rooted in the Cold War, politics remains, while stateless people remain invisible in the eyes of the law. It makes no sense.

As I researched further, I discovered that most European Union countries are signatories to the United Nations Convention Relating to the Status of Stateless Persons. The 1954 Convention establishes a legal framework for protecting the rights of stateless people. The United

States never signed this agreement. Why? Because the U.S. government operates under the assumption that statelessness cannot occur here, citizenship is granted to anyone born on American soil. But this narrow lens ignores the global reality.

The truth is, many countries do not grant automatic citizenship. People born in Myanmar, Palestine, the former Yugoslavia, and the former Soviet Union may not be recognized by any country, leaving them in legal limbo. They have no passport, no home country, no nation willing to accept them. This reality contradicts the American assumption that statelessness is a non-issue.

It was difficult to accept that my condition had a name—statelessness—and yet, there was no policy here to acknowledge or address it. Even the act of renouncing U.S. citizenship reflects the government's aversion to creating stateless persons. To renounce U.S. citizenship, one must leave the country and do it from a foreign U.S. embassy. The process requires proof of citizenship or residency in another country, payment of a fee, and acceptance of the fact that renunciation is final. Without another nationality, the U.S. will not approve the request, because they don't want to be responsible for creating stateless individuals.

And yet, people like me, who never renounced any citizenship but were left behind by collapsing governments, do exist. We are born into statelessness, not by choice, but by geopolitical collapse. Still, the U.S. has no mechanism to accommodate us. Instead, we're detained, criminalized, and ignored.

What disturbed me further was the inconsistency of citizenship laws. A child born in the U.S. to diplomats or military personnel may automatically become a citizen, even if they leave the country days later and never return. That person can walk into a U.S. Embassy years later, present a birth certificate, and claim a passport. Meanwhile, those of us who have fled war, persecution, and poverty to genuinely rebuild our lives here face impossible hurdles.

The U.S. immigration system is not just broken—it's outdated and illogical. We have never properly addressed statelessness. We've kept laws on the books that are relics of a different era, like the Cuban Adjustment Act, and used them selectively. And in the case of Cuba, we punish the country with economic embargoes while simultaneously offering Cubans special pathways to legal status. Ordinary Cubans—who have nothing to do with geopolitical disputes—are caught in the middle.

To me, statelessness is a human rights violation. No one should live without an identity, without a nation, without a place to belong. We create endless rules about immigration, borders, detention, but deny people the right to move freely and find a home. I understand the legal arguments, but emotionally and morally, I believe this: your country is not where you are born. It is where your heart feels at home. Being born somewhere doesn't mean that place is your country—it may mean nothing more than an accident of geography.

The truth is, we are overdue for change. Our immigration system must be re-examined and rebuilt. The issue of statelessness must be acknowledged and addressed. Outdated laws must be either revised or removed. If we truly want a fair and humane immigration system, we must first start by recognizing the people who have been left out entirely—people like me.

The Interrogation

My time in detention at the Corrections Corporation of America (CCA) was nothing short of surreal. The absurdity of the situation became most apparent when I found myself being interrogated by the CIA and FBI. It wasn't just the questions—they were ignorant, nonsensical, and driven by unfounded assumptions. What they didn't know—or perhaps refused to understand was that being stateless wasn't a matter of choice. It was a punishment, a branding of sorts, and the system had failed me in ways I couldn't have predicted.

One early morning, I was jolted awake by a guard. "The CIA is here to see you," she said. It was 4 a.m. The guard's tone was matter-of-fact, as though this were a routine occurrence. I had been through a lot, but nothing quite like this. I was led to a small room where two men were waiting. They were formal, serious, but it was clear that they had little understanding of the context that defined my life, my journey. They had a file in front of them, but they weren't looking at it—they were making assumptions based on a map, not history.

The first question was simple enough: "Do you know that Turkmenistan borders Afghanistan?" Of course, I knew that. I knew my geography better than anyone. I had lived there. But the absurdity came next. "Have you ever been to Afghanistan?" they asked. No, I hadn't. Afghanistan wasn't exactly a vacation spot—it was a closed-off country, sealed off by Soviet control. We didn't cross that border. It wasn't a road trip. But they refused to accept my answer, as if I were hiding something. They didn't seem to care about the larger political reality— Soviet Turkmenistan wasn't a breeding ground for terrorism.

Then came the question that floored me: "Do you know Osama Bin Laden?" I almost laughed. I had never been to Afghanistan, never even set foot in a country so foreign to me, so dangerous. Yet they asked me as if I could casually say yes. I was Armenian, Christian, and had fled from the violence between Armenia and Azerbaijan. How on earth could I know someone like Bin Laden? It didn't make sense, but they didn't care. They only saw a border, a geographical proximity, and a stereotype.

The questions continued. "Do you speak Arabic?" I replied truthfully, "No." But that wasn't enough. They didn't believe me. They brought in another person, someone who was fluent in Arabic, and I had to prove my innocence in the strangest way. This person interrogated me, watching my every move—my eyes, my face, searching for any sign that I was lying. Afterward, I was told that I didn't speak Arabic. I couldn't help but wonder, did they even know who they were questioning?

As if this wasn't enough, the conversation turned into something even more absurd. "Would you be willing to spy for the U.S. government in Iraq?" they asked. Iraq. A country I had no connection to, and certainly no interest in. The war with Iraq was just beginning, and here they were, asking me—someone with no citizenship, no ties to the U.S.—to spy in a foreign land. This was insanity. But the offer wasn't just about espionage; it was a thinly veiled attempt to get rid of me.

I didn't have citizenship anywhere. No country recognized me. I was stateless. So, they had no other options. They couldn't deport me, not without a citizenship to send me back to. They were cornered, and they thought they had found a solution: send me to Iraq, a country we were preparing to destroy, and see if I could disappear into the chaos. They didn't care what happened to me—after all, I was "nobody."

I refused, of course. I told them I couldn't spy for a government I didn't belong to. I wasn't even an American. And then they hit me with the most ludicrous response. They said that I could go undercover, dressed in a burqa, blending in as an Arab woman. This was the point where I almost couldn't keep my composure. A gay man, covered from head to toe, walking in Iraq? They didn't even seem to realize the dangers I'd face—not just from the authorities but from insurgents, from anyone who might approach me. The thought of it was beyond ridiculous. If I had walked in Iraq wearing a burqa, someone would've heard my voice and realized something was wrong—something would've happened to me.

They were willing to risk my life for what? A broken system, a set of assumptions, and a desperate attempt to find a solution to their problem. A stateless person, seen as expendable, was the solution. But I wasn't their answer. I wasn't a pawn in their game. I refused to cooperate with a government that saw me as a disposable object, someone to use when it was convenient and forget when it wasn't.

When they asked me if that was my final answer, I said yes. There was no other choice. I couldn't play their game. They could stare at me in silence, but I knew the truth: they had no respect for me, no respect for my rights, and no understanding of my life. I was just another statistic in a broken system, a system that couldn't even recognize what it was doing wrong. And all I wanted was to be seen for who I was: not a threat, not a pawn, but a person, a person with a complicated past, a refugee trying to survive, and a stateless individual who deserved far better than to be treated as an expendable pawn in someone else's war.

A New Beginning in Los Angeles

After what felt like an eternity, the day finally arrived for me to meet with my deportation officer at the Corrections Corporation of America. The wait was agonizing, but I had prepared myself for this moment. I requested a meeting, and soon enough, I was called in to discuss my case. I made it clear that I was stateless and had no criminal record. I referenced the Law of Zadvydas, which I had found in an immigration book, which stated that since all attempts to remove me from the United States had failed, I should be released within six months.

My officer carefully reviewed my case and assured me that he would recommend my release, though he couldn't guarantee the outcome.

Then, just before my birthday in February 2002, the moment I had been waiting for finally came. They told me I was free to go. The relief that washed over me was overwhelming—after spending so many months confined in a dormitory with forty other people, I could finally breathe the outside air again. It felt as if I had regained my freedom.

Upon my release, I immediately contacted Carmen, the owner of Intra-Tours, the travel agency I had worked for before. I asked if there was any chance I could return. To my relief, she welcomed the idea, but there was one obstacle: I didn't have a place to stay. Fortunately, Carmen offered me a temporary solution—her daughter's apartment. Since her daughter spent most of her time at her boyfriend's place, I was able to stay there until I could get on my feet. Eventually, I moved into my own apartment, but my legal troubles were far from over.

I was placed under an Order of Supervision, meaning I had to report to the immigration office every three months to update them on my well-being, employment, and efforts to find a country that would accept me. Despite my best efforts—bringing letters from various embassies in Washington, D.C., seeking political asylum—nothing seemed to work. The Order of Supervision was indefinite, which meant that every three months, I had to report or risk facing consequences, including potential re-detention. It was a burden, but I had no choice but to comply.

While continuing my work at Intra-Tours, I remained in contact with Michael. Our romantic relationship had ended long ago, but we still considered each other friends. I remember the conversation when he reached out, asking if there was a chance we could start over. I gently told him that the love I once felt had faded. I valued our friendship, but I could no longer see us being together. The betrayal, the lies, and my time in detention had changed me. It was over, and I had to move forward.

As time passed, I realized that Houston wasn't the place I wanted to be anymore after 12 years spent there. My acting career was still something I wanted to pursue, and I knew that Los Angeles was the center of the film industry. The idea of moving to L.A. seemed like a logical next step, but it wasn't without its challenges. I didn't have much in savings, so I needed to secure a job and find a place to live before making the move.

I was fortunate to find work at a travel agency in Beverly Hills, and after some searching, I found an apartment. With everything lined up, I knew it was time to take the plunge. The decision was daunting, but after all the upheaval in my life—moving from the Soviet Union, surviving detention, and constantly battling legal uncertainty—I realized that if I could make it this far, I could certainly manage a move from Texas to California.

I packed everything I had, including new items I had bought to furnish my apartment, as well as belongings I had left at Michael's place. The movers came, loaded everything onto the truck, and within a few days, I was ready to go. I said my goodbyes to friends who had supported me through thick and thin and purchased an airline ticket to Los Angeles. The move was a big step, but it was one I felt compelled to take.

When I arrived in Los Angeles, I wasn't sure if I would stay permanently. I wanted to see how everything unfolded—how the acting scene would treat me, if I would like living in the city, and if I would be able to build a life there. But my legal situation still loomed over me. I had to report to my deportation officer every three months, and since I was moving to California, I needed to be under the jurisdiction of immigration there. But given that I wasn't sure if my stay would be permanent, we made an agreement: I would continue to fly back to Houston every three months to report, until I made a final decision about whether I would stay in L.A. or return to Houston.

It was a new chapter in my life—one filled with uncertainty, but also a renewed sense of hope. I had survived detention, dealt with statelessness, and now, I was taking control of my future. The journey was far from over, but for the first time in a long time, I felt like I was moving in the right direction.

Struggling to Settle in Los Angeles

In 2007, I finally arrived in Los Angeles, California, ready for a fresh start. However, things didn't go as smoothly as I had hoped. The apartment I found online was much smaller than it had been described, and since I didn't have any friends in L.A. to check it out for me, I was stuck with it. The apartment was cramped, and some of my furniture, including a large leather couch, couldn't even fit through the door. For a while, it sat in the lobby outside my apartment. The location wasn't ideal either, but I quickly realized that online listings can be deceiving, and I had to make do with what I had.

Despite the apartment situation, I was fortunate to secure a job in Beverly Hills, continuing my work in the travel industry. The office was brand new, and the team was an eclectic mix of people from around the world. There was an Egyptian woman, a man from the Philippines, a girl from Ukraine, and later, another woman from Armenia. It was like the United Nations of travel agents, and working with such a diverse group of people was both interesting and rewarding.

Yet, I still felt the need for more space. I began searching for a larger place and eventually found a studio apartment in Koreatown, which seemed like a better fit. As I settled into my new life, I continued to pursue my passion for acting, applying for roles wherever I could. I even landed a few small parts in independent films, but nothing significant. One of the biggest obstacles, however, was balancing my day job with acting. Auditions, after all, are often scheduled during the day, and with my 10-to-6 work hours, it became increasingly difficult to make both work. Eventually, I gave up on acting—not because I lost interest, but because I became tired of the roles I was being offered.

The scene from the short film "Pandemic"

Being Armenian, my physical appearance, more Middle Eastern, often led people to cast me in negative roles, such as villains or antagonists, rather than more positive or dynamic characters. Over time, I realized that this typecasting was something that would stick with me if I continued pursuing acting, and it didn't appeal to me. After giving it a lot of thought, I decided to step away from acting for the time being, despite still harboring a deep passion for it.

Settling into Los Angeles was difficult. It was a big change from the life I had in Houston. Even though I knew Houston wasn't a place I wanted to stay long-term, I found myself questioning whether I had made the right decision. Every three months, as part of my Order of Supervision, I had to fly back to Houston to report to my deportation officer. For nearly eight years, I kept up this routine—flying back, reporting, and returning to L.A. It became part of my life.

My deportation officer, Walter, was kind to me and understood the challenges I faced. Over time, we built a rapport, and he allowed me to report by phone in some cases, especially if the cost of a flight was too high. He trusted me to report on time, and I always kept my end of the deal.

But there was one time when I needed to report in person. I called Walter to confirm my visit, and he told me that he wouldn't be available due to a personal emergency, but someone else would assist me. When I arrived at the immigration office in Houston, the officer who helped me looked at my file and asked why I was still reporting in Houston when I lived in California. I explained that I hadn't moved my case yet because I wasn't sure how long I would stay in L.A. I didn't want to make the change if I wasn't sure about my future there.

She made the decision to transfer my case to California, and from that point on, my Order of Supervision continued under the jurisdiction of L.A. Immigration. My new officer in California continued the same process, reviewing my efforts to find a solution and helping me work through my legal challenges. I continued sending letters to embassies, but they all replied the same way—my case had to be resolved in the United States, not in Europe or elsewhere.

I remembered, however, the idea I had entertained before leaving Houston—applying for asylum in Canada. But the fear of being detained there, not knowing how long it would take for my case to unfold, and the uncertainty of what would happen if Canada didn't grant me asylum made me abandon that thought. I didn't want to risk becoming stateless again, stuck in a detention center in a foreign country. That idea, like many others, slowly faded away.

Life in L.A. wasn't easy, but it was different. I was slowly starting to make it my own, though I still had a long way to go in adjusting to my new life, my ongoing legal battle, and the challenges that came with it. But with each passing day, I knew that this new chapter was one I would eventually find a way to navigate—one step at a time.

New Beginnings: Brewing Freedom in Los Angeles

Los Angeles, with its dynamic and ever-evolving atmosphere, quickly captivated me. The city was a kaleidoscope of contrasts: the swaying tropical palms, the expansive Pacific Ocean stretching along the coastlines of Santa Monica and Venice, and the bustling streets that hummed with an energy all their own. The climate, a stark departure from the oppressive heat and humidity of Houston, Texas, was a breath of fresh air—literally. For someone like me, whose skin was particularly sensitive to heat, the temperature in Los Angeles felt like a welcome reprieve, a gentle embrace of warmth without the overwhelming, suffocating humidity I had come to dread in Houston.

In Houston, the relentless heat had made everyday life a challenge. My skin reacted poorly to the intense heat, and I often found myself retreating into the cool refuge of air-conditioned spaces—the office, my apartment—rarely venturing outside. The city itself was not particularly pedestrian-friendly, and walking was often an arduous task in the sweltering climate. But Los Angeles, with its balmy, gentle breeze, seemed to offer the promise of a more harmonious existence. I began to envision a future here, a future where I could thrive in this new environment, far removed from the oppressive atmosphere of Texas.

Yet, there was a significant caveat: Los Angeles, for all its allure, was expensive. It was a city where every dollar earned seemed to slip away quickly, devoured by the high cost of living—rent, utilities, and daily expenses left little room for anything else.

Despite these financial challenges, I remained committed to maintaining a sense of style and presence. I adhered to a routine that had served me well in Houston: I made sure to present myself well. My wardrobe became a means of asserting my identity, a way to feel grounded in a city that was still foreign to me. I frequented high-end stores like Armani, Zara, and Gucci, hunting for deals on pieces that would ensure I always looked polished and put together.

Whether in the office or out socializing, my clothes became my armor, and I took care to always present the version of myself I wanted others to see.

The streets of Los Angeles, with their vibrant and diverse community, provided ample opportunity for me to connect with people, particularly within the city's gay community. There was an unspoken freedom in the air, an openness that allowed me to explore and express myself in ways I had never been able to back in the former Soviet Union. For the first time in years, I felt like I could truly be myself, unencumbered by the past, by societal constraints, or by the shadows of my previous life.

Amidst this newfound freedom, my mind turned toward entrepreneurship. I began to entertain the idea of opening a high-end furniture store, an endeavor I hoped would allow me to carve out a niche for myself in the competitive world of Los Angeles business. I tried to launch this venture, but it soon became apparent that I lacked the capital and infrastructure needed to establish a physical store and secure relationships with European suppliers. The dream of a furniture store was put on hold, and once again, I found myself searching for another path forward. My life in Los Angeles was filled with new beginnings, some of which flourished, while others withered away. But

I was resilient, determined to forge a new life, even if it meant navigating uncertainty.

I eventually found work in the travel industry once again, this time as a commission-based travel agent. The job, while offering flexibility, didn't provide the stability I had hoped for. Despite this, it became a means to an end, allowing me to continue my life in Los Angeles while I kept an eye out for new opportunities. It wasn't long before I stumbled upon a charming coffee shop in the heart of Hollywood, a discovery that would change the course of my life in ways I hadn't anticipated.

The coffee shop, Tiago, owned by Santiago, an Argentine entrepreneur, immediately struck me as a unique space. Santiago and his boyfriend had transformed what was once a simple internet café into a vibrant, welcoming space that specialized in high-quality, artisanal coffee. Santiago, who had a background in computer repair and web development, had purchased the café from its previous owner, who was Filipino. He saw potential in the space and set about reimagining it with a fresh vision: a focus on specialty coffee. This was a movement that was gaining traction in California at the time, one that emphasized not only the quality of the beans but the entire process behind crafting the perfect cup of coffee.

Specialty coffee was a revelation. It involved a meticulous approach to sourcing, harvesting, fermenting, drying, and roasting. Every step in the process contributed to the final flavor profile, and the concept of terroir—the unique characteristics imparted to the coffee by its region of origin—was central to the movement. The coffee shop's aim was to educate patrons about the nuances of specialty coffee, allowing them to taste the difference between beans from Africa, Brazil, and Central America. It was about appreciating coffee as more than just a drink; it was an art form. Santiago and his team worked tirelessly to perfect their craft, educating customers on how to taste coffee without adding sugar, allowing the complexities of the beans to shine through. This philosophy was revolutionary, as most people had been accustomed to drinking bitter coffee, often masked by the addition of sugar to counteract its harshness.

I began spending more time at this coffee shop, not just for the quality of the coffee but for the sense of community it offered. It became my refuge, a place where I could work, read, and escape the overwhelming thoughts of my past. The atmosphere was warm and inclusive, and Santiago's vision of the coffee shop as a hub for learning and connection resonated with me deeply. It was a space where people from all walks of life gathered—not just to enjoy coffee, but to share stories, engage in meaningful conversations, and connect with one another. In many ways, the coffee shop became my second home. It was a surrogate family in a city where I had no immediate relatives. The connections I made there—casual yet profound—helped me find a sense of belonging that I hadn't realized I was searching for.

In a city as vast and anonymous as Los Angeles, it was in that small coffee shop that I found a sense of community, a place where I could nurture both my professional and personal growth. Santiago's vision had not only redefined the coffee experience but also redefined my own experience of Los Angeles—a place where I could start anew, embrace my freedom, and build the life I had always dreamed of.

Sips of Freedom

As a frequent guest at Tiago Coffee Shop in Hollywood, I found myself drinking more and more coffee each day. Santiago, the owner, who had observed my regular visits, once casually asked if I ever thought about working there. At that time, I wasn't interested in a job. I enjoyed the atmosphere, the connections I made with the people, and the way the coffee shop served as a space where I could unwind. But as I spent more time in the shop, something began to shift inside me.

Processing coffee in Kona, Hawaii

My curiosity grew, and soon I found myself diving deep into the world of specialty coffee. I started to understand the artistry behind brewing a perfect cup—how the nuances of espresso extraction, the science of steaming milk, and the delicate balance of flavors in a cup could turn coffee into something much more than a morning ritual. I read about how coffee is harvested, how only ripe cherries are picked to ensure the best flavor, and how the processing methods, including fermentation and drying, affect the final product. I became fascinated by the complex relationship between the origin of coffee and the flavors it produces. Tasting coffee from Kenya, Colombia, and El Salvador, I was struck by how each region imparted its own unique characteristics into the beans.

This newfound knowledge sparked a desire to immerse myself further in this craft. I started seeing coffee less as a simple beverage and more as an intricate art form—one I could master. So, after some time, I asked Santiago if he had any part-time positions available. His response was positive, and soon I began working at Tiago's coffee shop, balancing my job at the travel agency by day and brewing coffee by night.

At the coffee shop, my focus was clear: I wanted to learn everything there was to know about specialty coffee. I enrolled in the Specialty Coffee Association of America's certification program, where I took courses in everything from the Barista Foundation to Coffee Brewing Foundations. I studied coffee chemistry, learning the delicate process behind making the perfect espresso and the techniques for steaming milk to create beautiful latte art. I spent countless hours perfecting my craft, wasting milk and coffee as I experimented with designs like rosetta, tulips, and hearts. But each successful creation felt like a small victory, a manifestation of the artistry that was so deeply tied to the coffee culture I was coming to love.

As I perfected my skills, I grew increasingly inspired by the pioneers in the coffee industry. I read books by James Hoffmann, former UK Barista Champion, and watched the competition of Michael Phillips, US Barista Champion, who later went on to win the World Barista

Championship. Their dedication to their craft encouraged me to push forward. I even dreamt of one day visiting coffee farms, experiencing the coffee harvest firsthand, and learning how skilled labor and care shape the beans that eventually reach my cup.

Los Angeles was home to a thriving coffee scene, with new specialty coffee shops opening up all the time. Shops like Intelligentsia Coffee, Verve Coffee Roasters, and Side Glass Coffee were pushing the boundaries of what it meant to serve high-quality coffee, and I made it my mission to visit as many of them as I could. I was particularly drawn to pour-over coffee—a method that required precision and care to highlight the natural flavors of the beans. With a specially designed kettle, I poured hot water over the grounds, taking time to extract the subtle, original flavors of the coffee. The experience was transformative. A cup of Ethiopian coffee could taste floral and honeyed, while a brew from Brazil might be more monotone and nuttier. Every origin told its own story, and it was exciting to learn how factors like terroir and processing methods could change the flavor profile.

I threw myself into the world of specialty coffee, attending retreats organized by the Specialty Coffee Association. My travels took me to Wisconsin, Hawaii, and other parts of the United States, where I further immersed myself in the culture of coffee. Each experience, each workshop, added depth to my understanding of this new craft, and I felt a growing sense of accomplishment.

In addition to becoming a skilled barista, I also found myself experimenting with baking. Inspired by the cakes my mother used to bake for us when I was a child, I began making cakes at the coffee shop in the evenings, perfecting my recipes and presentation. The first time I saw my cakes behind the glass display, waiting for the morning rush, I was filled with a sense of pride. The positive feedback from customers was overwhelming, and I felt validated in my new skills. For the first time in a long while, I felt like I was truly building something from the ground up.

Coffee harvesting and processing in Kona, Hawaii

The Tiago Coffee Shop had become more than just a place to work. It was my community, my family away from home. The connections I made with the people there, the lessons I learned about coffee, and the skills I developed all gave me a sense of purpose I hadn't experienced before. And while the challenges of my past—like the uncertainty surrounding my status—still loomed in the background, the world of specialty coffee provided me with a much-needed escape and a sense of direction.

Between Coffee and Complications

Life in Hollywood had become a strange mix of routine and chaos, but it was the coffee shop that provided me with a sense of purpose. Tiago, the specialty coffee shop owned by Santiago, had become more than just a place of work. It was a sanctuary, a haven where I could forget about the mess of my own life. Santiago, with his easy smile and laid-back demeanor, quickly became a close friend. His boyfriend, Adrian, on the other hand, was more complicated.

Adrian's jealousy was a constant presence in their relationship, often bubbling up in unexpected ways. Whenever Santiago would talk to other people, especially other men, Adrian's insecurity would surface. It didn't matter if the conversation was innocent; to Adrian, any interaction could easily be seen as flirting, and that would set off a storm of confrontation. The drama of their relationship seemed to spill out into the coffee shop and, inevitably, I became involved in their disputes. It wasn't something I wanted, but somehow, I found myself tangled in the mess of their emotions, trying to mediate between two people I cared about.

One evening, after yet another argument between the two, Santiago reached out to me. He needed space—a chance to clear his head. Adrian's jealousy had driven him to the point of emotional exhaustion, and Santiago needed to be away, even if just for a little while. He asked if he could stay at my apartment. "Just for a few hours," he said, "I need to think things through."

I didn't hesitate. I had been living alone in a small apartment just across the street from Tiago, a place that was both convenient and solitary. At $1,100 a month, it was expensive for the area, but its location was ideal for my new routine. I had recently quit my travel agency job, which I had grown tired of, and made the leap into full-time work at the coffee shop. The job was more inspiring, and the people I met at Tiago were like a new family.

My first cake at Tiago Coffee shop

My shifts at the coffee shop started in the afternoon, typically around 2 PM, and went until 9 PM when we closed. But my work didn't end there. After hours, I would stay behind to bake cakes and pastries, experimenting with different recipes and perfecting my technique. The act of baking was meditative, an escape from my lingering concerns about my immigration status. The simple act of creating something—even if it was just a cake—felt like I was building a small piece of stability in my otherwise uncertain life.

I hadn't been dating anyone since Michael. The trust that had been broken during my relationship with him had left me emotionally scarred. I simply wasn't ready to open myself up to someone new. The fear of being hurt again was too great, and the weight of my situation, as someone without a clear legal status, was too much to bring into a new relationship. It was easier to be alone. My loneliness was not something I feared; in fact, I found comfort in it. I had become accustomed to navigating life on my own terms.

But Santiago, ever perceptive, saw things differently. One day, as we were driving somewhere after closing the coffee shop, he asked me, "Why don't you have a boyfriend? You're a great guy, and I don't get why you're still single."

I hesitated, unsure of how much I should reveal. But I trusted Santiago, and after a long pause, I explained to him the pain of my past with Michael, the loss of trust, and the complications of my immigration status. "It's not that I don't want someone," I said. "It's just... I don't think I'm ready. And I don't want to drag someone into my mess."

Santiago nodded thoughtfully, his expression softening. "Your heart is closed," he said, "and I think you should give someone else a chance. Being alone forever... that's not the way to live. You're too good for that."

His words struck a chord, and I couldn't shake them. But the truth was, I wasn't ready. I wasn't sure how I could be when so many parts of my life were in turmoil. And even though I longed for connection, I was too scared to take that leap again.

During this time, I found myself drawn to a friend from the coffee shop, Sophie. She was British, charming, and full of life. She had a sense of elegance that was both captivating and calming. Sophie's life, like mine, was complicated. As a British citizen, she was only allowed to stay in the United States for 90 days at a time, after which she had to leave and re-enter. She spent the time in between in Dubai with her father, who ran a business there, and in Los Angeles, where she lived right next to the coffee shop.

Sophie, much like me, had a complicated relationship with her home country. She didn't like England and never wanted to date a British man. Her preferences leaned toward men from Morocco and the Middle

East, and she often shared stories about her adventures in both places. Her lifestyle was unconventional, but it was one that suited her. Sophie had no desire for anything permanent. She lived in a world of fluidity, moving between countries and relationships with ease.

Sophie and I often spent hours at Tiago talking about everything from love and loss to our dreams and disappointments. She listened, gave advice, and always offered me a different perspective on my life. While we both had our complicated pasts, there was an unspoken understanding that we were both searching for something, not necessarily love or stability, but maybe just a sense of purpose.

One afternoon, as I was spending time in the garden outside the coffee shop, I noticed how neglected the space had become. The plants were dying, and the area felt lifeless, much like the chaotic emotions that seemed to swirl around us in that coffee shop. I decided to change that. I bought plants and flowers, spent hours planting them, and turned the garden into a peaceful retreat. It was my way of contributing to the space, of creating something beautiful from the chaos.

Santiago, however, didn't fully understand why I had done it. He thought I was expecting something in return—maybe praise or recognition. But I wasn't. I had always been the type of person who did things because I wanted to, not because I expected anything in return. My actions came from a place of genuine care and love, something that was often misunderstood. But I didn't mind. I wasn't doing it for validation; I was doing it because it made me feel good, and I believed it would bring some peace to the shop.

As time passed, I continued to dive deeper into the world of specialty coffee. I started attending conferences, taking online courses, and immersing myself in everything coffee-related. The more I learned, the more I realized how much there was to discover. I even thought about entering the Barista Championship, but I hesitated. The idea of performing in front of judges, competing with other skilled baristas, terrified me. I didn't want to face the pressure of being judged. I just wanted to make great coffee and perfect my craft. The idea of fame or money never crossed my mind. I simply wanted to improve.

My first made pie

Hollywood, with all its dreams of fame, was right around the corner. I would often walk around the Boulevard and see the strange mix of people—tourists, aspiring actors, and musicians all trying to make their mark on the world. Many of them lived in their cars, moving from one audition to the next. They didn't rent apartments; they slept in their vehicles, showered at the gym, and did their laundry at laundromats. It was a harsh reality for those chasing the dream of stardom. It wasn't glamorous, but it was real. And it was a reminder that the pursuit of success in Hollywood came at a steep price.

Through all the ups and downs, I found a sense of peace in my work at Tiago. The chaos of my life—my unresolved immigration status, my emotional walls, the tension between Santiago and Adrian—all seemed to fade away when I was behind the counter, making coffee. The coffee shop became my refuge, a place where I could pour my heart into something simple yet meaningful. And in that simple act of brewing coffee, I began to realize that maybe, just maybe, I was brewing more than just drinks. I was brewing my own future.

Wandering Beyond the Coffee

Before moving full-time to the specialty coffee shop Tiago in Hollywood, while still juggling responsibilities at the travel agency, I seized every opportunity to escape Los Angeles and explore the diverse corners of the United States. Each holiday presented a chance to discover a new facet of this vast country. Among all the places I visited, California itself offered me some of the most memorable and meaningful escapes.

Santa Barbara, California

Santa Barbara quickly became one of my favorite destinations. The city had a distinctive colonial charm, shaped by its Spanish heritage. Walking down its cobblestone streets, flanked by whitewashed buildings with red-tile roofs, I felt transported to a different era. The intricate architecture of old churches and the peaceful rhythm of the town invited contemplation. There was something magical about Santa Barbara—a peaceful elegance that contrasted the fast- paced energy of Los Angeles.

Then I stumbled upon Solvang. Nestled in the Santa Ynez Valley, Solvang felt like a secret European village tucked away in California. Its Danish-style buildings, windmills, and quaint bakeries offered a glimpse of a world I had long dreamt of visiting. Having never been to Europe, this slice of Denmark felt surreal. It had the warmth and enchantment of a fairytale, and walking through it felt like crossing not just a physical boundary, but a portal into another continent.

Dutch Harbour, Alaska

But perhaps the most profound journey I embarked on during that time was to Alaska. I had always held a quiet fascination with Alaska, particularly because of its unique history as a former Russian territory. It felt like a forgotten connection to the land of my ancestors. The idea of setting foot in Sitka, the old capital during the Russian period, excited me beyond measure.

Barrow. Arctic Circle, Alaska

I decided to visit Alaska in the winter. It was a bold decision, and as I would later discover, not a particularly well-prepared one. I packed lightly, bringing only a trench coat and a few sweaters. When I arrived in Barrow, one of the northernmost towns in the world, locals greeted me with a mixture of amusement and concern. One Eskimo asked me, "Are you from Hollywood?" with a laugh, clearly amused by my city attire in such unforgiving weather.

Despite the cold, Barrow was a revelation. The Arctic Ocean lay frozen, stretching endlessly into the horizon. The town had one school, one store, a single police station, and a resilient population living in harmony with the harsh environment. Seeing igloos up close, learning how they were constructed, and observing the local customs gave me a profound appreciation for human adaptability. It was like stepping into a documentary, but with all five senses awakened.

Barrow. Arctic Circle, Alaska

My Alaskan journey continued from Anchorage to Fairbanks aboard a long, slow train winding through snow-covered Denali National Park. The stillness of the white wilderness, the haunting beauty of the frozen forests, and the occasional wildlife sightings made the trip feel sacred.

Aleutian Islands, Alaska

Another unforgettable experience was my visit to the Aleutian Islands. While not as brutally cold during spring, they still held the remote, untouched beauty of the frontier. Fields of wildflowers greeted me alongside the coastlines, and I encountered many foreign workers, especially Filipinos, who had come to the islands to work in the seafood industry. Their presence there, so far from home, reminded me of my own journey and what it means to seek something better.

In Sitka, I felt another emotional pull. Here, the echoes of Imperial Russia still lingered. The Russian Orthodox church stood proudly against the Alaskan backdrop, and I heard stories about the Old Believers—a sect of Russians living traditional lives, similar in many ways to the Amish. Their long beards, old-style clothing, and commitment to preserving a centuries-old way of life intrigued me. It felt like I had found a hidden piece of Russia inside America.

Hawaii, too, became a frequent destination. I visited the islands three times, each time falling more in love with the tropical serenity. The beaches, the rhythm of island life, the warmth of the people—everything about Hawaii drew me in. It was the perfect contrast to the intensity of Los Angeles or the sprawl of Houston. Hawaii offered a healing, soothing presence that I came to crave.

These journeys, though brief, nourished my soul. They reminded me there was more to life than the daily grind and personal struggles. They opened my eyes to the diversity of human experience and landscape within the borders of a single country. Each trip was a small act of freedom—a reclaiming of joy and curiosity despite the burden of my unresolved immigration status. These were the moments that stitched together a patchwork of belonging in a country that never fully accepted me, but that I nonetheless chose to explore and love in my own quiet way.

The Passport That Wasn't

December 2011 arrived in Los Angeles like a quiet sigh. The streets sparkled with lights, palm trees wrapped in Christmas garlands, and shop windows glowed with festive decorations. The holidays were approaching—Christmas, New Year's—but I wasn't in a celebratory mood. The weight of my statelessness bore down on me more heavily during these moments. Everyone around me seemed to be making travel plans, going home to family, flying to winter wonderlands or warm beaches. I, on the other hand, remained tethered to one place by the invisible chains of legal limbo.

Still, I longed to go somewhere. I'd already visited many parts of the United States—Puerto Rico, Hawaii, Alaska, the West Coast, the desert—but this time, I wanted something more remote. Not another crowded city filled with high-rises and noise. I craved solitude, discovery, a feeling of stepping off the edge of the known world.

That's when I stumbled across American Samoa.

It was everything I was searching for: remote, beautiful, and technically within the United States. As a U.S. territory, it offered a legal grey area—a place I could reach without a passport, just with my California driver's license. I'd never been to the South Pacific. It felt like the closest I might ever get to Australia or New Zealand, distant lands I had always dreamed of but never had the chance to visit.

Before deciding on this trip, I had spent months—maybe years—researching any possible way to get a passport. A real passport. I combed through forums, blogs, obscure websites, hoping for a loophole, a backdoor, something. That kind of desperation leads people down strange paths.

One day, I found a website offering help with Canadian, U.S., and European documents. The site looked official enough. Not flashy, but just credible enough to make me believe. I started chatting with someone on the other end. I poured out my story—my statelessness, my desire for freedom of movement, my need for something, anything, that could help me live a normal life. He said he could help me get a Canadian passport. It would cost money, of course, but it was possible. It seemed too good to be true.

And it was.

He asked for a deposit—$600, maybe more, I don't remember the exact amount now. What I do remember is the wiring instructions: send the money to Ukraine via Western Union. I didn't question it. I was naive, hopeful, maybe a little reckless. I sent the money. And I never heard from him again.

All my messages were ignored. The site disappeared. That small flicker of hope went out like a candle in the wind. I felt stupid. Used. Ashamed. But it wasn't the end of my search.

Sometime after that, I found something that felt different: the World Service Authority, based in Washington, D.C. They offered what they called a "World Passport." It sounded like a fantasy, but the more I read, the more intrigued I became. The organization was founded by a former WWII bomber pilot, Garry Davis, who had renounced his U.S. citizenship after fighting in World War II. He dreamed of a world without borders, a place where citizenship didn't define your humanity. He had created a passport that declared its bearer a "World Citizen."

I learned he had walked into the U.S. Embassy in Paris, surrendered his citizenship, and emerged with only his world passport, only to be immediately detained by French authorities who didn't recognize it. His story resonated with me: someone disillusioned by the limitations of nations, dreaming of something bigger.

So, I applied.

The passport looked legitimate. It had my name, date of birth, place of birth—everything but a listed nationality. It read simply: World Citizen. I paid $160 for it, and when it arrived, I held it in my hands like it was gold. But it was something. It was more than I had before.

Now, with my California ID and this symbolic document, I felt ready to take the next step. American Samoa was calling.

I packed my bags. It wasn't much—I traveled light—but I included both the world passport and my driver's license. Just in case. I had no idea then that this journey, so carefully considered and yet seemingly so simple, would become a turning point in my life. It was meant to be a peaceful escape for the holidays, a quiet adventure to a distant island.

But instead, it would mark the beginning of one of the most difficult chapters in my life—a chapter written not with ink, but with fear, confusion, and the endless struggle of someone who belonged nowhere.

The passport that wasn't real. The trip that changed everything. The quiet island that became a storm.

American Samoa was waiting.

The World Passport I received felt like something real, something that gave me a sense of identity. It came as a printed booklet—just like any regular passport—with pages for visas and stamps.

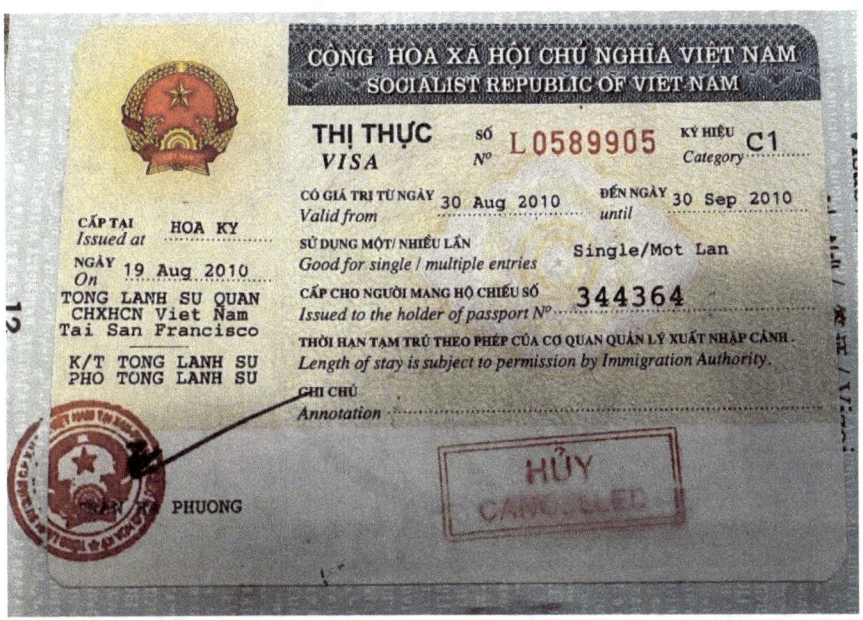

A Vietnam visa issued in my World Passport

At the time, I had no idea the World Passport wasn't widely recognized. I didn't come across any critical information about it. What I *did* see were photos online—people showing stamps in their World Passports from countries that had accepted it for entry or visas. That gave me hope. It seemed real enough. It gave me a sense of belonging.

What I didn't realize at the time was that this passport was controversial. Later, I'd learn that it's often criticized for being misleading—looking official, yet not accepted by most governments for international travel. But back then, I didn't know that. For me, it symbolized something bigger. It gave me a sense of security. As a stateless person, it felt like I finally had *something* in my hand—some kind of document that represented me.

So, I planned to use the World Passport while traveling within the U.S., instead of just relying on my driver's license. Not necessarily because I thought it was required, but because I wanted to feel like I had a passport—like I belonged somewhere.

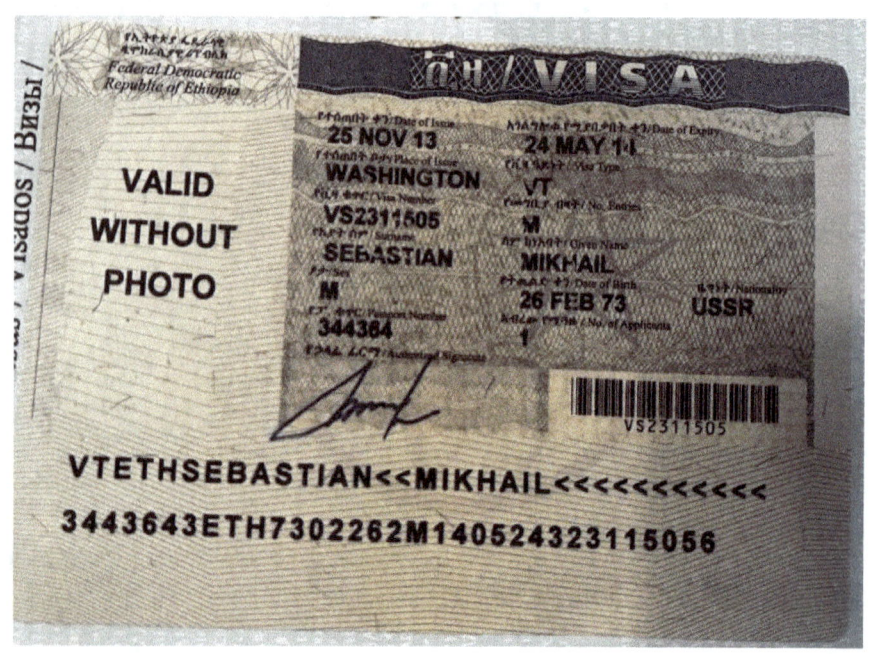

An Ethiopian visa issued in my World Passport

I thought back to my previous trip to Puerto Rico, which is a U.S. territory. There, all I needed was my ID. So naturally, I assumed the same rules would apply for American Samoa. I read that it was also a U.S. territory, and that was enough for me to feel confident. What I didn't understand back then was that Puerto Rico is an *incorporated* territory, and its people are U.S. citizens.

American Samoa, on the other hand, is *unincorporated* territory and its people are U.S. nationals—not citizens. But to me, it all sounded the same. I had no idea how crucial that difference would turn out to be.

With my documents in hand, I packed lightly for what I thought would be a four-day New Year's trip. I told my coworkers I'd be back soon. The only way to get to American Samoa was through Hawaii, since Hawaiian Airlines is the only carrier flying to Pago Pago.

At the Los Angeles airport, I went to the Hawaiian Airlines counter and handed over my driver's license. The agent asked if I had a passport, which threw me off—I didn't think I'd need one. Still, without hesitation, I handed her my World Passport.

She didn't seem to notice anything unusual about it at first. But when she tried to scan it, she ran into a problem—she couldn't find any information about my citizenship or nationality. I explained that I was stateless and gave her my Employment Authorization Document (EAD), which I renewed every year as part of my order of supervision. I think she mistook it for a green card (permanent resident) or something similar, and eventually, she issued my boarding pass.

I flew to Honolulu without issue. Once there, I looked for my connecting gate to Pago Pago, the capital of American Samoa, and noticed something strange: a sign next to the gate labeled it as an *international departure*. That confused me. Why would a flight to a U.S. territory be treated like an international one?

I asked the gate agent, and she told me that while American Samoa is indeed a

U.S. territory, it operates its own immigration system. So, technically, it's treated like an international destination.

That was a red flag. I started panicking. I knew this could cause trouble for me. My first instinct was to ask the agent to remove my luggage so I could stay in Hawaii and return to Los Angeles later. But by then, the gate area was crowded—people were pushing to board— and in the chaos, I somehow found myself swept onto the plane.

I sat down, terrified. My gut was screaming that I'd made a mistake. This wasn't going to be like Puerto Rico. But part of me still held onto hope. I had printed information that clearly said American Samoa was U.S. territory. I told myself I'd be okay.

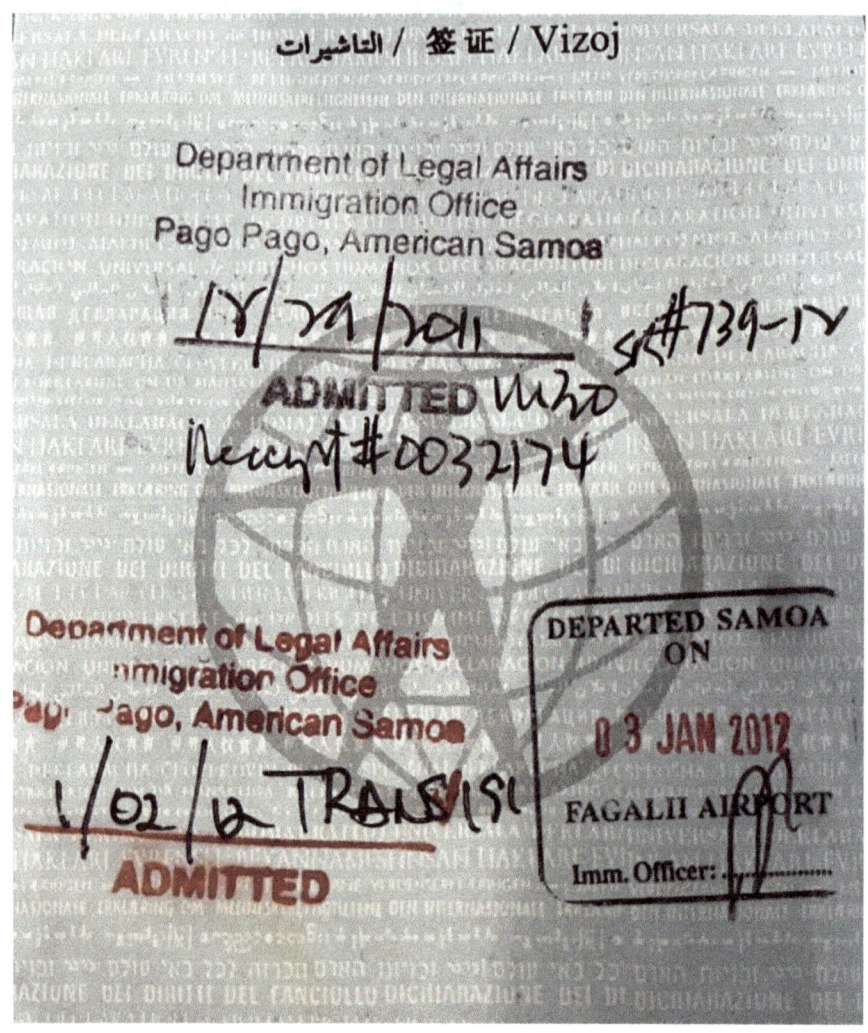

Entry stamp to American Samoa in my World Passport

When we landed in American Samoa, we had to go through local immigration. I handed them my World Passport. They looked it over, clearly unsure of what to do with it, and brought me to a back office for further questioning. The officer asked if I had anything else to show, so I gave her my California driver's license and my employment card.

From what I could tell, she assumed I was a permanent resident based on those documents. She stamped my World Passport and let me through.

And just like that, I found myself in American Samoa. In a completely unfamiliar place, thousands of miles from Los Angeles, with no idea that this short trip would lead to a major turning point in my life. It will become my curse and eventually define my fate.

American Samoa

American Samoa

American Samoa lies about 14 degrees south of the equator and just east of the International Date Line. It's the southernmost U.S. territory and the last place in the country to see the sunset each day. And just like that, I found myself there, still holding onto hope that everything would go as planned, but also a little terrified. Even though I was nervous, I felt ready. I had my documents prepared and was confident I could explain my case on the way back to Los Angeles: I hadn't left the U.S.— I was in a U.S. territory.

I checked into a hotel and began to explore. American Samoa was small, nothing like Puerto Rico. There weren't many tourists. It was hot, humid, and tropical, and with my sensitive and oily skin, the heat became unbearable. I was constantly sweating. The place felt isolated, far removed from everything I knew.

The capital, Pago Pago, had a small port where cruise ships occasionally docked. Tourists came off the ships for a few hours, wandered around, and left. There wasn't much to see beyond some scattered vegetation, a few undeveloped beaches, and flying foxes— giant bats protected by the National Park Service. It didn't feel like a tourist destination.

Apia. Western Samoa

Most of the people I met there were either on temporary assignments for the U.S. government or young professionals—lawyers fresh out of law school—looking for experience. That's when I learned about Western Samoa, or what is now simply called Samoa. I assumed it was just another island in the same chain, and I thought I could take a short trip there before flying back to L.A.

The day before my return flight, I decided to go. I took a short flight from Pago Pago to Apia, the capital of Samoa. When I arrived, they looked at my documents and my driver's license. But again, they asked for a passport. I didn't understand why—I still thought this might be U.S. territory, or that maybe they were just following stricter rules. So I handed over my World Passport. They stamped it without issue.

Apia. Western Samoa

Apia, in contrast to American Samoa, was more developed and tourist-friendly. It felt livelier, more modern, and definitely more welcoming. I saw tourists from Australia everywhere. Compared to the emptiness of American Samoa, Samoa felt like a real travel destination.

One of the most striking differences I noticed between American Samoa and Western Samoa was the physical appearance of the people. Though they share the same language, culture, and ancestral roots, their lifestyles have shaped them in visibly different ways. In Western Samoa, most people I saw were tall and slim, with a natural grace in the way they moved. Meanwhile, in American Samoa, people tended to be much larger in size, often overweight.

Curious about the contrast, I started asking locals about it. The most common explanation I heard was diet. In American Samoa, fast food is cheap and widely available—McDonald's, in particular, seems to be a popular hangout spot.

Burgers, fries, and sugary soft drinks had clearly become a staple in daily life. Many spent long hours there, eating not out of necessity but convenience and affordability.

In contrast, in Apia, the capital of Western Samoa, the lifestyle felt slower, more grounded. People mostly ate vegetables, chicken, and traditional island foods.

McDonald's, I was told, existed but was considered expensive, and many locals preferred to avoid it. The difference in diet was clear not only in people's size, but in their overall energy.

Market in Apia. Western Samoa

Apia itself was charming and full of character—a small city with friendly, welcoming people and a laid-back vibe. I spent a lot of time just walking around, observing daily life, comparing the rhythms of the two Samoa's, and learning from the little details that often go unnoticed.

After a short stay, I flew back to Pago Pago to connect to my flight to Los Angeles. At the airport, I handed over my driver's license again, and once more, they asked for a passport. I gave them the World Passport. The agent scanned it, then paused and asked if I had any other documents. I said no. She told me to wait and went to speak with her supervisor.

That's when I started to panic.

Her supervisor came over and said they had never seen this kind of passport before, and they needed to check with immigration. The moment she said "immigration," my heart sank. I knew something was wrong. This felt like the same warning sign I had seen earlier—when the gate in Honolulu said "International Departure" and the agent told me American Samoa ran its own immigration system. It was all happening again.

They scanned my documents and sent them to the U.S. immigration office in Honolulu. When they got a response, the agent returned and told me, "I'm sorry, but we're not allowed to board you on the flight."

I pleaded with her. I tried to explain that I wasn't entering the U.S.— I was returning to the U.S. I hadn't left the country. But she explained that, technically, American Samoa is outside the U.S. immigration zone. Even though it's a U.S. territory, because it runs its own immigration system, every passenger flying to Hawaii is required to clear U.S. immigration, as if arriving from a foreign country.

I was stunned. I couldn't process it.

She told me the immigration office flagged my name because I had an outstanding deportation order from years ago. Since the U.S. government couldn't remove me—because no country would accept me—I had remained under an order of supervision. But by voluntarily traveling to American Samoa, I had triggered that order. According to immigration, I had now "self-deported."

It felt like my entire world crumbled in that moment. I was in shock. I cried. I begged. I tried to talk to the supervisor again, but she told me there was nothing she could do. The immigration office had made the final call. She told me to go to the Attorney General's office the next morning to try to resolve the situation. But the flight was leaving that night, and the office was already closed.

I stood there, watching the plane take off. The same flight that was supposed to take me back home—to L.A.—now soaring into the sky, leaving me behind. I was stranded. I had barely any money left—I had only packed and planned for a short vacation. I was exhausted, terrified, and overwhelmed.

A dark thought crossed my mind—should I try to make a run for it? Climb the fence, board the plane anyway? But I knew I couldn't do that. I'd get arrested. And it wouldn't solve anything.

So, I just stood there, staring at the tarmac, watching the plane disappear. I felt like I was losing everything again—my apartment, my belongings—just like what happened in Houston, when I was detained and everything I had was gone in an instant. I thought I'd escaped that nightmare. But here I was again, lost, alone, and terrified.

Exiled in Flight

Just like that, I lost everything—again.

In 2001, I was apprehended by immigration authorities while working at Intra-Tours and placed in immigration custody at the Corrections Corporation of America. That arrest marked the beginning of a downward spiral.

Years later, in 2011, I was banned from entering the United States. According to immigration, I had "self-deported" when I left the U.S. mainland, even though I was under a prior deportation order from 1996 for voluntary departure. I lost my apartment in Houston, Texas, along with many of my belongings.

And now, once more, I was losing everything. I lost my apartment in Los Angeles. My belongings. My stability.

It was terrifying. Surreal. I didn't know what to do.

I was trapped. An exile—this time in American Samoa, a remote U.S. territory in the South Pacific.

As the plane took off, I stood there on the tarmac, stunned. Hopeless. A taxi driver approached me, thinking I was a tourist looking for a ride. But I explained my situation: I was trapped. He helped me return to the same hotel I had stayed at when I first arrived.

At the hotel reception, I tried to explain what had happened and asked if I could stay just one night. It was already late. I promised to sort things out the next day. The reservation agent took pity on me and gave me a room.

I barely slept.

The next morning, terrified, I stored my luggage with the hotel and went straight to the Attorney General's office, hoping for answers.

They were just as shocked and confused as I was.

After some time, I was introduced to Valerie Lawson, a Canadian woman working as an assistant to the Attorney General of American Samoa. I later learned that her husband worked at the Bank of Hawaii, and she had moved to American Samoa with him. A qualified, experienced lawyer, she had joined the AG's office to assist with legal matters.

Valerie reviewed my documents—my employment authorization card, my driver's license, and most puzzling of all, my World Passport.

"What is this?" she asked.

I explained everything—my statelessness, my situation.

She made some calls, trying to make sense of it. I sat in the waiting area, desperate for news.

I called Tiago Coffee Shop, where I worked, and spoke to Santiago. I told him I was stuck and didn't know when I'd be back. They were shocked too—they had expected me back in four days. The shop was short-staffed. They asked me to keep them posted. I had no idea then that I would be gone for a year and a half.

When Valerie returned, she told me the World Passport was not recognized by any country as a valid travel document. Some people may have entered countries with it, but there was no evidence they were ever allowed back.

She was shocked that American Samoa had admitted me using that document.

"Why American Samoa?" she asked. "The ticket here costs around $1,700. No tourists come here."

I explained my statelessness, how I had traveled to Puerto Rico before with no issues, and how I simply wanted a vacation outside the U.S. mainland. I came across American Samoa without realizing how complex and isolated it was, especially its independent immigration system.

She said to return the next day. In the meantime, the office arranged for me to stay again at the hotel, likely for five days or so, until they figured out a plan. They hadn't expected me to stay long.

Back at the hotel, I was finally able to rest. They provided food. I messaged everyone I knew, explaining what had happened. Confusion and fear echoed back to me from every corner.

The next morning, I returned to the Attorney General's office. Still no answers.

As I sat there, I noticed something that fascinated me. Several men—biologically male—were working in the office, dressed in feminine clothing and high heels. Their mannerisms were feminine, but their bodies were clearly masculine.

It surprised me. I had only seen drag queens perform in clubs, never working openly in professional settings like this. But in American Samoa, it seemed normal.

Later, I learned they were part of the fa'afafine community—a cultural identity in Samoa, distinct from Western ideas of gender. It was something completely new to me, and it sparked a deep curiosity. Fa'afafine is a recognized third- gender identity in Samoan culture, referring to individuals who are assigned male at birth but are raised and live as female. Unlike the Western concept of transgender identity, *fa'afafine* exists within a unique cultural framework—one that has long embraced gender fluidity as part of its traditional social structure. This role is not only accepted but often respected, deeply woven into the fabric of Samoan society for generations.

American Samoa

Amidst my personal crisis, I was also beginning to learn about the world, about identity, and about how different people live, survive, and find belonging, even in exile.

The curiosity about the men dressed as women continued to occupy my thoughts, even as I tried to rest and process the overwhelming sense of being trapped. I hoped that, at least, there might be someone in American Samoa who could help me resolve my situation, so that I wouldn't have to face it alone.

American Samoa

As I spent more time in American Samoa, I began to realize that their culture was different from anything I had encountered before. What I learned from the locals—and through my own observations— was fascinating. In American Samoa, if a family had multiple sons and no daughters, the youngest son would be raised as a girl. The same applied if a family had only daughters: the youngest daughter might be raised as a boy. This wasn't seen as strange; it was simply the way things were done. It was a practice that helped balance gender roles in a way that was considered normal within their culture.

This cultural norm was quite different from anything I had ever known. In American Samoa, even though homosexuality wasn't openly

accepted—there were no gay clubs or visible LGBTQ communities—
it was accepted for boys to be raised as girls and for girls to be raised as
boys. The family would protect these individuals, and it was not seen as
abnormal or out of place.

I found this new reality both fascinating and unsettling as I sat in the
Attorney General's office, waiting for news about my own situation.

Valerie, still working tirelessly to understand what had happened to
me, made calls to the mainland and tried to navigate through the
confusion. But there were no answers yet. Just when I thought the
situation couldn't get any more surreal, two unexpected officers arrived.
Valerie had contacted them, and they were now here to interview me.

They introduced themselves as FBI agents and explained that they
were investigating the unusual circumstances surrounding my case.
They were baffled—someone with a World Passport, traveling to
American Samoa, with a history of deportation issues, yet possessing
valid documents for work and living in the U.S. was unprecedented.

The agents asked me to follow them to the FBI office, where they
began questioning me about my identity, my legal status, and why I had
chosen American Samoa. I explained that I had traveled to many places
within the United States, including U.S. territories like Puerto Rico. I
was simply looking for somewhere remote, a place that felt different
from the mainland but still within the United States, and that's how I
ended up here. I had no idea this would turn into such a nightmare.

Then came the unexpected line of questioning:

"Have you been to any websites about fake passports?"

I was stunned. I didn't know what they were talking about. I had
visited countless websites during my search for legal documents, but
none about fake passports. After some prodding, I realized they were
referring to a website where I had once been scammed.

I explained to them that I had been desperate to find legal
documentation, and I had stumbled upon a website promising to
provide a Canadian passport. The person I communicated with had

initially suggested a passport under a different name, but later agreed to issue it under mine. They asked for a deposit of $600, which I sent to Ukraine via wire transfer. After that, I never heard from them again. I was scammed, but I didn't know it at the time.

Attorney General Office of American Samoa

I told the FBI agents everything I knew, hoping that my transparency would clear up any misunderstanding. They asked if I could provide them with the details of the wire transfer so they could trace the person who had scammed me.

I logged into my Wire account and provided them with all the information: the name of the recipient, the transfer date, and who had picked up the cash. I also explained my concerns that if this scammer was using multiple identities, there could be many others who had fallen victim to the same fraudulent operation.

After reviewing everything, the FBI agents were satisfied with my honesty. They confirmed that I had no involvement in any criminal activity, and they cleared me of any wrongdoing.

They escorted me back to the Attorney General's office and contacted Valerie to inform her that the situation was resolved. But my situation wasn't over. It was far from it. Valerie encouraged me to relax and wait until they called me, but I couldn't. I was desperate to get back to my life, to return to Los Angeles, to my job at the coffee shop, to my apartment, to some semblance of normalcy. I refused to leave the office. I couldn't just sit and wait. I needed answers, and I needed them now.

Trapped Between Borders

Day after day, I returned to the Attorney General's office in American Samoa, sitting there from morning until the office closed. I was trying to hold onto some shred of hope that something would change, but with each passing day, I became more and more consumed by the overwhelming weight of my situation.

Some people in the office seemed uncomfortable with me being there for so long, unsure how to help me. Others simply didn't know what to do. Valerie eventually approached me with a suggestion: perhaps I could volunteer to occupy my time. But at that moment, volunteering was the last thing on my mind.

How could I think about helping others when I felt so lost? This wasn't just a temporary setback; this was my second time being trapped. First, it was the immigration authorities who had detained me, but now, I was exiled in a place where I had no legal standing. I had lost everything twice over—my apartment, my belongings, my sense of stability. And now, I was banned from re-entering the U.S. mainland. The stress was unbearable.

Valerie's suggestion to volunteer came from a place of kindness, but she couldn't fully understand what I was going through. She wasn't in my shoes. She hadn't been a refugee fleeing war, or someone struggling to come to terms with their identity in a world where their very existence was criminalized. She didn't know the trauma I had endured, from being apprehended and detained in 2001 to facing deportation again, now in exile.

At the time, the idea of volunteering felt insignificant compared to the crushing weight of my reality. I was in a foreign place, with no way to return home, and every aspect of my life seemed uncertain.

As the days passed, Valerie informed me that the Attorney General's office could no longer afford to keep me in the hotel. They were trying to find a local family who could take me in temporarily until my situation was resolved. The office would cover the costs, but I couldn't help but feel the weight of this shift. This wasn't just about finding me a bed; this was about my life being reduced to a series of bureaucratic decisions.

The more I thought about it, the more I realized that the blame wasn't solely on American Samoa's Attorney General's office. It was also on Hawaiian Airlines, which had allowed me to board the flight to American Samoa without verifying the validity of my travel documents. Had they stopped me at the gate, I would have never found myself in this predicament. And yet, they were not held accountable.

Valerie continued to push, writing letters to various U.S. government agencies, trying to find a solution. The responses she received were consistent: because of my previous deportation order, and because I technically "self-deported" by leaving the U.S. mainland, they couldn't process my return. My case was closed, and American Samoa was left holding the responsibility.

What I didn't realize at the time was that American Samoa wasn't like other U.S. territories. Though American Samoans are U.S. nationals and hold U.S. passports, they can't easily transition to U.S. citizenship. Foreigners who enter American Samoa can't get residency, and locals who want U.S. citizenship must leave the island, live on the mainland for several years, and then apply. The laws were complex, and the more I learned, the more confusing everything became.

American Samoa

Despite Valerie's best efforts, including sending letters to Congress and contacting the Department of Homeland Security, no answers came. The decision was final: I could not return to the U.S. mainland. My case was closed, and my ties to the United States were severed.

It felt like a final goodbye to a place that, despite all its flaws, had once been my home. I was exiled, with no way back.

The Battle of Waterloo: My Exile Begins

The moment I arrived in American Samoa, I felt like I was facing my personal Waterloo. Much like Napoleon Bonaparte, who was defeated at the Battle of Waterloo and exiled to the remote island of Saint Helena, I found myself defeated by the immigration system, exiled to a place where escape was impossible, and the path forward uncertain. My exile was not one of military conquest, but one of bureaucracy, broken systems, and the weight of a government and society that seemed to have forgotten about people like me.

The United States government, the immigration authorities, and the maze of rules and regulations became my battlefield. I was stranded at the edge of the world, facing an unpredictable and overwhelming reality.

From the moment the sun rose each day, the heat of American Samoa hit me like a wall. The humidity, the stillness of the air, the suffocating heat—it was almost unbearable. The sun rose at six in the morning, and by eight, it felt like the island was already cooking under its oppressive rays. No wind, no relief, just the unrelenting heat. The physical discomfort mirrored the turmoil inside me. I had made the decision to come here, and now I was paying the price. In those moments, I couldn't help but blame myself for my hasty decision to fly to American Samoa. If only I had thought through the consequences, if only I had been more careful, I might not have ended up in this suffocating isolation. But there was no turning back. I was in exile, trapped in a place where the world seemed as oppressive as the climate.

After days of uncertainty, I was told the Attorney General's office had found a family that would take me in. Their names were Tupu and Susana Tao, a couple who lived on the outskirts of what could only be called the "city center" of American Samoa. The house was large, two stories, and had a certain rustic charm. Inside, I was introduced to their children—three girls, with the oldest studying in Hawaii. They also had a young granddaughter, left in their care while her mother pursued her studies in the U.S. I was struck by the kindness of this family. They provided me with food, shelter, and some semblance of normalcy in the midst of chaos.

But the refuge was temporary. I had no real escape. The heat in the house was suffocating, especially since there was no air conditioning. The walls seemed to trap the heat, and I found it nearly impossible to find any peace or respite. My thoughts were constantly interrupted by the oppressive heat, and I began to realize how little control I had over my situation. I asked for a fan to circulate the air, but it felt like a small comfort in a much larger storm.

The days blurred together. The constant diet of rice and chicken became both a physical and emotional reminder of my situation. I had grown up with access to fresh fruits, vegetables, and a variety of foods, but here I was, stuck in a cycle of monotonous meals. The chickens, scrawny and wild, were not like the tender birds I had known before. They roamed freely around the yard, and anyone could catch one for dinner. I began to feel like I had stepped back in time to a simpler, more communal way of life, one that reminded me of the Soviet Union, where everyone was connected, yet at the same time, no one had the freedom to live as they wished.

The family's way of life was alien to me, yet there was an odd comfort in their generosity. Despite the challenges, I began to form bonds with them, learning their customs, their daily rhythms. But no matter how much they gave me, I couldn't escape the fact that I was still an outsider, an exile in a land far from home. And the question that hung over me each day was: How long would this last?

During my time in exile, I began to learn more about the history of American Samoa and the complexity of its status within the United States. I learned that American Samoa was not like Puerto Rico or any other U.S. territory. While it was part of the U.S. in some ways, its people, though holding U.S. passports, were not granted full U.S. citizenship. Their unique status made it difficult for anyone, including myself, to fully understand how I could possibly fit into this system.

American Samoa had been divided from Western Samoa in the early 20th century, and the U.S. had taken control of the eastern part, making it a strategic military outpost. Over time, the Samoans were granted U.S. national status, but their path to U.S. citizenship was more complex than most people could understand.

This realization added a layer of complexity to my situation. I had come to American Samoa for vacation, seeking refuge from a busy city, only to discover that the very rules and systems I was trying to navigate were not as straightforward as I had imagined. The more I learned, the more I realized how little I knew about this place. American Samoa was both part of the U.S. and apart from it, creating a unique web of laws and expectations that left me feeling even more isolated. This understanding did not provide me with an easy answer, but it did give me a deeper understanding of my circumstances.

Exile, it seemed, was not just about physical separation from the world I knew—it was about being trapped in a system that refused to acknowledge my humanity. Each day, I faced new challenges: the oppressive heat, the isolation, the broken promises of resolution from the U.S. government. But I did not give up. I continued to fight for a way out, even when it seemed like no solution would come.

My time in American Samoa was not just a struggle for survival in a foreign land. It was a battle with myself, with the system, and with the idea of being stateless in a world that demands identity. Each day was a battle, and like Napoleon, I couldn't help but feel as though I was being sent to a place where escape was no longer possible.

A Lifeline in Exile

As I continued my exile in American Samoa, I found some solace in the kindness of Tupu, the man of the house. Tupu worked at the port, handling customs for the cruise ships that docked in the harbor. Every day, without fail, he would give me a ride to the only place in American Samoa where I could find something resembling hope: McDonald's.

McDonald's wasn't just a fast-food restaurant—it was the only place on the island that offered free Wi-Fi.

There, I could connect to the world beyond the island and send out SOS messages to anyone who might hear me. I was desperate, trying to reach out and find a solution to my statelessness, to figure out my next step.

By then, I had stopped caring about returning to the United States. I had spent years paying taxes, abiding by the laws, and contributing to the country without ever breaking any rules, yet the U.S. had shut its doors on me because of an immigration system that left people like me stranded in limbo. There was no law, no clear path to rectify the situation for someone like me. My only hope was to reach out to the rest of the world, hoping that someone, somewhere, might offer a way out. Tupu, despite his own struggles, helped me when he could, sometimes giving me small amounts of money, whether from a win at the local lotto or just out of generosity. He understood my situation, and though it was hard for him to grasp why a person could be stateless, he was sympathetic and always tried to help.

My days became a monotonous cycle of sitting at McDonald's, using their Wi- Fi to connect with the outside world. Tupu would drop me off every morning before heading to work, and I would stay until the sun set. Each day, I would write, tweet, send emails, and blog—anything to transmit my SOS messages. I was determined to reach someone who could help, anyone who would listen. I began to realize that my only shot at finding a solution was to use my voice, my story, and the power of the internet to spread my message as far and wide as possible. I needed to find someone who cared about the plight of the stateless, who could offer me a path forward.

The days spent in McDonald's were long, stretching from morning to night, but they became my refuge. I would often hear stories from the people around me—locals and tourists alike—about American Samoa, its unique political and social system, and the history that had shaped this place into what it was. I was still trying to make sense of everything, to understand the complexities of a territory that was part of the United States in some ways but separate in others.

As I spent more time in McDonald's, I struck up conversations with some of the locals, including a representative from the local government. I learned that American Samoa's relationship with the United States was far more complicated than I had initially thought. There were layers of history, politics, and cultural identity at play that I had not fully understood.

I was told that American Samoa had been deliberately kept separate from Western Samoa for a variety of reasons, the most significant being its sovereignty and its relationship with the United States. American Samoa had resisted the imposition of a federal immigration system, similar to what Puerto Rico had experienced, fearing that it would lose its autonomy and the special privileges it enjoyed. If American Samoa were to be incorporated fully into the United States, it would lose its status as a semi-autonomous territory, and the people would have to pay property taxes, face mortgages, and bear the same burdens that Hawaiians and Puerto Ricans had experienced when their lands were annexed.

Unlike Hawaii or Puerto Rico, where the government and its people were forced to accept U.S. rule, American Samoa had managed to maintain control over its land and resources. The land in American Samoa belonged to the people, and no one had to pay for mortgages or taxes on it. You could build a house by the ocean, and it would cost you nothing more than the materials. This was an incredibly important part of their way of life, and they were unwilling to lose it. They feared that if they joined Western Samoa or became fully integrated into the U.S., they would lose their land and freedom.

American Samoa's desire to remain separate from Western Samoa also stemmed from a fear of losing the benefits of the U.S. national status. By staying a U.S. territory, American Samoans retained their unique U.S. passports, which allowed them to travel freely without the visa restrictions that a Western Samoan passport would impose. For them, the U.S. passport was a vital asset—a symbol of their connection to the outside world and a lifeline to mobility.

The split between American Samoa and Western Samoa was not just political; it was also about identity. American Samoans did not want to lose the privileges that came with their relationship to the United States. They wanted to maintain their sovereignty while still being part of the broader American sphere. It was a delicate balance, one that many felt was worth preserving, even if it meant staying divided from their Pacific neighbors.

As I came to understand the complex dynamics of American Samoa, I began to realize that my quest for a solution to my statelessness was intertwined with these larger political struggles. The American Samoan people were caught between their desire for sovereignty and their connection to the United States, just as I was caught between my desire for belonging and my status as a person without a country. My search for help continued at McDonald's, writing messages, reaching out to organizations, individuals, and anyone who could offer assistance. But as I sat there day after day, I couldn't help but wonder: Would anyone ever hear me?

The Frustrating Wait: Hopelessness and Confusion

As the days turned into weeks, my situation grew more complicated. I continued visiting Valerie, but each time I was met with the same grim reality: there was no immediate hope. The U.S. government was still refusing to offer a solution, and American Samoa, with its ties to the U.S., couldn't accept me back. I had no legal status, no way to return to the United States, and the possibility of finding a country that would accept me seemed further out of reach with every passing day.

Despite the bleak outlook, I tried to connect with people in American Samoa. One person I became somewhat close to was a bodybuilder originally from Western Samoa. He had moved to

American Samoa to work, and we communicated about my predicament. It was difficult for him to understand how my situation could even be possible. How could someone be caught in such a bureaucratic nightmare? The more I explained my story, the more I realized how hard it was for people to grasp the complexity of my statelessness.

I watched, day after day, as tourists poured out of cruise ships and flocked to McDonald's, not only for the food, but for the air conditioning and Wi-Fi as well. While they were relaxing, waiting to leave, I couldn't help but fantasize about boarding one of those cruise ships and escaping the island, anywhere, as long as it was away from this place. The idea of stowing away crossed my mind, but I dismissed it quickly. I didn't want to involve Tupu, and I knew attempting to escape in such a way would have dire consequences.

I continued living with Tupu's family, making friends with his daughters. The older girl had a school project on the Russian Revolution, and I helped her research, using my knowledge from growing up in the Soviet Union. I kept myself busy, trying to maintain some semblance of normalcy, but it felt like I was in a holding pattern, unable to move forward or back. I was trapped—physically, emotionally, and politically.

One day, I remembered something from my past—the letter I had sent to the United Nations High Commissioner for Refugees (UNHCR) when I was detained in Houston, Texas. I decided to reach out again, hoping they might be able to offer some help. To my relief, I finally received a response. They had been investigating my case, communicating with embassies and organizations from the former Soviet republics to determine my status. After a long process, they confirmed that I was officially stateless according to the UN's definition.

This letter, confirming my statelessness, was sent to Valerie and eventually to a congressman from American Samoa. The hope was that it might open doors for further discussions with the U.S. government.

But despite all the efforts, it felt like everything was stuck in a loop. The meetings and attempts to move forward were stalled in bureaucratic limbo. Month after month passed, and I was still stuck on the island with no clear path forward.

Throughout this long, drawn-out process, there was one person who remained a consistent source of support: Lindsey Jenkins from UNHCR. She was in charge of statelessness cases and helped me navigate the bureaucratic nightmare I was facing. Lindsey kept in constant contact, updating me on the progress of my case, and kept pressing the U.S. government, particularly the Department of Homeland Security, to take action.

Lindsay Jenkins
Assistant Protection Officer, UNHCR

Despite her efforts, the reality was sobering. I was still trapped in American Samoa, with no way to return home, no passport, and no rights. Statelessness, I began to realize, was a form of human rights abuse. I was abandoned, caught in the gap between nations, unable to find refuge anywhere. Everyone is entitled to citizenship, to a passport, to a country that claims them as their own—but I had nothing. I was invisible, without identity, without protection.

I continued to send out my SOS messages, hoping that someone, somewhere, would hear my cry for help. But the replies were few and far between.

Meanwhile, I learned that Hillary Clinton had recently spoken in Geneva during the Day of Human Rights, where she was asked about statelessness. Her response was disheartening. She mentioned that the United States was a major donor to the United Nations, but never acknowledged the stateless crisis that was happening within its own borders. It seemed like the U.S. government, despite its advocacy for human rights globally, was ignoring the suffering of stateless individuals like me.

It was infuriating. Here I was, on American soil, stranded without a country, without rights, and yet the U.S. government was more focused on its role as a donor to international organizations than on addressing the human rights violations happening within its own territory. It felt like a betrayal, not just to me, but to the very ideals the U.S. claims to uphold.

McDonald's: My Refuge and Window to the World

McDonald's became my unexpected refuge in American Samoa. It wasn't just about the food or air conditioning—it was my only connection to the outside world. Day after day, I found myself there, sometimes just sitting with a cup of coffee, hoping for a breeze, a familiar face, or some hint of change. Over time, the employees and regulars began to recognize me. They didn't know the full story, but they saw I was different—someone clearly stuck in a strange place with nowhere to go.

Locals would occasionally approach me, curious about who I was. There were no articles about me in the local newspaper, no official statements—but word travels fast in small communities. People felt sorry for me, but didn't know how to help. Their own hands were tied.

As an incorporated U.S. territory, American Samoa could only do so much. Any decisions about my fate rested with Washington.

Still, McDonald's offered comfort. It was air-conditioned, open, and oddly communal. When I needed a break from the psychological weight I carried every day, I'd escape into that space, watching tourists wander in from the cruise ships, not to see the island, but to fill their bellies with burgers and Coca-Cola, hiding from the heat and waiting for their departure.

Sometimes, when the weather allowed—if the heat softened or rain cooled the air—I ventured outside. That's when I met a man I'll call John. I don't remember his real name, but I remember his kindness. He was an American who had moved to the island years ago, married a Samoan woman, and started a family. One of his sons was serving time in the local jail. I think that's what made him more empathetic—he knew what it meant to feel powerless in the face of systems.

John had heard my story through the grapevine and wanted to help, even if only by giving me a temporary escape from my reality. He took me hiking. We explored the mountains and beaches of American Samoa. The higher we climbed, the cooler it got. Shade from thick tropical trees created a different world—lush, alive, and quiet. For a few moments, I felt like I could breathe again.

We found crabs along the shore, examined plants I'd never seen before, and talked about life. I was always fascinated by biology growing up in the Soviet Union, and this island felt like a living classroom. I tried to learn the local flora, what plants might be used for healing, and how nature thrived here so freely.

John's generosity reminded me that kindness still existed—not transactional, not forced, just human. He didn't want anything from me. He just wanted to help someone in pain. It was humbling. In the mainland United States, people are often closed off, busy chasing careers, money, or status. But here, John—like many others—valued connection. His gesture opened my eyes.

Spending time with locals gave me a new perspective. American Samoa, though a U.S. territory felt like another world entirely. People lived simply. They weren't chasing wealth or fame—they cherished family, community, and faith. Sundays were for church—beautiful hymns filled the air. The islanders found joy in what they had, and their happiness came from togetherness, not possessions.

It reminded me of aspects of life in the former Soviet Union—the sense of communal responsibility, the closeness of family, the pride in language and culture. American Samoans preserved their language, spoke it every day, and passed it to the next generation. English may have been the official language of government, but Samoan was the language of the heart.

They were grounded in their identity. Their strength came from their unity, from their shared values and history. It was both familiar and completely foreign to me. It was something I had lost, or perhaps never truly had.

As I walked those mountain paths or sat in McDonald's, I began to think more deeply about life, about choices, about fate. I'd always heard of the "law of attraction"—that we bring into our lives what we put out into the world. I started wondering: Did I attract all this? Did I bring this exile upon myself?

Could I have chosen not to go to American Samoa?

The more I reflected, the more I realized that perhaps everything in life—good or bad—is drawn to us by some invisible force. If we attract chaos, perhaps it's because there's chaos inside us. But if we seek peace, clarity, and kindness, we can begin to pull those things toward us, too.

Meeting John, seeing the generosity of strangers, finding calm in the trees—it all showed me that there is good in the world. And maybe I could find a way to keep drawing that goodness into my life.

Recollection of Memory

I'm doing my best to gather as much information as I can about everything I went through—especially the time I spent in Azerbaijan, Armenia, and Russia. My memory is a bit blurry in places, but I'm trying to reconstruct it all as accurately as possible. A lot of the trauma I experienced, especially during my time in the detention center in Texas and later in American Samoa, has impacted my ability to recall everything clearly. Still, I feel it's important to get this story right.

I remember that my family fled to the Armenian Soviet Socialist Republic in the 1990s. I'm not entirely sure if that was during my time in school in Armenia or shortly after, but I believe it was after. I spent around four months in Armenia while my parents tried to find a way to settle there. But settling wasn't easy—there was a massive influx of Armenian refugees fleeing Azerbaijan, and Armenia itself was still reeling from the earthquake. The country wasn't in a position to help all the displaced people coming in.

Since Armenia didn't work out, we went to Russia in the early 1990s to try and build a new life. But again, it didn't go as planned. We couldn't settle there either. Eventually, we returned to Azerbaijan, but it wasn't long before things became worse. The cruelty and violence between Armenians and Azeris escalated even more. That's when we started the process of moving to Turkmenistan—but it happened in stages. It wasn't a one-time move. We had to go back and forth, moving things, trying to find someone willing to exchange apartments with us. I was attending university at that time, which made everything more complicated. I started university in 1991, and by 1992—maybe even earlier—we had already moved to Turkmenistan.

I think we left Azerbaijan for good around 1989 or 1990, before the full collapse of the Soviet Union. I still do not remember the years when everything happened. The conflict between Armenia and Azerbaijan had already turned violent. There were killings, rape, and all kinds of atrocities. That's why we escaped in the first place.

As for statelessness, I want to say a few things about that. Statelessness isn't just a legal condition. It's a human rights issue. And in the United States, the human rights of stateless people are regularly violated. The U.S. government has waged a quiet war against stateless individuals, refusing to adopt any meaningful legal protections. They continue this war in silence, without acknowledging the damage they cause.

The United Nations adopted the 1954 Convention Relating to the Status of Stateless Persons—a treaty aimed at protecting people like me. The U.S. government refused to sign it. That decision alone says a lot. It's as if the U.S. spat in the face of the UN and the rest of the world. Every time the issue of statelessness is brought up in international conferences, U.S. officials like Hillary Clinton love to remind everyone that the U.S. is the major donor to the UN. But what does being a "major donor" have to do with protecting stateless people living in the U.S.? The answer is—nothing.

It's as if the U.S. is saying: "We're paying the bills, so don't tell us what to do."

When I was nine months into my confinement in American Samoa, I had already spent 16 years of my life in the U.S., building a future. And yet, the country that preaches about human rights in China was violating my rights on its own soil. The same country that was built by immigrants had turned against them. The same country that calls on others to treat stateless people with compassion had no compassion for those already within its borders.

I wasn't just stuck—I was being mentally and physically broken. I wasn't allowed back into the U.S. I wasn't given help to go anywhere else. I was left in limbo, stuck in a U.S. territory, invisible and unwanted.

I know I'm not the only one. There are other stateless people who feel the same pain, the same abandonment. You can't just sit and wait for some official to wake up one day and fix this. We have to speak up. We have to fight.

Immigration and Customs Enforcement treated stateless people like third-class humans—like we didn't matter. The emotional exhaustion, the hopelessness, the endless waiting—it was unbearable. I was confined, with no way in and no way out. I was tired of being at the mercy of a system that didn't care.

Invisible People

While still stranded in American Samoa, I kept fighting. I wrote, I blogged, I sent messages—crying out for help in any way I could. I never imagined, growing up in the Soviet Union, that one day I would become a person who belonged nowhere. Statelessness was never something I even considered. It wasn't a concept I understood—until I was living it.

Then, somehow, I found myself in the United States—the most powerful country in the world. A country that claims to be a global protector of human rights. But this same country has no laws, no regulations, and no system in place to address statelessness. Despite all its resources and power, it cannot figure out how to protect those who have no country. Statelessness is mankind's most silent crisis.

After World War II, the international community came together to prevent such suffering. The 1954 Convention Relating to the Status of Stateless Persons was the first significant step in that direction. Later came the 1961 Convention on the Reduction of Statelessness. The U.S. left its fingerprints all over these efforts, but refused to take any responsibility. It never ratified either treaty.

And here we are, decades later, still turning our backs on stateless people. Still denying rights and protection. Still pretending the problem doesn't exist. So, what happened to the inalienable rights we supposedly hold sacred—life, liberty, and the pursuit of happiness? How can the

U.S. lead the world in human rights advocacy while ignoring the most vulnerable population within its own borders?

There are an estimated 12 to 15 million stateless people worldwide. Many live invisible, unprotected lives. Some are used by criminal gangs as pawns, because no state will claim them. They have no documents, no country, no voice. They're perfect targets for exploitation. Some might even turn toward violence, not because they are evil, but because they've been abandoned, erased, and stripped of all dignity.

And in the United States, our immigration laws don't just ignore statelessness—they enable its abuse. Despite advancements in science, education, and global cooperation, we still lack the most basic understanding and compassion for stateless people. Our government continues to detain us, confine us, and deny us a legal path forward—all while focusing media attention on "illegal immigration."

But here's the truth: most stateless people entered legally. We had visas. We followed the rules. We didn't "sneak in." We simply became unwanted by our former states, and the U.S. had no process to deal with that.

I remember one case from my time in detention in Houston, Texas. A Nigerian man was in a similar situation—his government refused to recognize him.

Eventually, U.S. authorities obtained a mysterious one-way travel document for him, apparently from the old INS. They tried to deport him via KLM Royal Dutch Airlines, routing through Amsterdam. But once the plane landed in Amsterdam, he escaped custody, ran to a police station at the airport, and applied for asylum in the Netherlands. What happened next, I don't know. But that story stayed with me. Because it showed the lengths people have to go just to be seen as human.

While the U.S. government condemns statelessness in Asia, Africa, and the Middle East, it completely ignores the issue at home. So, here's my question: Can the stateless population of the U.S. get a pass into whatever alternate reality the Department of State, the Department of

Justice, the Department of Homeland Security, and ICE are living in? Because what we see, what we endure in the real world, is absolutely unjustifiable.

Statelessness is a condition that deprives individuals of all positive rights. It forces us into a world where state sovereignty trumps human rights. In my case, that meant six months in immigration detention, denied legal status, exiled and confined in American Samoa, against my will. I was refused travel documents to seek asylum in Europe. I was trapped.

The U.S. must amend its Immigration and Nationality Act to include statelessness as a ground for protection and settlement. And it must finally ratify the 1954 and 1961 UN Conventions.

Compare this with Europe:

- In the United Kingdom, recognized stateless persons can apply for a special passport.

- In the Czech Republic, a stateless person can apply for nationality after five years of permanent residency.

- In Sweden, even asylum seekers who don't meet traditional protection criteria may still be granted residency, for reasons like integration or adaptation.

Stateless individuals there can also receive travel documents under the 1954 Convention.

- Even Syria, which turned its country into a civil war, was able to grant citizenship to thousands of stateless Kurds in 2011.

If Syria could find the moral courage to acknowledge and address statelessness, what is the United States waiting for?

Breaking News

Life in American Samoa dragged on in a strange, repetitive rhythm. Each day started the same: I would walk to the Attorney General's office to check with Valerie, still hoping, still asking if there was any update about my case.

Afterwards, I'd return to McDonald's, my makeshift office, to write, send messages, and keep pushing out calls for help into the void of the internet.

At one point, I had a glimmer of hope. The Congressman of American Samoa, Eni Faleomavaega, got involved. He sent a formal letter to the Department of Homeland Security (DHS) asking them to intervene in my case and allow me to return to the U.S. mainland. But the response from DHS—under Secretary Janet Napolitano at the time—was a denial, layered with legal acrobatics that only deepened the absurdity.

First, DHS argued that by traveling from the mainland United States to American Samoa, I had voluntarily self-deported. That made no sense—American Samoa is a U.S. territory, not a foreign country. But when American Samoan officials challenged that logic, DHS shifted its argument.

They claimed that my brief trip from American Samoa to neighboring Western Samoa (now known as Samoa)—and my subsequent return—meant I had crossed a U.S. border. And since American Samoa allowed me to re-enter after visiting Western Samoa, DHS claimed that the territory had effectively taken full responsibility for me. According to them, I was now American Samoa's problem, not theirs. They insisted that I should not have been allowed back into U.S. territory in the first place.

It was all a smokescreen. A deliberate effort to complicate things, pass the buck, and avoid taking responsibility.

American Samoa is not a foreign nation. It is part of the United States. So, if I returned from Western Samoa to American Samoa, I was back on U.S. soil. But instead of addressing my case, DHS used these flimsy technicalities to justify leaving me stranded.

It reminded me of a more recent case—one involving a Salvadoran man, married to a U.S. citizen, with legal permission to remain in the United States. Despite his status and the court's protection, he was mistakenly deported to El Salvador's notorious prison for gangs and criminals. When a federal judge ruled that the U.S. government had to bring him back, the government argued that it was too late—he was already deported and outside their jurisdiction. But if they could deport him, they could also bring him back. They simply chose not to.

And that's what happened to me. The U.S. government made up excuses not to bring me back. First, they claimed I self-deported. Then, they blamed my trip to Western Samoa. Finally, they washed their hands of me entirely, saying American Samoa had accepted me, so now I was their responsibility.

But I refused to give up. I told myself: I will fight until my voice is heard.

And eventually, someone listened.

A journalist named Moses from GlobalPost saw my SOS tweets and contacted me. He was intrigued by my story and wanted to write about my situation. That article was the first time my case was made public. From there, everything started to move.

After GlobalPost, more media outlets reached out—National Public Radio (NPR), Salon.com, Huffington Post, and even local media from American Samoa, New Zealand, and the Northern Mariana Islands. My name began circulating. My story began to spread.

I remember getting a phone call from NPR. They wanted to do a live interview. It was around September 2012, if I remember correctly. I was told to go to a local radio station to connect with NPR's Washington office. The interview aired under the title: Stateless and Stranded in American Samoa.

Living in limbo. Denial of human rights to stateless persons in the United States

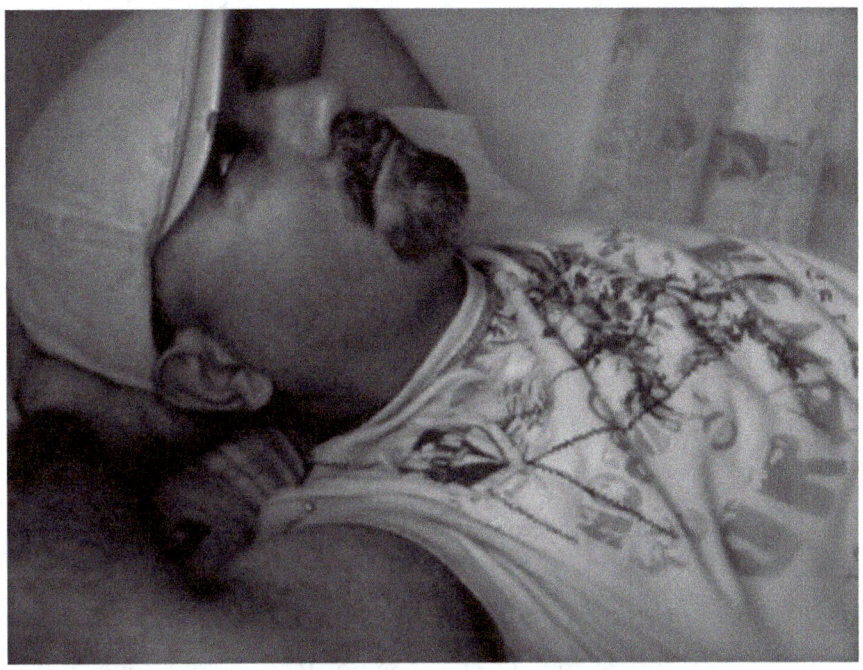

That NPR piece sparked even more attention. Salon.com asked me to write a personal letter detailing my experience. I titled it Vacation from Hell. It wasn't meant to be catchy—I just wanted the world to understand the nightmare I was living.

In a strange twist, I started to become well-known in American Samoa. People began recognizing me, talking about me. I was becoming somewhat of a local celebrity—not because I wanted fame, but because I refused to be silent. I didn't want attention. I only wanted help.

But somehow, through all the hardship, the despair, and the endless bureaucratic runarounds, I had managed to make my voice heard.

Hope in the Shadows

While I was living with the American Samoan family, who, as I mentioned before, were incredibly generous, understanding, and kind, we created a kind of makeshift routine. In the evenings, we'd often gather together as a family.

We watched movies and cartoons with the children, shared meals, and talked about life. Sometimes the conversations turned serious: we discussed world affairs, life in the U.S., and the complicated relationship between American Samoa and the United States.

I learned a lot just by observing and listening. American Samoa is a small island with limited opportunities, especially for young people. After finishing high school, many of them leave for Hawaii or the mainland United States to pursue education or careers. One thing that stood out to me was how many young American Samoans chose to enlist in the U.S. Army. Military service was a common path—it offered benefits, a sense of purpose, and a way out. Some stayed in the Army for their careers. Others returned to the island or settled on the mainland after their service.

But not all was hopeful. American Samoa faces serious public health challenges. Obesity, diabetes, and kidney issues requiring dialysis are widespread. Much of this stems from the diet: fried foods dominate, and fast food—especially McDonald's—is a staple. I rarely saw anyone eat vegetables or fresh fruit. For many, McDonald's wasn't just a convenience—it was a cornerstone of daily life, a place to hang out, grab a quick bite, or just pass time.

Despite these challenges, the people of American Samoa were incredibly warm and compassionate. I remember one night clearly: I had stayed late at McDonald's, working as usual, and by the time I left, the buses had stopped running. I didn't have enough cash for a taxi, and walking home would have taken over an hour in the dark. I was stranded. A Samoan woman saw me standing outside and asked if I needed help. I explained my situation, and without hesitation, she paid for a taxi to take me home. That moment of unexpected kindness stayed with me.

During the day, when I couldn't afford transportation, I would walk home. The walks became something spiritual for me. They gave me time to think—even if that thinking was often heavy and filled with worry. My mind was constantly occupied. Even when I tried to sleep, I felt like I wasn't really resting. My body was in bed, but my thoughts kept spinning. I'd wake up exhausted, as if I hadn't slept at all.

There were days I felt completely broken. The psychological toll was immense. At one point, I fell into such a dark place that I seriously considered ending my life. I felt like I couldn't endure the uncertainty and isolation anymore. I was 39 years old, alone on a remote island, and every door I tried to open seemed bolted shut.

Still, I kept fighting. I sent messages, made phone calls, and tried every possible route. I was willing to go anywhere at that point—any country that would take me. I just needed a travel document that would allow me to board a plane and leave. I even reached out to the United Nations High Commissioner for Refugees (UNHCR), asking if they could help relocate me to a third country.

The response was cautious but not without hope. They told me my case was complicated and that relocating me would be extremely difficult. Before they could even consider that option, they would need to exhaust all possible avenues with the U.S. government. Only if the U.S. completely refused to take responsibility would they start searching for another country that might accept me, which would mean even more delays.

In the meantime, I had no choice but to continue waiting, reading, writing, surviving. Slowly, cautiously, hope began to return when the UNHCR agreed to advocate on my behalf. I was in contact with two people from their office: Lindsay Jenkins, Sr. Protection Officer and Charity Tooze, who I believe was a senior communications officer at the time.

Charity told me that the UNHCR was in direct contact with the Department of Homeland Security regarding my case. I remember her saying: "Our hope is to continue to advocate on Mikhail's behalf. I'm not in a position to say whether or not the wheels of bureaucracy will turn fast enough, but I do know that we are doing what we can to reach out on his behalf." She also pointed out that my situation highlighted the struggles of over 12 million stateless people around the world.

When the UNHCR stepped in, I felt, for the first time in a long while, that I wasn't entirely alone. And as media coverage of my story continued to grow—across the United States and beyond, I became known as the stateless man stranded in American Samoa. It was never the kind of recognition I wanted, but it was a step toward being seen, toward being heard.

Exiled Within Exile: Silence, Identity, and Survival in American Samoa

Living with the American Samoan family who took me in was, in many ways, a blessing. Their kindness, generosity, and patience gave me a roof, a sense of safety, and a window into their daily lives. We'd often gather as a family to socialize. Sometimes we'd sit together, talking about the world, about Samoan culture, traditions, daily life or simply share a meal. These moments were comforting. They helped distract me from the ever-present uncertainty of my own situation.

But one part of me remained hidden.

I never spoke about my sexuality. I kept that part of my identity buried deep inside, behind layers of practiced silence and years of learned caution. I didn't know how people would react, especially the man of the house. He once made a casual but negative remark about gay people. That single moment was enough to lock the door on any possibility of honesty.

Still, I sensed they had suspicions. Susana, the wife, asked me a few times whether I had a girlfriend or if I planned to marry and have children. Her questions were gentle, almost probing, as if she was offering me a small opening to share. But I couldn't walk through that door. I answered vaguely and deflected. The fear of rejection—or worse—was too great.

People notice things you don't see in yourself. Sometimes it's in your voice, your posture, your walk. After recording myself on video, I began to see what others might have seen—maybe a hint of softness in my tone, or something in my stride that betrayed what I worked so hard to hide. But that's just who I was. I couldn't change it, and I had no reason to be ashamed of it. Still, survival demanded silence.

Unlike in the United States, I didn't see any sign of an LGBTQ community on the island. No clubs, no open expressions. Maybe it existed quietly, like an underground current. But I didn't seek it out. I didn't have the space to explore that part of myself—not in that moment, not in exile. My focus was survival. And in many ways, American Samoa reminded me of the places I had left behind— Azerbaijan, Turkmenistan—where fear, secrecy, and threats of violence followed anyone who didn't conform.

In Turkmenistan, I had been beaten at university—attacked simply because I was perceived as different, as not masculine enough. I kept my head down there too, just as I did now. It was a painful form of self-erasure, but it was the only way I knew to stay safe.

During this time, my laptop became my lifeline. It was more than a machine—it was my pen, my paper, my voice, and my escape route. I sent messages to journalists, to lawyers, to human rights organizations. I tweeted SOS pleas into the digital void, hoping someone—anyone— might respond.

And someone did.

The UNHCR kept in contact with the Department of Homeland Security on my behalf. I was doing everything I could from my end— writing, calling, advocating. And they were doing the same from theirs.

Still, the process moved slowly, and the weight of uncertainty never lifted.

I often thought about others in my position. I wasn't just fighting for myself. I was fighting for those who didn't have the tools, the voice, or the platform. At the time, estimates suggested that around 4,000 stateless people were living in the United States. But no one really knew the true number. Many lived in hiding, afraid to surface, knowing that once their name entered the immigration system, they could be detained indefinitely, caught in a legal limbo with no way forward and no way back.

I knew this firsthand. When I was detained in the immigration center in Houston, I learned the harsh economics of exile. The U.S. government paid the private facility $150 per day for each immigrant held inside. Detention had become a business—one that profited from people like me. Not criminals. Not threats. Just human beings trapped in a system that had no place for them.

So, I stayed in American Samoa, quietly surviving. Walking sometimes for hours when I couldn't afford the bus. Sleeping with my mind racing, only to wake up exhausted. I smiled when I needed to, hid my pain when I had to, and kept writing—writing to escape, to remember, and to hold onto hope.

Medical Emergency in Exile

By the end of October or maybe early November 2012, nearly a year into my confinement in American Samoa, I found myself facing a new and urgent crisis—one that went beyond paperwork and legal limbo. I needed surgery.

The diagnosis came during a visit to the LBJ Tropical Medical Center in Pago Pago. I had started to feel discomfort in my lower abdomen. Something wasn't right. My testicles were swelling, and the pain was growing worse by the day. At first, I ignored it, thinking it would go away. But it didn't. Eventually, I went to the hospital, where I was seen by Dr. Vladimir, a Russian doctor working at LBJ. There was something comforting about hearing Russian again, even in that moment of vulnerability. He examined me and diagnosed me with an inguinal hernia and interdigital mycosis. The hernia required surgery, but the hospital lacked the facilities and specialists to perform the operation safely. I needed both a neurologist and a haematologist—neither of whom existed on the island.

That's when desperation took hold.

I reached out to everyone I could. I pleaded with the local American Samoan government, the U.S. federal government, the United Nations, and even the local newspaper, Samoa News. I contacted the Office of the Attorney General and begged for them to send me off the island, just anywhere I could get proper treatment. At that point, I didn't care where—Hawaii, Los Angeles, anywhere but there. I could not bear another day in exile, not like this.

It had already been nearly a year since I arrived in American Samoa, and the stress was becoming unbearable. I was smoking heavily, my anxiety was consuming me, and my body, now literally, was beginning to break down.

Initially, my case was being handled by an assistant attorney general named Valerie, who had been supportive and understanding. But then she left—her husband got a new job, and she had to move with him. That's when Vincent Cruz, a new assistant attorney general, took over. I reached out to him, hoping he might be able to help push for a solution.

Instead, I read his words in Samoa News. He said the Attorney General's Office had done all it could and that there was little they could do to help a stateless person like me. He said, "American Samoa cannot deport someone unless another country has given permission for that person to enter."

But that wasn't entirely true. And I knew it.

According to international law, specifically under conventions related to deportation, expulsion, and removal, a stateless person can be deported to the country of their last habitual residence if they have no nationality. In my case, that was the United States, where I had lived for 16 years. It wasn't just a technicality. It was my life. My roots were there. My identity, my community—everything I had—was in the U.S. That's where I had built my life before I fell through the cracks of immigration and statelessness.

But my arguments fell on deaf ears. No one seemed willing to challenge the system. Everyone was "waiting for a decision by the federal government." I appreciated the effort, I truly did. But meanwhile, I was in pain, physically and emotionally deteriorating with each passing day.

I kept fighting, kept sending emails, kept making noise. My laptop—my only real tool—became a lifeline, a megaphone, and my only companion. I was just trying to stay alive, to stay sane, to survive this silent war with bureaucracy and geography.

Eventually, I would get the surgery. But not there. Not in Pago Pago.

It would take more time—months more—before I finally left American Samoa. And only after my return to the mainland United States was I able to receive the medical care I needed. I underwent laparoscopic hernia surgery in the state of Massachusetts, after I had settled on the small island of Martha's Vineyard. It was there, in that peaceful corner of America, that I finally began to piece my body and my life back together.

But during those long months in American Samoa, with my health failing and no answers in sight, I felt abandoned by systems that were supposed to protect the vulnerable. I was left in limbo, caught in a place where I didn't belong, unable to move forward or go back. My body became a metaphor for my condition—ruptured, strained, in need of urgent repair.

And yet, somehow, I kept going.

Framed in Exile

At some point in late 2012, as I continued navigating the ever-tightening labyrinth of statelessness from within the confines of American Samoa, I found myself in communication with the United Nations High Commissioner for Refugees (UNHCR) more frequently. My main contact there was Lindsey Jenkins, the Assistant Protection Officer. She had been following my case for months, advocating on my behalf with compassion and consistency.

One day, Lindsey told me something unexpected: UNHCR was considering producing a short documentary about me. Their goal was to highlight the issue of statelessness in the United States—something still so rarely acknowledged—and the film would potentially be screened during Human Rights Day, possibly even at the White House.

At first, I hesitated. I didn't want to be on camera. I didn't want to be portrayed like some kind of exhibit—an exotic animal in a zoo, on display for others to gawk at, pity, or pass judgment on. I worried about how the video might affect my case. What if the wrong words, the wrong framing, made things worse?

David Baluarte
Mikhail's Lawyer

But ultimately, I agreed. Not for myself, but out of respect for the efforts the UNHCR had invested in trying to help me. They had gone far beyond their mandate, trying every possible channel to get me out of the limbo I was stuck in. I felt it was my way of honoring their efforts—to allow them to tell my story so others might be helped too.

And then, something even more meaningful happened. Lindsey Jenkins connected me with a lawyer. Not just any lawyer, but someone who was dedicating his life to the legal fight for stateless people like me. His name was David Baluarte. At the time, he was an Associate Dean and a Clinical Professor of Law at Washington and Lee University in Virginia. He took my case on pro bono, and from the moment we connected, I knew I was finally being guided by someone who understood the magnitude of what I was going through.

David didn't just see a lost case or an immigration puzzle. He saw a person whose life had been unmade by invisible borders. He knew this was unprecedented—and he wasn't afraid to say it. I remember people constantly comparing my situation to Viktor Navorski, the character Tom Hanks played in The Terminal. A man trapped in transit, stateless and directionless, caught between the cracks of nations and bureaucracy. But this wasn't fiction. This was my life.

When the film crew finally arrived in American Samoa, I met Patrick and Jennifer, two kind, compassionate Americans working on behalf of the UNHCR. For a brief moment, it felt like someone had opened a window in the suffocating room I had been locked in for so long. They interviewed me, filmed scenes of my day-to-day life, and gave me space to share my truth. Sometimes I got too emotional and couldn't finish a thought. We would pause and try again. They were patient, never pushing, never judging.

They stayed for about a week. When it came time for them to leave, I went to the airport to see them off. I stood by the departure gate, holding back tears—and then failing to hold them back. Watching them board that plane, something inside me cracked. I was happy for them, of course, but I was also devastated. I longed for what they had: the freedom to come and go, the ability to leave.

Before Patrick left, he gave me a gift—something simple but deeply meaningful. He helped me upload episodes of a British comedy series called Miranda. He knew I needed a distraction, something to lift me, even briefly, out of my mental darkness. What he didn't know was how effective that gesture would be.

After they left, I began watching Miranda every night. I laughed—genuinely laughed—for the first time in months. The absurdity, the awkwardness, the joy of the characters on screen—it allowed me to forget where I was. For 30 minutes at a time, I wasn't a stateless exile trapped on a remote island. I was just someone laughing at a joke. Someone human again.

Patrick was gay. That detail matters—not just because it gave me someone I could privately relate to, but because it reminded me I wasn't completely alone. There was someone else who understood what it felt like to exist in a space where you couldn't be fully seen or accepted for who you are. He made me feel safe, understood, and momentarily seen in a world that had tried to render me invisible.

That week, with the cameras rolling and kind people listening, became one of the most healing moments of my entire exile. Not because it changed my circumstances, but because it reminded me that I still mattered. That somewhere out there, people cared. That the fight to be seen, to be heard, and to be free was not mine alone.

A Voice Beyond the Island

When Patrick and Jennifer left American Samoa, they took with them not just footage and interviews, but a part of my story—a cry for help captured in pixels and frames. They were headed back to edit the documentary that would, as I was told, be shown during Human Rights Day, possibly at the White House. For me, it was more than just a film—

it was a lifeline, a chance for the world to see what statelessness looks like in the flesh.

When the video was finally completed and I received the link, I felt a surge of hope I hadn't felt in a long time. It wasn't just about me anymore. My story now carried the weight of others—those who, like me, were living in the shadows of the legal system, without identity, without protection, without a home. I knew that people around the world, in the U.S. or elsewhere, who had endured statelessness could see themselves in my story. Maybe this video would help amplify our collective voice.

Without wasting a second, I downloaded it. I saved it like a treasure—something sacred. Then I started sending it everywhere: media outlets, human rights organizations, immigration lawyers, advocates, and newsrooms. I was desperate for someone to see it, to take it seriously, and to do something, not just for me, but for all of us who lived without a country to call our own.

The video began with a shot of the hotel where I stayed on the day I arrived in American Samoa—December 29, 2011. Back then, I was just another traveler. I had come for what was supposed to be a four-day vacation. I had no idea those four days would turn into nearly a year of entrapment.

The documentary told my story with brutal honesty. It included interviews with people who had come to play crucial roles in my life, like Lindsey Jenkins of the UNHCR and my lawyer, David Baluarte. Lindsay, Assistant Protection Officer at UNHCR, explained the legal foundations of my statelessness in a way I never could:

"Mikhail was born in the former Soviet Union. He and his family, due to threats and discrimination based on their ethnicity, fled from one republic to another. Because of their flight, they never fulfilled the residency requirements needed to gain citizenship in any of the post-Soviet countries. Eventually, Mikhail came to the United States in the late 1990s to seek asylum."

David explained how I had received permission to travel to American Samoa without fully understanding where I was going or what the consequences might be. And once I was there, the system simply didn't know what to do with me.

"American Samoa has no idea what to do with Mikhail. He's stuck there, by all accounts, in a McDonald's, sending messages for help around the world."

The footage cuts between moments of my own interview and commentary from Lindsey and David, showing the legal and humanitarian crisis of statelessness through the lens of one man's lived experience. Lindsey emphasized the larger implications:

"Mikhail's case highlights the lack of legislation in the United States for stateless individuals. There's no framework to grant them citizenship or even permanent residency. What's happening to Mikhail should never happen again."

She also reminded the audience of the promises made:

"In December 2011, at a ministerial meeting in Geneva, the U.S. reaffirmed its commitment to preventing statelessness. And yet, people like Mikhail remain forgotten, unprotected, and ignored."

One moment from the video stayed with me the most. A haunting line:

"Our own courts have found statelessness to be a punishment more primitive than torture."

That sentence echoed in my head for days. Statelessness wasn't just about lacking a passport or an ID. It was about existing without the most basic human recognition. It was about walking through the world unseen, uncounted, and unwanted.

In the final scene of the documentary, my voice cut through the silence:

"I want the U.S. government to bring the issue of statelessness to life. To know that stateless people exist in this country—and to understand the grief, the difficulty, and the fear that come with that. I want them to allow us a pathway to become permanent residents, and eventually, citizens."

That was my hope—that someone in Washington, someone watching that documentary, would hear those words and act. That our suffering would finally be acknowledged. Those policies would change. That no one else would ever have to go through what I did.

And maybe, just maybe, this video—this small but powerful piece of my story—would be the beginning of something bigger than me.

From Purgatory to Possibility

After the UNHCR video was produced and began making its way around the world, I refused to sit still. Every second mattered. I was still stuck in American Samoa, but my story was no longer confined to the island. I sent that video everywhere I could—across every corner of the globe, to every media outlet, human rights group, and advocacy platform. It was my SOS, not only for myself but for others like me.

Then came a glimmer of unexpected hope.

I was contacted by someone at CNN. He told me he worked closely with Christiane Amanpour, one of the most respected and acclaimed international journalists. He asked if I was still in American Samoa. I replied, "Yes." He said CNN was interested in my story but still needed confirmation. Even that small gesture—a possibility—lit a spark in me. I had watched CNN for years. To be featured on their platform was not just a dream; it was a shot at being heard.

I sent them the video UNHCR had produced and explained the context in detail. I told them what American audiences rarely heard: media in the U.S. talked endlessly about illegal immigration, but no one spoke about statelessness. No one knew what it meant to live without a country, to have no legal identity, to belong nowhere. In America, people are born citizens by right. Statelessness is a foreign concept to them.

But it is very real—and very painful.

I explained that some regimes collapse, others actively choose not to protect certain groups. They strip people of nationality, often out of cruelty or indifference. We had to start talking about this. We had to break the silence.

To my surprise and relief, CNN agreed.

Then came Christiane Amanpour's powerful coverage on CNN International in her program Imagine a World. She opened it with a haunting line:

"Imagine a world where there's no place like home—and home is no place at all."

She described my situation: how I had been trapped in American Samoa for a year, in what looked like paradise, but felt more like purgatory. She spoke about my past—how I fled Azerbaijan after the Soviet Union collapsed, how I tried to find safety in Turkmenistan but couldn't stay because I'm gay and homosexuality is illegal there.

She explained how I ended up in the U.S., and how, holding a Soviet passport from a country that no longer exists, I was barred from international travel.

Then came the fateful trip to American Samoa—a U.S. territory— where I was allowed to go. But when I took a short side trip to neighboring Western Samoa, I unknowingly stepped into an independent nation. That's when everything changed. When I tried to return to American Samoa, I was denied reentry to the U.S. mainland.

So, I was stuck. Living with a local family of eight. Sending out desperate messages for help from the Wi-Fi at McDonald's.

Christiane closed the segment by saying:

"Like the other 12 million stateless people worldwide, all Mikhail Sebastian wants is to go home."

The video went viral. The floodgates opened. Suddenly, I was receiving messages from all over the world—not just from stateless individuals who saw themselves in my story, but from supporters, advocates, and ordinary people offering encouragement. Other stateless people reached out asking for advice, asking what they could do. Many were afraid to go to immigration offices out of fear they'd be detained. They felt helpless. And now, because of that video, they weren't alone anymore.

Then came the moment that truly shifted the ground beneath my feet.

UNHCR told me that the original video had been shown at the White House. And shortly after, the U.S. Citizenship and Immigration Services reached out to them. They said they wanted to look into my case, not with promises, but at least with interest.

Weeks passed. I waited, hoping. Then came the news I never thought I'd hear:

The U.S. had decided to grant me humanitarian parole.

It was like a meteor falling from the sky. I could hardly believe it. I was going home.

When the document arrived in American Samoa, Susana, Tupu's wife, and I were literally chasing down the delivery truck—either DHL or UPS, I can't even remember. We just needed that piece of paper.

And then it was in my hands.

I opened the envelope, saw the official document, and screamed with joy. We rushed home, where we celebrated, danced, laughed, and cried. It was pure happiness.

The next step was to book a flight. Hawaiian Airlines, incredibly, allowed me to use my original round-trip ticket, even though it had expired nearly a year ago. Maybe it was guilt on their part—they had made an error in boarding me in the first place, failing to check my documents properly. Whatever the reason, they didn't penalize me. They simply reissued the ticket.

I packed. I said my heartfelt goodbyes to the incredible family who had taken me in. They had become more than hosts; they were my family, and they always will be. Even now, I hope someday to return to American Samoa—this time as an American citizen—to thank them, face to face, for what they did for me when I had nowhere else to go.

At the airport, I finally received my boarding pass. I walked toward the plane with tears in my eyes. As the aircraft lifted off, I looked out the window at the island below.

I whispered, "Goodbye, American Samoa."

I was flying to Honolulu—back to the United States. A new chapter was beginning. I was filled with excitement, gratitude, and a bit of anxiety. Where would I live? Would people remember me? What about my old job? My life had been on pause for nearly a year and a half. And now, the play was resuming—scene unknown.

This was the start of a new life. A new adventure. After exile.

Return to the United States: A New Beginning

When I finally arrived back in the United States, my first point of entry was Honolulu, Hawaii. As soon as I stepped off the plane, immigration officials were already waiting for me. They had to process my arrival, which included taking fingerprints and photographs. Although I still had my driver's license, it wasn't a valid document for international entry, especially not after a year-long exile. The only other identification I had was my World Passport.

Even though I was granted humanitarian parole, I hadn't fully understood the limitations of what that meant. Humanitarian parole is typically granted for extraordinary circumstances—like if a close family member is seriously ill and someone needs to be there to assist. It's a temporary measure, usually valid for six months to a year. After that, the person is expected to leave. But in my case, leave for where? I couldn't go back to American Samoa, and I had nowhere else to return to. That part of the document I didn't dwell on. The only thing I saw, the only words that mattered to me in that moment, were: Permission to enter the United States.

At immigration, when they asked for my documents, I handed them my driver's license first, knowing they wouldn't accept it. Then I gave them the World Passport, even though I was aware by then that it wasn't recognized by the U.S. authorities. As expected, they rejected it. Instead, they stamped a separate immigration form—a small but precious piece of paper—that documented my entry under humanitarian parole. And with that, I was processed and cleared to board my next flight to Los Angeles.

Landing in Los Angeles was surreal. After everything I had gone through, I wasn't sure where to go next. So, instinctively, I went to Tiago, the coffee shop where I had worked before leaving for American Samoa. I thought maybe I'd see familiar faces, maybe even some support. But things had changed. The energy was different. I no longer felt welcome.

I approached Santiago and Adrian, my former boss and colleague. While I was stranded in American Samoa, I had reached out to them because I didn't know how long I'd be stuck. At first, I thought it would only be a few days, maybe a couple of weeks. But as things dragged on and my return became uncertain, I asked Santiago for a huge favor: to go to my apartment, collect my belongings—clothes, furniture, everything—and store them somewhere safe. I had no one else in L.A. to ask. I trusted him.

But when I returned and asked about my belongings, they seemed confused. Then they told me—flatly—that everything had been given away. My furniture, clothes, even the designer jackets I had saved up for—all gone. I don't know if they donated my things or kept them for themselves or handed them to friends. No one took responsibility. No one apologized. They just said, "We didn't know if you were ever coming back."

But I had never told them I was never coming back. In fact, I had stayed in contact. I had shared updates, told them I was still trying to work out my case. I never gave permission for them to discard my life. At the very least, they could have reached out one last time to ask me what to do.

That moment was devastating. Everything I had built in Los Angeles, all the things that gave me comfort and identity—erased. But as painful as it was, I reminded myself: material things can be replaced. What mattered most was that I had made it back. I was safe. I was free.

After losing nearly everything during my detention in Texas, and again during my exile in American Samoa, I made a quiet promise to myself: No more shopping for designer clothes. The risk of losing everything again was just too high. And honestly, after what I'd been through, all I wanted was stability—somewhere to sleep, food to eat, a way to start over.

In the same building as Tiago, there was a music producer named Marco—an Italian guy I knew from when he used to come in as a customer. When he saw me, he was surprised but kind. I explained my situation: I had just returned, had no money, no home, and nowhere to go. Without hesitation, Marco offered to let me stay at his new condo in Los Angeles until I could get back on my feet, find a job, and rent a place of my own.

That act of generosity meant everything.

And so, my new life in Los Angeles began—again. I was starting from scratch, but at least this time I had shelter, support, and the determination to rebuild. My next mission was to find a job, return to the coffee world I loved, and piece together the life that had been scattered by borders, bureaucracy, and exile.

A Roof, a Room, and a Bit of Grace

Marco was a charming and intelligent man, kind-hearted and generous, with a refined presence that came from years in the music industry. He had worked with well-known celebrities and had earned a reputation for his talents as a music producer. At the time, he was in his late 40s and had a long-distance girlfriend, Paola, who worked at a post office in Italy. She would occasionally fly in to visit him in Los Angeles, stay for a while, and then return home.

Though Marco's condo had two bedrooms, and I had my own room, I often felt uncomfortable whenever Paola was around. I didn't want to intrude on their space, but I had nowhere else to go. And we never really discussed how long I was supposed to stay. I didn't ask, and he didn't say.

Marco never asked me to pay rent—he understood my situation and knew I didn't have the money. Still, I wanted to show my appreciation, so I began cleaning his entire apartment once a week. I'd do a deep clean of the living room, kitchen, both bedrooms—everything. It was my quiet way of saying thank you for his generosity and for giving me shelter when I had none.

Meanwhile, I started job hunting. I eventually found work at a small coffee shop, but the pay was low and the hours were inconsistent. It wasn't nearly enough to rent even a modest place in Los Angeles—one of the most expensive cities in the country. Back at Tiago, I had enjoyed a salary and some financial stability.

But in the specialty coffee world of L.A., baristas were expected to have deep knowledge and skill, yet were paid poorly—$8, maybe $9 an hour. Worse, there were no guarantees of full-time work. Most of the time, you'd only get a few shifts a week, just four or five hours at a time.

The idea of getting two jobs felt daunting, especially without a car. Commuting across the sprawling city by public transportation made everything harder. I was exhausted even just working one job. The months dragged on. Nearly a year passed, and I still hadn't saved enough to afford a place of my own.

Eventually, Marco approached me. Gently but firmly, he said it was time for me to move out. I had overstayed my welcome, and I understood. I had no resentment. I just needed to figure out my next move.

Soon after, I found a job at a coffee shop in Santa Monica. The pay was finally enough to let me rent a shared apartment in Hollywood. It wasn't ideal—I was living with a roommate and commuting across the city—but it was a step forward. I had a bit more independence and some stability.

I also worked for a while at Intelligentsia, one of the most respected names in specialty coffee. But it was my time at a smaller café—Refinery Coffee in Santa Monica—that made the biggest difference. The pay was better than most other places, and I was finally able to save a little money.

But the longer I stayed in L.A., the more alien it felt. The city that had once been full of promise and connection now felt cold and unfamiliar. I walked the same streets, but everything had changed—especially me. I no longer belonged. I had lost friends I trusted. I felt unwanted. And deep down, I knew I needed to leave.

At the time, I had a friend in Puerto Rico, Sebastian Legner, whose father owned a coffee farm. I reached out and asked if I could come stay during harvest season, hoping to immerse myself in the life of a coffee farmer—something I had always wanted to experience. After some conversations and with his father's blessing, they agreed. They would offer me a place to stay, meals, and a small stipend of around $100–$150 a week.

I said goodbye to California and boarded a flight to Puerto Rico.

The farm, Pomarrosa, was nestled high in the hills—a paradise far from the chaos of L.A. It was surrounded by rows of coffee trees, fruit-bearing plants, and vegetable gardens. It felt like another world. A peaceful retreat in the middle of nowhere. For the first time in a long while, I felt disconnected from the pain and pressure of everything I had endured. I didn't want to think about Los Angeles anymore. I didn't want to revisit the loss or betrayal or disappointment. I just wanted to be—to exist quietly, simply, and purposefully.

In Puerto Rico, I found a new kind of refuge. I was still stateless, still living in limbo, but at least I was surrounded by green hills, honest work, and the smell of fresh coffee cherries drying in the sun.

The Coffee Alchemist of Pomarrosa

Picking coffee cherries in Pomarrosa

At Café Pomarrosa, nestled deep in the hills of Puerto Rico and far removed from the bustle of San Juan, I quickly immersed myself in the life I had always envisioned—harvesting coffee, picking ripe cherries, and exploring the mysteries hidden within each varietal. I arrived as a wanderer, but I stepped onto that farm with purpose. From the very next day, I began experimenting.

Puerto Rico doesn't offer the same high-altitude terroir that countries like Ethiopia or Colombia are known for—its elevations are modest, and that has a significant impact on flavor potential. Still, I saw potential. Different varietals of Arabica were growing at Pomarrosa, and I was determined to understand how Puerto Rican coffee could express itself through nuanced processing.

Sorting coffee beans. Pomarrosa

I drew inspiration from Aida Batlle, the iconic producer in El Salvador known for her meticulous and innovative approach to coffee processing. Though El Salvador's altitudes provided more ideal conditions for Arabica, I believed that her methods could be adapted—and perhaps reveal something unique when applied to Puerto Rican soil.

I began by replicating several processing methods:

- Traditional Washed Process: A 12-hour dry fermentation followed by washing the parchment and drying it on raised beds or patios.

- Kenya-Style Process: A 48-hour dry fermentation, with the beans washed every 12 hours using fresh water and a wooden paddle, then soaked in clean water for 24 hours before drying.

- Burundi Process: This involved a 24-hour dry fermentation with intermittent washing every 12 hours, followed by a 24-hour underwater soak—again with washing at regular intervals—before drying.

- Natural Process (my favorite): The cherries were floated to remove defects, then dried whole, allowing the beans to absorb sugars and flavors from the mucilage as they slowly cured under the sun.

Each method told a different story in the cup. While some yielded surprisingly complex and fruity profiles, others fell flat, constrained by the island's limitations—its lower elevation, its soil chemistry, and the varietals available.

But that was the whole point. You cannot coax a Pacamara to taste like a Geisha. You can't expect Catimor to perform like a Caturra. Each variety reacts differently to processing, and terroir matters. Puerto Rico isn't Kenya, and it isn't Brazil. Even the same process, applied to the same varietal, can result in entirely different flavor outcomes in different regions. Soil pH level, climate, rainfall, disease resistance, and microbial activity all play a role.

Still, I believed that with care, experimentation, and respect for the bean, Puerto Rican coffee could shine.

I wasn't just chasing flavor. I hoped that if these experimental lots turned out well, the farm could eventually sell the coffee at a higher price, giving local producers a chance at sustainability.

Puerto Rican coffee is expensive. Unlike in other coffee-producing nations, laborers in Puerto Rico must be paid hourly under U.S. labor laws. That alone drives up the cost. Many American roasters opt for cheaper beans from Central America or Africa, where wages are much lower and the supply chain is more flexible. As a result, most Puerto Rican coffee is either consumed locally or sold to specialty buyers overseas, particularly in Japan and other parts of Asia, where there's a stronger market for exotic, high-priced coffee.

But even with the high cost, typical Puerto Rican coffee can taste flat, often similar to lower-grade lots from Honduras or Guatemala.

That's not because the beans are bad, but because the production lacks innovation, and the terroir can only do so much without proper handling. The challenge is to elevate the profile of the coffee without inflating the price beyond what the market can bear.

Sebastian Legner, my friend and host, was a generous soul. He assisted me every step of the way, encouraging my curiosity, feeding both my body and my mind. He had an extensive collection of coffee literature, which he gladly shared with me. In my free time, I devoured book after book, learning everything I could about botany, processing, and global coffee economics.

He also loved to cook. Our days often ended with shared meals and cups of freshly brewed coffee, comparing notes and chasing flavors late into the night. Occasionally, we would leave the farm to visit San Juan or explore other parts of the island—brief escapes that reminded me of the world beyond the hills.

This chapter of my life was more than an agricultural experiment. It was a period of learning, healing, and quiet transformation. For once, I was not just surviving—I was contributing, creating, imagining. I was using my hands and my senses to transform raw cherries into something beautiful and expressive. And even as a stateless person, I found a temporary sense of purpose rooted in the soil of an island I never imagined I'd call home.

A Morning Like No Other

Waking up at Café Pomarrosa in Puerto Rico was like stepping into a dream I had long been chasing. The sounds of birds filled the morning air with melodies that felt like whispers from nature itself. It was surreal, like the countryside scenes I used to imagine as an escape—far from the chaos of big cities, far from people, far from the noise. Just animals, trees, and me.

The days began with a cup of beautifully brewed Puerto Rican coffee, and even when it rained, I refused to stay inside. I was determined to work. Motivated by purpose. Picking cherries under a grey sky still felt like liberation. My time on the farm wasn't just an agricultural experiment—it was also healing. After everything I had been through, I needed that rhythm. I needed to start again.

But even as I embraced this peaceful new chapter, a storm still lingered behind me—my legal status.

After I was allowed to return to the mainland U.S. from American Samoa under humanitarian parole, my attorney, David Baluarte, immediately contacted the Department of Homeland Security and United States Citizenship and Immigration Services (USCIS) to address my case. The parole allowed me to re-enter, but only for one year. The fundamental question remained: What happens when the year is over? Where do I go, as a stateless person?

What I hadn't expected was to be labeled a fugitive. Before I took the fateful flight to American Samoa, I was under an Order of Supervision in Los Angeles. Leaving the U.S. mainland without formal permission meant I was flagged.

Upon receiving the parole, I was told to contact USCIS to clear up the confusion, removing my name from any watchlists, just to be allowed to board the return flight.

It was surreal. Fugitive? I didn't even know what to think anymore. I had no country, no home—and now I was being accused of fleeing?

David worked tirelessly. He found a way forward: since my original political asylum case from 1996 had been denied and I had since "executed" my deportation by leaving the U.S. in 2011, my case was considered closed. That meant I was now eligible to apply for a new asylum case.

This time, I didn't want to hide. I was ready to tell the truth: I am gay, and I cannot live safely in Turkmenistan.

In Turkmenistan, homosexuality is criminalized. Gay men can be imprisoned for up to five years. Social stigma, harassment, and threats are part of daily life. At the university, I was constantly scrutinized—for how I walked, talked, and even breathed. Every day felt like a quiet battle, waiting for the next confrontation. I knew I had to leave.

America wasn't immediately safe for me either. It took years before I truly understood that it was a country where I could be openly myself. Filing the new asylum application with David's help felt like coming out not just on paper, but in spirit.

We submitted the claim, citing the dangers I faced as a gay man under an authoritarian regime in a Muslim-majority country. I had lived in the U.S. for over 18-19 years by then. I paid taxes. I contributed. And I had endured more than most people could imagine.

Eventually, I was called for an interview with a USCIS officer in Anaheim, California. It lasted around two hours. David and several of his law students joined me. We presented everything, laid it all bare. Then we waited.

While the asylum case was still pending, I left Los Angeles for Puerto Rico, chasing not just peace, but purpose. One morning, as I picked coffee cherries under the sun with birds swirling in song around me and butterflies flickering through the trees, my phone rang. It was David.

He didn't waste a moment.

"Your asylum was granted."

I froze, holding a cherry in my hand.

In that instant, I felt something I hadn't felt in years—relief, recognition, maybe even joy. I was finally granted asylum in the United States. I was eligible to apply for a green card. But I had to wait one year without leaving U.S. territory.

When I told David I was in Puerto Rico, he laughed and said, "I told you—no more islands!"

We both laughed, but I reassured him: "Don't worry, this one's incorporated."

Despite the victory, there were still limitations. Even though I had lived in the

U.S. for over 18-19 years and paid taxes all those years, none of that time counted toward citizenship because I had no legal status. I would now have to wait one year to apply for permanent residency, and then wait another five years before I could apply for U.S. citizenship.

That was the law. It didn't matter how much of my life I had already given to this country.

But that morning, standing in the middle of the coffee farm, covered in cherry pulp, hands sticky from the sweetness of the fruit, I no longer felt invisible. I had a chance. I had protection. I had a place, even if just temporarily.

And above all, I had hope.

The Pause Between Places

When the news arrived that my asylum had been granted, I was on a coffee farm in Puerto Rico, knee-deep in experiments on post-harvest processing. I had no doubt what it meant, but I didn't celebrate. Joy didn't come rushing in. The trauma I had carried for so long—losses both material and invisible—had hollowed me out. I had lost hope so many times before. My first instinct was not to rejoice, but to plan.

According to U.S. immigration regulations, I would be eligible to apply for permanent residency after one year. Then, I could request a travel document—something granted to people like me, who have no passport, no nation. It's not a passport, not even close. It's valid for only a year and serves a narrow function: to allow someone like me to leave the U.S. and return. I began to imagine a route out—a path to a European country where I might start again, this time as a stateless person seeking asylum under frameworks that better recognized my condition. But I didn't know what to do exactly. The plan was hazy. Everything was.

In the meantime, life on the island offered other diversions. A barista competition was taking place nearby, and I signed up to judge. Back when I lived in Los Angeles—before that strange, surreal exile in American Samoa—I had participated as a technical judge in a regional barista competition. This one in Puerto Rico was different. The category I judged was called Coffee in Good Spirits, where competitors crafted drinks mixing coffee and alcohol. It was a joy—something I hadn't felt in a long time. I was learning again, sharpening my senses, rediscovering my place in the specialty coffee world.

But the harvest season was coming to an end. Mr. Legner, the owner of the farm, gently let me know I wouldn't be able to stay once it was over. We had many conversations, sitting with Sebastian and his father, a German immigrant who had carved out a life on this mountain slope. We talked about fermentation, drying curves, water activity levels, and all the micro-details that can make or break a specialty coffee. There was a sense of quiet purpose in those talks, but I knew my time there was limited.

I didn't want to go back to Los Angeles. That chapter was finished. I didn't want to start over in a place where I had already lost so much. I began looking for another corner of the island, somewhere to breathe.

Eventually, I found it—a second coffee farm, tucked higher up in the mountains, surrounded by wild orange trees, lemons, and lush coffee plants. When the season ended, everyone else left. I stayed behind, alone.

A friend offered me a small house there—nothing grand, just walls and a roof. He asked if I'd repaint and do some maintenance in exchange for staying. I agreed. He also gave me a dog. I named him Amadeus, after the great composer Wolfgang Amadeus Mozart. In the silence of that farm, Amadeus became my only companion.

Each morning, I woke early, brewed my coffee, cooked breakfast, and walked the farm with Amadeus at my side. We discovered waterfalls, traced riverbanks, and wandered among unfamiliar plants. There was something healing in that routine. He listened to me as if he understood. When I spoke of my confusion, my pain, my longing, he simply sat there, ears perked, eyes locked on mine.

And that was enough. That silent companionship meant everything.

Amadeus was more than a dog—he was my only friend, my witness in "paradise." He would trot beside me through the fields, chase lizards through the coffee trees, and then curl up at my feet in the evening as I read or sat in silence. When the wind moved through the trees at night and the stars stretched endlessly above, he stayed close, a small heartbeat against the vastness.

Sometimes, as I watched him sleep, I'd think about that barista competition again—the clatter of tampers, the hiss of steam wands, the aroma of finely-tuned espresso blends mingling with spirits. There was something beautiful about it all, something deliberate and human in the way people measured seconds, temperature, and grams. It was one of the few spaces where I felt seen, where skill and precision could speak louder than status or origin. In that room of baristas, for a brief moment, I wasn't stateless. I was just a judge. A peer. An equal.

But then I'd return to the present: the quiet, the solitude, the questions that hovered over me like a cloud.

I kept planting, kept working the land, trying to root myself in a place that wasn't mine. The soil accepted me, at least. The trees didn't ask for paperwork. The dog didn't care where I was born.

And yet, beneath the calm, the truth remained: Puerto Rico was not my destination—it was a pause, a breath between storms. The economy was unforgiving. Jobs were scarce. Even as a skilled barista, the wages weren't enough to live on, and the rent could crush whatever stability I had left.

I was grateful for the island's embrace, for the farm, for Amadeus. But I knew it couldn't last.

As the days passed, I began to feel the ground shifting under me again. The question I had carried for so long returned in full force: Where do I go from here?

There were no answers. But there was motion. There was breath. There was a garden taking root in foreign soil, and a dog who sat by me while I dreamed aloud.

Maybe that was enough for now.

A Temporary City, A Permanent Choice

Back on the coffee farm in Puerto Rico, as the harvest drew to a close and the income dried up, I found myself once again facing the unknown. I spent long evenings searching online for jobs across the United States—California, Alaska, even New York, though I had always disliked that city. New York had a certain romance in the imagination, but to truly live there, not just survive, you needed more than an income. You needed freedom. You needed enough to pay the rent, yes, but also enough to go out with friends, buy a decent meal, and not panic every time you checked your bank account. New York wasn't a place for the poor. It was a city for those who could afford to live above the edge of survival. That idea vanished quickly.

I kept searching. Other states, other cities. But nothing came together.

When the last assignment on the farm was finished and there was no more money coming in, I had no choice but to leave. With nowhere else to go, I returned to the one place I had tried so hard to leave behind: Los Angeles.

I had no savings, so I found a cramped shared apartment in Hollywood. It had been turned into a kind of Airbnb-style hostel—a one-bedroom split with two bunk beds, four strangers sharing a room, a kitchen, and a bathroom. After years of living alone, it was claustrophobic. I missed my independence, my quiet. I couldn't unwind, couldn't call it home.

Still, I had no other choice.

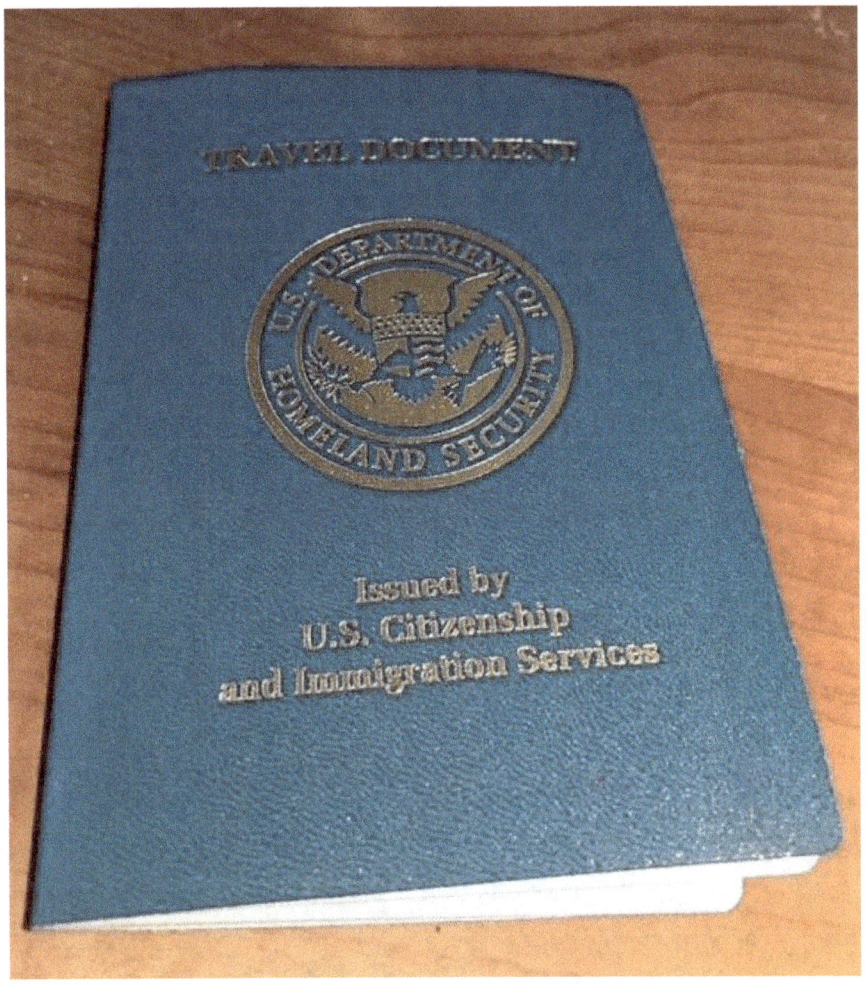

Refugee Travel Document

While searching for work, I decided to let go of old wounds, especially those connected to my previous job and strained relationships. But there was one place I couldn't give up: Tiago. That coffee shop had been a refuge for me during my earlier years in Los Angeles. It was more than a workplace—it was where I relaxed, read, met people, and felt part of a community.

Now I returned not as an employee, but as a customer. I would sit quietly in my usual corner, reading the news, writing in my journal, observing life around me, and applying for jobs.

Eventually, I found one in Santa Monica, back in the coffee industry. The pay wasn't great, but it kept me afloat. Still, I knew L.A. wasn't where I belonged anymore. It was a stopgap. I began to search again, this time with less urgency and more intention, trying to imagine where I could finally settle and rebuild.

During this time, I reached out to Lindsay Jenkins, the Assistant Protection Officer for UNHCR in Washington. I told her everything— that I wanted to leave the United States, that I was exhausted, mentally broken, worn down by the years of uncertainty and confinement. I said I was considering using a travel document to leave and seek asylum in Europe as a stateless person.

She was alarmed.

She urged me not to make any rash decisions. She insisted on flying to Los Angeles to meet in person.

We met at Tiago, in that familiar corner where I had spent so many hours lost in thought. She listened patiently as I poured out my frustration, my pain, my hopelessness. And then, with quiet conviction, she reminded me of everything I had already survived—everything I had built here.

"You've come this far," she said. "You've endured so much. Why throw it away now?"

She explained that if I left, I would be abandoning the asylum I had fought so hard to obtain. I'd have to start the cycle all over again in a new country, with no guarantee of safety, no certainty that I wouldn't be detained again. She told me to wait until I received my permanent residency. Wait the five years. Become a citizen. Then I could decide where I wanted to live. But don't leave now, not like this.

Her words struck a chord. I struggled to control my emotions, to hold back the overwhelming tide of everything I had been carrying. I began to rethink my decision, to question whether escaping again would solve anything.

She was right.

This was my life now. I had built something here. Despite the traumas, the isolation, the bureaucratic nightmare—I had survived. I had learned to live independently, to earn my own way, to navigate a society that had never been built with someone like me in mind.

The United States was not perfect. But it was the only place that had ever given me a real chance.

It taught me freedom. It gave me the tools to think and act on my own terms. It gave me the chance to exist without permission, to dream without borders.

In the end, I realized something profound:

The United States wasn't just a country I had landed in—it was the key that had unlocked every door I had never been allowed to touch.

And despite everything, it was home.

The truth was, despite all the hardship, I had a life here. A hard-won, independent life. In the United States, I learned how to stand on my own. I learned how to earn, how to live, how to think for myself. No one could take that away from me.

The United States had given me something no other place had: freedom, in the truest sense of the word. Freedom to define who I was, to rebuild after I had lost everything, to dream again. It gave me the chance to live, not as someone asking for permission, but as someone claiming their space in the world.

Yes, it had broken me. But it had also shaped me.

This country was my test. And, in many ways, my triumph.

And maybe that's what freedom really is: not a life without struggle, but the power to keep going in spite of it.

The Island I Never Knew I Needed

Martha's Vineyard. Edgartown

After weeks of uncertainty and searching for direction, I came across an intriguing job posting while scrolling online from my small room in Hollywood. A café with the unusual name Behind the Bookstore—located on Martha's Vineyard Island, Massachusetts—was looking for a Coffee Director with a background in specialty coffee. I had never heard of the place. Martha's Vineyard? It sounded familiar in that distant, postcard kind of way, but it was completely outside my realm of experience.

I had been to Massachusetts before, but never to this island. Out of curiosity, I began searching for photos and information. What I saw on the screen surprised me—charming New England homes, sailboats dotting the Atlantic, winding lanes and colonial architecture that looked more British than American. There was something both quiet and dignified about the place. I didn't know anyone there. I had no connections. But something told me I should apply. So, I did.

At the time, I was still working as a barista at a café inside the Los Angeles Museum of Contemporary Art. The pay was modest, but it helped me get by. Still, I knew I couldn't stay in LA much longer. I was searching for a way out—not just from the physical space, but from the cycle of low-paying jobs, expensive rents, and a sense that time was passing without direction. When I submitted my application to Behind the Bookstore, I didn't expect much. But within days, I received a response. A phone interview was scheduled with Andrea, who handled hiring for the café.

Behind The Bookstore Cafe. Edgartown, Martha's Vineyard

We spoke for nearly an hour. It was one of those rare conversations where everything flowed naturally. She was warm and professional, and by the end of the call, she told me that I'd soon be meeting the owners of the business. I assumed that meant another video call or a phone interview down the line. I had no idea they'd show up in person.

It was during Nowruz, the Persian New Year, and I was behind the register at the museum café. The place was buzzing—full of families, tourists, locals, all celebrating the holiday. I was taking orders, focused and moving quickly, when I noticed a man waving at me from across the room. He looked like someone out of a storybook—silver hair, soft eyes, a full beard, like a scholarly version of Santa Claus. I waved back politely, not sure who he was, and continued working.

After my shift ended, he approached me with a gentle smile and introduced himself as Jeffrey. Beside him was his wife, Joyce. "We're the owners of Behind the Bookstore," he said. "You applied for the Coffee Director position. We wanted to meet you."

I was stunned. No warning, no appointment—just a spontaneous arrival. But there was something about their presence, their energy, that felt genuine. They didn't come to interrogate or test me; they just wanted to see who I was, to get a sense of the person behind the résumé. We spoke briefly about my work, my love for coffee, and the island I'd never heard of. They explained that the role was seasonal, running from mid-April to mid-October, aligning with the tourist flow during the warmer months. The pay was generous, much better than anything I was earning in Los Angeles, and it came with housing options.

I'd never considered seasonal work. I'd never thought of Massachusetts as a place to start over. But something inside me started to shift. A quiet voice saying: Maybe this is the new beginning you've been waiting for.

The next day, Jeffrey invited me to meet again in Santa Monica. We sat at a small café and spoke for hours. He was calm, soft-spoken, thoughtful—the kind of person who listens more than he speaks. I liked him immediately. There was no pressure, no urgency. Just a sincere conversation about the possibilities of this new chapter. He told me about the person who held the job before me, a Korean-American man named Kim, who had moved on to pursue ceramics.

They needed someone to take the reins—and they believed I was that person.

I thought it over that night. I didn't ask anyone for advice. I didn't call friends or consult anyone from the coffee world. I simply talked to myself, the way I always had in times of transition. My inner voice and outer voice had a long conversation. I knew I was tired of barely surviving in L.A., of living in overcrowded apartments with strangers, of working so hard just to stay afloat. The offer felt like a small miracle—a door opening when so many had slammed shut.

When I called Lindsay Jenkins from the UNHCR to tell her the news, she was ecstatic. "You have no idea how lucky you are," she said. "Do you know how special Martha's Vineyard is? It's where the Kennedys vacationed. It's a presidential island—a Democratic haven. It's beautiful. It's peaceful. You're going to love it."

Her excitement added a layer of magic to my decision. For once, I didn't feel uncertain. I didn't feel like I was running away from something. I felt like I was running toward something.

So, when Jeffrey extended his hand and said, "Welcome aboard," I shook it firmly and said yes. I didn't know what awaited me on that island, but I knew it was time to go. And for the first time in a very long time, I felt like something in the universe had aligned in my favor.

The Island Beyond the Map

Martha's Vineyard. Edgartown

And just like that, April arrived.

My flight was booked. I was heading to a place I'd only seen in pictures—a place that looked like something out of a postcard. I was flying to Martha's Vineyard. I didn't go alone. The café had hired a new chef for the season, and we traveled together to the island. As the plane descended, I pressed my forehead to the window, curious and uncertain about the place that would become my new home.

It was April 15, 2015, the day I first set foot on Martha's Vineyard. The air was cold and sharp, the sky shifting moods between wind and rain. This wasn't the Martha's Vineyard I had seen in online photos, full of sunshine, yachts, and cheerful vacationers lounging by the ocean. The island was still in hibernation. It wasn't ready to receive tourists yet, and suddenly I understood—seasonality. That word finally clicked.

Back in Los Angeles or Puerto Rico, I never really thought about the seasons in this way. But here, the rhythm of life was different. The tourist season really began in June and slowed down by October. April, on the other hand, was still grey and sleepy. But even under the clouds, I could feel something quietly magical in the air.

We arrived in Edgartown, a charming coastal village where the café was located. The town felt like a whisper from another century—white clapboard houses, picket fences, cobblestone streets, and salt-tinged winds. The bookstore stood at the front of the property, and tucked just behind it, hidden from the road like a secret garden, was the café: Behind the Bookstore. The name made perfect sense now.

Aquinnah. Martha's Vineyard

It was small, cozy, and undeniably charming. Inside, there was barely enough room for a handful of tables. But outside—outside—there was a lovely garden enclosed by trees, flowers, and string lights. It looked like a place that didn't belong in the real world. It was something from a fairytale. And I loved it instantly.

As I stood there, taking it all in, I felt a rare sense of arrival. Like the universe had quietly opened a door just for me. I thanked Jeffrey in my heart for taking a chance on me. And I thanked God, too, for guiding me to that job posting, to this island, to this moment.

The Atlantic stretched beyond the shoreline, powerful and cold. I would often walk along the coast, letting the salty wind hit my face, staring into the vastness of the ocean. "Here I am again," I thought. "Another island. Another chapter." But this time, the island was part of the United States. This wasn't like American Samoa, where my statelessness had defined every moment. No—this place was different. I felt welcomed. I felt like I belonged.

And then, just like that, I got to work.

As the Coffee Director, this was my space. My domain. No one was going to tell me how to run it, what beans to buy, or how to build the program. I began ordering everything we needed—cups, saucers, brewing tools. I had already tasted dozens of coffees in Los Angeles and knew what I wanted to bring in.

But I also had a vision—an international one. I wanted to introduce our customers to specialty coffee roasted not just in the United States, but all over the world. Roasters from Sweden, Germany, and Italy. Kenyan beans roasted in Milan. Ethiopian coffees roasted in Berlin. Each roaster had a unique philosophy, a different approach to roast profiles, and I wanted to show how terroir and technique could transform the same green coffee into wildly different experiences.

It was exciting. It was creative. It was mine.

Of course, like any café, there were challenges. The small-town energy meant gossip sometimes traveled faster than espresso shots. There was drama, personality clashes, and occasional tension. But I wasn't interested in arguments or power struggles. I didn't want to fight—I just wanted to work, to create, to serve beautiful coffee in a beautiful place. But I also didn't want anyone stepping into my space or questioning my work. I had fought too hard to get here. I was territorial—protective, even defensive, when it came to what I had built.

Behind The Bookstore Cafe (BTB)

As I settled into the café, I started to understand Jeffrey more. He wasn't just a typical business owner. He was observant, methodical, and always present. One day, while I was dialing in the espresso machine, I noticed him sitting quietly in the corner, watching me work. He had been there for hours. Finally, he said, almost casually, "So... how was American Samoa?"

I paused.

I hadn't told him about that. Not directly, at least. But I knew then— he had Googled me. He had read my story online. The detention, the statelessness, the exile. At first, I didn't want to talk about it. But eventually, the story came out. We talked about it. He listened.

And while I appreciated his interest, I didn't like the feeling of being watched. "Don't you want to go for a walk?" I asked him once. "Or do something else?"

"No," he said, smiling. "Why? You trying to get rid of me?"

"It's just… when you're sitting there watching me all day, it makes me uncomfortable. I feel like I'm being tested. Like I have to prove myself."

That honesty broke the ice between us. After that, something shifted. We clicked. Over time, our relationship deepened into something more meaningful than boss and employee. We became like family. The kind of family I had always longed for—not bound by blood, but by understanding.

And so, in that garden café behind a bookstore on a tiny island I hadn't known existed, I found a new version of home. I was no longer just surviving. I was creating. I was living.

Coffee, Culture, and Control

Martha's Vineyard. Edgartown

One of the very first conversations I had when I arrived to take charge of the coffee program at Behind the Bookstore in Martha's Vineyard was about customer service. It's a concept that carries almost mythical weight in the United States—this idea that "the customer is always right." Everywhere I'd worked, people repeated it like gospel. But in my experience, that phrase was one of the biggest lies in American business culture.

Whoever came up with that slogan must've been drunk—or desperate. I understood the historical context, maybe. Back when competition was fierce, and small businesses had to do everything possible to attract and retain customers, such a slogan might have served a purpose. But now? It had become a toxic excuse—an open door for manipulation and entitlement.

I had already seen it in Los Angeles, working in coffee shops where people placed wrong orders and later demanded free replacements, claiming it wasn't what they asked for. The truth was simple: if you order a cappuccino and I make you a cappuccino, and then you change your mind and decide you wanted a mocha, that's on you. The customer, in that case, is wrong.

And if you're wrong, I'm not going to pretend otherwise just because you handed over $4 for a drink. I'll own up to any mistakes we make on our end, of course. I'll fix them. But I won't bow to false ideas of politeness or fake service just to appease someone who is clearly in the wrong. That kind of performance isn't in me. It never was.

Martha's Vineyard. Edgartown

In America, customer service often feels like theatre. A fake smile. A cheerful voice. Pretending like you're genuinely thrilled someone walked in the door. I couldn't be part of that performance. It wasn't honest, and I'm someone who believes in what's real. Truth. Integrity.

If a customer deserved kindness, they'd receive it. If they deserved correction, they'd receive that too. That was the principle I brought with me to Martha's Vineyard.

That's how we built the foundation of our service: rooted in fairness, not in fantasy.

As the season approached, the island began to change. The cold and quiet of April gradually gave way to a pulse of energy. One of the most unique things I discovered about Martha's Vineyard was the way it drew people from all over the world, especially young people, mostly from Eastern Europe, who came to work temporary jobs during the summer through exchange programs. They were students, many of them studying at the American University in Bulgaria or other institutions in Romania, Serbia, Albania, Croatia, and Russia.

They came on special visas, eager to earn money to pay for their education and experience the United States. After the summer, most of them would travel a bit—New York, Chicago, maybe Los Angeles—before flying home. I had never encountered that kind of workforce before, and it opened up a whole new cultural dimension for me. I got to learn about their worldviews, their histories, and their habits. And it also taught me a lot about leadership and conflict.

When it came time to hire for the café, I didn't want to just interview people one by one and make quick decisions. I preferred to gather a group, observe their energy, see how they interacted, and figure out who was best suited for which job—barista, server, register, kitchen, runner. I took my role seriously, especially when it came to training baristas. This wasn't just about pushing buttons on a machine—it was about learning craft, service, and precision.

But with the new staff came challenges—many of them cultural. Most of these students came from post-communist societies, and their work ethic, understanding of hierarchy, and approach to rules were shaped by that history. Some of them brought with them a kind of casualness, even laziness, that didn't sit well with the pace and expectations of our café.

There were times when they didn't take orders seriously, cut corners, or questioned basic procedures. I understood where it came from— these weren't bad people. But I had to draw the line. This wasn't Eastern Europe. This wasn't back home. This was our café, our business, and things had to be done a certain way.

It wasn't easy. They took criticism personally. Any correction was seen as a personal attack. But I had to break through that. I wasn't attacking them. I was defending the standard, the work, the atmosphere we were creating.

I never mixed friendship with business. That was something I learned early in life, especially growing up in the Soviet Union. Friendship was sacred.

Business was a responsibility. The two don't belong in the same cup. I could be friendly, yes. I could even enjoy time outside of work with my team once in a while. But I never let anyone confuse that for true friendship, or think that familiarity meant the rules didn't apply.

Some called me tough. Others said I was difficult. Maybe I was. But I had earned that toughness. It came from experience, from surviving systems that broke people. And I wasn't about to let anyone, no matter how well-intentioned, undermine what I was building. I had struggled too long to get to that moment: to be in charge of something meaningful, to have the freedom to create, to finally work without the shadow of my statelessness hanging over me.

I had a job to do. And I did it well. Whether people liked me or didn't, agreed with me or not—that didn't matter. I wasn't there to be liked. I was there to create something excellent. And I did.

Jeffrey: The Mentor I Never Had

Jeffrey was a man who radiated confidence. It wasn't just because he was the owner of multiple businesses or because he had money—it was the power of control. Jeffrey had a quiet authority, the kind that made you respect him, not because he demanded it, but because he commanded it through his actions and demeanor. He ran the business his way, and we followed because we understood that, at the end of the day, he was the one paying our salaries, not the other way around.

But despite that commanding presence, Jeffrey was also generous in a way that few are. He wasn't just a boss; he was someone who trusted the people he hired to do their jobs. He knew that if he hired the best, he didn't need to micromanage. He gave us the freedom to run the coffee shop as we saw fit, but with the understanding that any major decisions, like ordering new equipment or introducing new ideas, had to pass through him for approval. And more often than not, he would back our choices if he saw the value.

This balance of trust and control worked. While we were empowered to make decisions, we also knew we were doing so under the guidance of someone who had been through the ropes and understood the business inside and out. He wasn't just a boss in the traditional sense; he became a figure of support, someone who listened and offered advice when needed, without ever feeling like he was asserting dominance just for the sake of it.

In many ways, Jeffrey felt like the father I had longed for. Not the kind of father who spoils you with wealth, but the kind who guides you, who shares wisdom earned from years of experience. The kind who warns you when you're about to make a mistake, not because he wants to control you, but because he knows the cost of those mistakes all too well.

That wisdom was something I deeply appreciated. At 22, when I first arrived in the United States, I was young and naive. I didn't know much about how things worked, especially in the business world. But as the years passed and I found myself in positions of responsibility, I understood more. And now, as I look back, at the age of 52, I often think about those formative years. The wisdom Jeffrey shared with me is something I hope to pass on to the younger generation. It's up to them whether they accept it, but my task is to offer it, just as Jeffrey did for me.

Of course, our relationship wasn't without tension. There were moments when we disagreed, times when I lost my job for a brief period, but we always reconciled. The business was bigger than any single argument, and we both knew that. Even though Jeffrey didn't work directly in the coffee shop, he understood the bigger picture—how every small detail, every decision, affected the whole. For those of us working on the ground, the coffee shop became a second home. We spent more time there than anywhere else, and every decision felt personal. But Jeffrey understood that, and his support made all the difference.

Over time, I came to see Jeffrey not just as a boss, but as part of the family. I met his wife, Joyce, and his daughters, Sasha and Natalie. They welcomed me with open arms, made me feel like I truly belonged, even though we came from different worlds, with different backgrounds and different beliefs. The core of their family, though, was something I could relate to: the shared bond of respect, understanding, and support.

Jeffrey's intelligence and unique approach to life shaped how I viewed the world and, eventually, how will I run my own coffee business, if I would have one. I learned from him not only how to run a coffee shop but also how to be more patient, more deliberate, and more willing to listen. He taught me how to keep emotions in check and focus on the practical reality of running a business, rather than acting impulsively. It wasn't always easy, but it was the right lesson.

I'm grateful to work for him. Jeffrey didn't just teach me about the business part of running a cafe. He taught me about life, about navigating challenges, and about resilience. And most importantly, he showed me that I wasn't just some lost cause. I could rise, even when it seemed like I was failing. We both understood that failure wasn't the end—it was just part of the battle. And battles, as Jeffrey taught me, are meant to be won.

Joyce: The Quiet Guidance of a Mother

If Jeffrey was a father figure in my life, then Joyce was undoubtedly the mother I never had. She had a quiet strength about her, far less vocal than Jeffrey, but in her silence, she spoke volumes. Her presence was a calming one, and though she didn't use many words, her eyes conveyed everything. A glance from Joyce could communicate more than an entire conversation—whether it was acceptance, disapproval, or a silent but firm instruction. It was a language I came to understand well, and over time, I learned to read it.

When I arrived behind the bookstore, Joyce was in charge of the charming little bookstore located just in front of the main road. It was a place like no other—an escape into a world of stories and novels, tucked away in an old building with beautiful tile stairs. The bookstore was a labyrinth of literature. Every corner revealed something new— travel books on one side, business volumes on another, and the forbidden works stacked in quiet nooks. There was a children's section, a fiction corner, and a cozy space where you could sit, read, and lose yourself in the worlds within those pages. The bookstore wasn't just a place to buy books; it was an experience, and Joyce was the heart of it, ordering new releases, organizing events, and ensuring every book was in its place.

Joyce was less controlling than Jeffrey, but she was no less dedicated. She worked quietly, allowing others to do their tasks while always keeping a watchful eye on everything. She was far from the stereotypical 'boss' figure. Instead of barking orders, she created an atmosphere where you knew your role and your responsibilities without needing constant reminders. When she spoke, it was rarely to tell you what to do. Instead, she would offer suggestions, guidance, or—when necessary—gentle corrections.

One moment that stood out to me, though, was a lesson I learned through a mistake. There was a regular customer, Harriet, a British woman who came into the coffee shop with her friends. One day, Harriet walked in, and I noticed she appeared to be pregnant. I simply said, "Congratulations," thinking it was a kind gesture. However, Harriet didn't take it that way. She reacted angrily, accusing me of calling her fat. I was shocked—this wasn't at all what I intended. I had only meant to offer congratulations, assuming she was pregnant, but she clearly felt offended. She even went so far as to tell others not to come to the coffee shop because of what I'd said.

It wasn't until Joyce stepped in that I truly understood the cultural misstep I'd made. Joyce calmly pulled me aside and explained the situation. She told me that in the United States, it was considered inappropriate to comment on a woman's appearance, especially regarding pregnancy, unless you were certain. I hadn't meant to offend Harriet, but I had inadvertently done so. Joyce didn't lecture me in an angry or confrontational way. Instead, she gently explained the cultural nuances that I didn't understand yet. She helped me see that in this new world, I needed to be more mindful of how my words might be received.

What struck me about Joyce was her ability to teach without judgment. Unlike Harriet, who was quick to anger, Joyce's approach was nurturing and patient. She understood that I came from a different background, one where such a comment wouldn't have been seen in the same light. Joyce didn't criticize me harshly or make me feel like I'd done something unforgivable. She simply guided me, showing me the path forward, and allowed me the space to grow. It was this approach that made her not just a boss, but a mother figure—one who nurtured, corrected, and helped me find my way.

Joyce's wisdom wasn't always in her words but in her actions. She didn't need to raise her voice to make her point; she simply led by example, showing me how to handle situations with grace, patience, and understanding. And in those moments when I needed it most, when I felt like I had failed or made a mistake, Joyce was there, offering the kind of guidance that only a mother could provide—gentle but firm, understanding yet clear.

Sasha: A Guiding Light in My Journey

Sasha was a lovely soul, the kind of person whose presence could calm the stormiest of days. When I first arrived, she was helping her mother at the bookstore—working the register, assisting customers, and, most notably, sharing her love for books. Sasha had an enthusiasm for reading that was contagious. She didn't just recommend books; she engaged with the customers, explaining what she'd read and offering insights into the stories that had captivated her. She was a gentle spirit, but in her own quiet way, she was also incredibly tough.

What I appreciated most about Sasha was her role as my confidant. In a family where there were occasional tensions, especially between me and Jeffrey, Sasha was the one person I could turn to when I needed someone to talk to. There were times when I felt misunderstood, or when my disagreements with Jeffrey left me feeling like I was at a crossroads. During those moments, Sasha was always there to listen, never to judge but always to offer perspective.

I never sought Sasha out to influence her father. She wasn't a pawn in a game of family politics. No, Sasha was my sounding board, a person who simply listened and helped me process my frustrations. Over the years, I had come to understand Jeffrey in my own way, but Sasha knew him in a much deeper, more personal way. She had insight into his thoughts, his motivations, and his approach to situations that helped me navigate the complexities of my own feelings and actions. She'd offer guidance on how to approach challenges in ways that were less confrontational, reminding me that sometimes it's okay to admit defeat, but always with the goal of moving forward.

Sasha became like a life coach to me. She was the one I turned to when life felt heavy, when I was dealing with trauma or struggling through tough times. I always knew that no matter what, Sasha would be there to help ease the burden, to help me find perspective, and to make me feel welcome again. She wasn't just a friend; she was a sister I never had. The bond we shared was unique and precious, one that I truly cherished.

Beyond our conversations, Sasha was also the one who organized gatherings at the family home, inviting friends and family to spend time together. I loved these gatherings. They were light-hearted affairs where I could let loose, make everyone laugh with my silly comments, and simply enjoy the company of others. I would often act as the center of attention, the little clown, trying to entertain the whole "circus." The fact that people laughed—whether at me or with me—was enough to make me feel good. It was a reminder that there was joy to be found, even in the simplest of moments.

Through my time with Sasha, I learned a great deal about people. I came to understand the different walks of life and how decisions were shaped by circumstances. I saw how people could be manipulative, how some could pretend to be your friend while working behind your back, and how others might not have the courage to confront you directly. But Sasha was never like that. She was straightforward, honest, and courageous. She never hesitated to say what needed to be said, even if it could hurt. And when she did, she would always acknowledge it first, making sure I understood that her words were coming from a place of care, not malice.

Sasha was a rare person, with a unique blend of intelligence, kindness, and courage. She became my guardian, my guide, my philosopher, and my anchor. Whenever I was lost in my thoughts, unsure of my next step, I knew I could turn to her for advice. And when she spoke, I listened. Because I knew her advice came from a place of deep understanding and wisdom. I trusted her, and in turn, she helped me find my way.

Island of Solitude: A Stateless Journey Through Martha's Vineyard and Beyond

Aquinnah. Martha's Vineyard

When I first arrived on Martha's Vineyard on April 15, 2015, it felt like stepping into another world. The island, distinct from anywhere I'd been in the United States, immediately caught my heart. What drew me to Martha's Vineyard was not just its natural beauty, but its unique character. The island lacked the usual American chains that defined many places I had known—no McDonald's, KFC, Starbucks, or sprawling department stores. Instead, every business was locally owned, which created a deep sense of individuality and charm. There was an authenticity to the island that felt rare, even in a country as vast as the United States. It was a place where the rhythm of life seemed slower, more intentional, and less driven by the demands of consumer culture.

It reminded me of a forgotten corner of America, untouched by the mass commercialization that had taken over so many other places.

However, this island paradise came at a steep price. Living on Martha's Vineyard was expensive, beyond what I had imagined. There were no apartment complexes or affordable rentals, and most people owned their homes—large, expensive houses, with prices starting at a million dollars and climbing far higher. The majority of the workforce, especially the seasonal employees, were students, many from Eastern Europe. They worked hard during the short summer season, but finding a place to live was a challenge. The lack of rental properties meant that housing was scarce, and renting even a single room in a house could cost an eye-watering amount. It was a place where living costs were astronomical compared to most parts of the United States, and finding affordable housing was a luxury few could afford.

Despite the financial strain, Martha's Vineyard offered something that made it worthwhile—the chance to live on an island that felt worlds away from the typical American experience. The island's charm was undeniable. The weather in the summer was warm and inviting, and there was something almost magical about the landscape. The stunning cliffs of Aquinnah (also known as Gay Head) were my favorite part of the island—an area that seemed surreal, a perfect blend of natural beauty that reminded me of parts of Ireland, yet with a strange, almost otherworldly energy. It felt like standing at the edge of a world unto itself, disconnected from everything else.

The town of Oak Bluffs was another special place on the island—a vibrant, colorful community that felt like a vineyard heaven. The historical architecture, the cottages painted in bright pastel colors, and the quiet charm of the town gave it a timeless quality. As I spent more time on the island, I came to know the local people and regular customers at the coffee shop where I worked. Over time, many of them became close friends. The connections I made during my time there became a significant part of my life, and I grew fond of the place, of the people, and of the rhythm of island life.

Even though the island's beauty was captivating, the cost of living and the seasonal nature of the place meant that my time there had its limitations. When the busy tourist season ended, Martha's Vineyard became quieter, colder, and more introspective. Many of the stores, including the coffee shop where I worked, closed for the season. It was during this downtime that I made a life-changing decision. The sense of stability that I had been craving was elusive, and my ongoing struggles to find work and make ends meet in places like Los Angeles had left me yearning for something different.

With the coffee shop shutting down and work becoming less predictable, I decided to take advantage of the free time to travel—something I had always dreamed of doing but never had the opportunity to pursue. I had already been waiting for years to be naturalized as an American citizen. According to U.S. immigration laws, I would have to wait five years after receiving my political asylum status and permanent residency before I could apply for citizenship. In the meantime, I had the chance to explore the world, to see places I had only read about, and to experience different cultures. This was an opportunity to fulfill a childhood dream that had been lying dormant for far too long.

But there was a significant challenge: as a stateless person, I didn't have a passport. In fact, my previous experience with a World Passport issued by the World Service Authority was something I had left behind after my time in American Samoa. So, I turned to another option—the U.S. refugee travel document. This travel document, issued by the United States, allowed stateless people like me to travel abroad and return to the U.S. It was valid for one year and, for many countries, it acted as a legitimate travel document. Some countries, like Belgium, Germany, and the Netherlands, accepted the travel document for visa-free entry. However, other European Union countries required additional paperwork, specifically a visa. This created a delicate balancing act.

The last thing I wanted was to risk traveling to a country where I could enter without a visa, only to find myself in trouble later on for not having the right documentation when moving on to another country. The complexities of international travel for someone in my position were numerous, and the potential pitfalls were real. But the opportunity to see the world, to experience its diversity and history, was too enticing to ignore.

In the end, the choice to travel was not just about the places I would visit but also about the freedom it offered me—freedom from the struggles I had faced in the past and the uncertainty that had marked much of my life. It was about embracing the unknown, seeking a sense of belonging in new places, and finding a new adventure beyond the constraints of statelessness.

Beyond The Vineyard

As the end of the season in 2015 approached on Martha's Vineyard, I began to feel a sense of reluctance at the thought of leaving. The island had become more than just a seasonal job; it had become a place I didn't want to part from. I found myself drawn to the idea of experiencing winter and snow, something I had never truly known on the island. The island's businesses, particularly restaurants and cafes, were preparing to close for the off-season, a cycle that seemed inevitable. The thought of the coffee shop I worked at shutting down for the winter made me hesitate.

I approached Jeffrey, the owner of the café, with an idea. What if we kept the café open for the winter? It was a novel concept, as no business on the island had ever attempted to operate through the cold months. After some consideration, we decided to give it a try. The challenge was that we didn't have enough indoor seating. In the summer, we used a large tent to cover the outdoor patio, allowing guests to sit under the tent, sheltered from the rain, or enjoy the fresh air when the weather was clear. The café, with its vibrant flowers, music, and warm atmosphere, was a charming and lively space in the summer, but in the winter, it would be a different story. Still, we decided to add four tables inside and give it a shot, despite knowing the winter months would be tough.

But despite our best efforts, we quickly realized that the winter season didn't draw enough customers. The business wasn't generating the profits needed to sustain itself, and the idea of keeping the café open year-round was short-lived. It was a disappointment, but it was also a moment that pushed me toward my next adventure. By then, I had obtained my travel document, which would allow me to leave the United States. That's when I stumbled across an opportunity that seemed too perfect to pass up.

The Specialty Coffee Association was organizing a trip to Ethiopia— the birthplace of coffee—and I knew I had to be part of it. It was a rare chance to immerse myself in the coffee-growing regions I had long read about.

Yirgacheffe, Sidamo—these were the names of regions I had always admired for their exceptional coffee, and now, I had the chance to experience it firsthand. I immediately applied, knowing that this would be the first time I would travel outside of the United States in years.

Ethiopia was the first country I would visit after my time in the U.S., and it felt like a monumental step. It was my first taste of Africa, and I was both nervous and excited. The trip would take me to Addis Ababa, where I would learn about coffee culture from the ground up. I was struck by how women were the primary coffee preparers in Ethiopia, something I had never seen before. As I traveled around Addis Ababa, I felt the weight of history in the air. Ethiopia, with its ancient traditions, felt like stepping into another era. It wasn't like the modernized world I had known—it was raw, real, and full of life.

During the trip, I toured coffee farms, learned about processing methods, and tasted coffee in ways I never had before. The experience was both humbling and inspiring, and I felt a deep connection to the land where coffee had originated. The more I traveled through Ethiopia, the more I was drawn to its culture and people. Ethiopia became a place that would hold a special place in my heart, and I would return twice more to experience its diverse regions and coffee cultures.

However, while in Ethiopia, I found myself captivated by another country: Rwanda. I had read about the tragic history of Rwanda's genocide, the horrors of 1994, and the years of suffering that followed. I watched Hotel Rwanda, and the stories of survival, loss, and resilience left a profound impact on me. There was something about Rwanda that called to me, something deep in my soul that told me I had to visit the country.

So, I took a side trip to Rwanda. The moment I arrived at the airport and started the drive around Kigali, I knew this was a place that would change me. Before heading to my hotel, I made sure to visit the Genocide Memorial in Kigali, to pay my respects to the victims of the 1994 genocide. It was a sobering experience, but one I felt compelled to do.

Rwanda was everything I had imagined—and more. The country, known as the "Land of a Thousand Hills," was strikingly beautiful, with lush greenery and rolling hills that stretched as far as the eye could see. The weather was perfect, the air crisp and fresh. The people were kind and welcoming, and I was struck by how clean the country was, far cleaner than I had ever expected. In fact, Rwanda would go on to be the cleanest country I had ever visited in Africa.

I fell in love with Rwanda almost immediately. The beauty of the landscape, the warmth of the people, and the resilience of the country resonated deeply with me. Over the course of my travels in Africa, I would visit many countries, but none left an impression on me quite like Rwanda. I promised myself that I would return, and I did—every year. Rwanda became a place I could not forget, a country that captured my heart in a way I never anticipated. It became my soul's home, and I knew that every year, I would make my way back to Rwanda, where a piece of me would always remain.

Edgartown, Martha's Vineyard

Horse farm. Chappi Island. Martha's Vineyard

Martha's Vineyard

Martha's Vineyard

The Roads Beyond

Rwanda opened my eyes to a different kind of world. A world where daily life was shaped not by excess and convenience, but by endurance, community, and quiet dignity. Traveling there challenged many of my assumptions—about wealth, about happiness, and about what it means to live a meaningful life. It gave me a deeper understanding of how different life is outside the United States, especially in places like Africa, where struggle is constant, but hope, remarkably, still persists.

In Rwanda, I witnessed people navigating lives without the safety nets that many in the developed world take for granted. People worked their land, grew their own food, and raised their families in homes built by hand. And despite these hardships, there was something radiant about the Rwandan spirit. People smiled often. They were eager to talk, to help, to offer kindness—even when they had little to give.

Havana, Cuba

The contrast with life in the United States was striking. In the U.S., even people living modestly—able to pay rent, stock their fridges, drive a car—often felt unhappy, discontent with their lives, weighed down by the sense that they were never doing enough, never having enough. But in Rwanda, people made do with less, and somehow, they radiated more.

I promised myself I would return—and I did. Every year since, I returned to Rwanda. There was something about the place that I couldn't shake loose from my soul. It became a kind of spiritual anchor for me, a compass point of calm and connection in an otherwise chaotic life. Rwanda had become a part of me.

When I returned to Martha's Vineyard after that first trip, the season was winding down. The cafe was preparing to close, as most businesses did during the long off-season. But for the first time in my life, I experienced snow.

Havana, Cuba

It was Christmas Eve, 2015. I stood in the street, watching the island transform into a silent white wonderland. It was magical. I ran into the snow like a child, laughing, tossing it in the air, pressing it against my face. After so many years spent in warm climates—Texas, Los Angeles, Puerto Rico—it felt like a dream. In the Soviet Union, where I grew up, New Year's—not Christmas—was our holiday. But it, too, was always associated with snow. This snowfall brought back those memories. For a moment, I was a boy again.

After we closed the shop, I didn't linger on the island. I had caught the travel bug, and I wasn't ready to sit still. So, I packed my bag and left for Ecuador, where I spent a month exploring the country, immersing myself in the culture. From there, I traveled to Guatemala, El Salvador, and Panama. Each country left its mark on me in different ways, but one stood out above the rest—Cuba.

Havana at night

Cuba had long held a place in my imagination. Growing up in the Soviet Union, we were raised with a strong sense of camaraderie with Cuba. It was presented to us as a sister nation, standing firm against U.S. imperialism. I'd always wanted to visit, to see the reality behind the propaganda—both Soviet and American.

Despite the U.S. embargo and the restrictions placed on American citizens, I realized I might be able to go, since I was not a U.S. citizen yet—just a permanent resident traveling with a refugee travel document. I wasn't sure whether those same restrictions applied to me, but I was willing to take the risk.

Before I went, I connected online with Philip Oppenheim, a British businessman and former member of UK Parliament, who had spent years working with Cuban coffee farmers. He was developing a brand called "Alma de Cuba", helping improve the quality and production levels of Cuban coffee. We spoke about the challenges and potential of Cuba's coffee industry, and he shared insights that fascinated me.

Hotel Nacional de Cuba

He told me that, incredibly, Cuba was producing less coffee than it had in the 1960s. The industry had stagnated, crippled by outdated equipment and limited resources. But the potential, he insisted, was still enormous. Cuban coffee had a strong following in countries like Japan and Germany, and when the embargo eventually lifted, he predicted a surge in demand from the U.S. market.

Philip also explained how Cuba's geography made it an ideal place for coffee cultivation—mountains near the sea, rich volcanic soil, and cool growing conditions with ample sunlight. He painted a picture that made me even more eager to go.

And so, I went. From Boston, I flew to Panama, then on to Havana.

As soon as I landed in Cuba, I felt the strange familiarity of a place preserved in time. The old cars, the colonial buildings, the warmth of the people, the complexity of the culture—it was both a step backwards and a step into something uniquely Cuban. I was there not just as a traveler, but as someone eager to understand how coffee culture was evolving on the island. Thanks to my connection with Philip, I got a window into that world.

The trip was everything I hoped it would be—educational, emotional, unforgettable. And it reminded me once again that no matter how far I traveled, how many stamps filled my travel document, my journey was never just about geography.

It was always about people. About stories. About places that change you.

And Rwanda—Rwanda was still calling me back.

Cabaret Show, Havana, Cuba

When I landed in Havana, Cuba, it was close to midnight. I had no hotel booking, no Airbnb reservation. At that time, due to the U.S. embargo, you couldn't book an Airbnb even if you wanted to—and finding a hotel room was equally challenging. Everything felt uncertain, but not unfamiliar. I had been in similar situations before.

My Spanish—learned partly on the job at a grocery store in Texas, mostly surrounded by Mexican coworkers, and through community college classes in Houston—was just enough to get me by. It had helped me across Central and South America. Cuba was no different.

Outside the airport, I approached a taxi driver with a vintage Oldsmobile from the 1950s or early '60s. It looked like something from a museum, like I had stepped into a preserved piece of mid-century Americana. These cars, once symbols of U.S. luxury, were now icons of Cuban resilience. I asked the driver if he knew any place I could stay— somewhere safe, simple. He made a phone call.

Minutes later, he took me to a modest apartment not far from Havana's city center. A woman and her elderly mother greeted me warmly—they had a one-bedroom apartment they were renting out, a typical casa particular. It was clean, welcoming, and came with breakfast each morning. I was grateful.

Before traveling, I'd done my homework. I knew U.S. credit and debit cards wouldn't work in Cuba, so I had brought enough cash— new, crisp bills only. Torn or worn currency wouldn't be accepted. And the exchange rate was steep. The government charged a 13% commission to exchange U.S. dollars, a penalty absent for other currencies like euros or Canadian dollars. I made sure to exchange my money at the airport.

Tropicana show in Havana, Cuba

Online forums had warned travelers about shortages—basic items like soap, toothpaste, or even toilet paper. Wanting to be respectful, I packed a few rolls of toilet paper in my bag. But when I offered one to the woman renting me the apartment, she looked at me, confused. "Why did you bring this?" she asked, almost laughing. "We have plenty." I smiled, a little embarrassed. Sometimes, even the best research can't replace real human interaction.

They treated me like family. Each morning, they prepared me breakfast—coffee, fruit, bread, and eggs. And with that, my journey through Cuba began.

I wandered Havana's streets, soaking in the colors, the sounds, the stillness of a place stuck in time. The city was a living museum. The Spanish colonial architecture, faded but dignified, echoed with history. Buildings crumbled under the weight of time and neglect, casualties of a nation blocked from the global economy. Renovations were slow and scarce. Still, the beauty was undeniable.

I had come not just as a traveler, but with a deep personal interest. Growing up in the Soviet Union, I'd always been aware of the special bond between Cuba and the USSR. To us, Cuba wasn't just another island—it was a comrade in ideology, in struggle, in defiance. I admired the revolutionary figures: Fidel Castro and Che Guevara, not as symbols of authoritarianism, but as people who dared to stand against imperialism, to dream of a world where education and healthcare were free, where workers had dignity.

Yes, the dream was flawed. Reality complicated things. The state took over private land. Small landowners became tenants on what was once theirs.

Entrepreneurs found themselves tangled in bureaucracy. The government tried to build socialism, but often at the cost of individual freedom. Still, the core idea—to build a nation where ordinary people could live with dignity—spoke to me.

I made it a point to visit the monuments of Che and Fidel, and to speak with everyday Cubans—restaurant workers, museum staff, shopkeepers. Many of them were warm and welcoming, willing to talk, willing to help. But there was also an undercurrent of hustle. Tourism had become a lifeline. Everyone, it seemed, had a side gig. A taxi driver might also be a musician. A hotel porter might rent out rooms on the side. Everyone was finding a way.

And then there was Cuba's peculiar economy—two currencies: the Cuban peso (CUP) and the convertible peso (CUC), which was pegged to the U.S. dollar.

Tourists paid in CUCs, locals were paid in CUPs. The average salary was astonishingly low. I met doctors earning $50 a month, teachers taking buses because they couldn't afford cars. Yet somehow, they survived.

Some had family abroad, especially in Florida, who sent money back home. Others ran small private restaurants or rented out rooms. The government had begun allowing small-scale entrepreneurship, cautiously testing the limits of reform. But it was still difficult. Scarcity was everywhere. A trip to the grocery store could be a scavenger hunt. But amid all of this, there was also a spirit of survival, of creativity, of humor.

The embargo felt cruel. Outdated. The Cold War had ended long ago, yet Cuba remained shackled by policies rooted in another era. And it was the people who suffered most, not the government.

Despite everything, Cuba was alive. Its people had endured. And I admired that.

Every street I walked felt like a step through history. Every conversation revealed another layer. And I realized then—this trip wasn't just about coffee, or politics, or nostalgia. It was about witnessing resilience. About understanding how people live when the world forgets them.

Cuba, for all its contradictions and hardships, had left its mark on me.

And I was just getting started.

Home Is a Room, Not a Country

While I was in Havana, Cuba, I embraced every opportunity the island had to offer. I visited the iconic Hotel Nacional de Cuba, famous for hosting distinguished guests like Winston Churchill and Ernest Hemingway. Walking through the grand lobby, admiring the old photographs on the walls, I felt transported to a bygone era. It was surreal to witness remnants of Cuba's glamorous past, once shaped by American influence: luxurious hotels, casinos, cabarets—all symbols of a different time, before the revolution.

Pinar del Rio, Cuba

That contrast between pre-revolutionary opulence and present-day survival under socialism struck me deeply. Cuba, despite its challenges, still preserves pieces of its cultural soul. I had the chance to attend a cabaret show—vibrant, colorful, and nostalgic. The dancers, adorned in feathers and glitter, brought an energy that was both romantic and exotic. In that moment, I felt like I was witnessing something sacred—something Cuba refused to let fade away.

My journey also took me to Pinar del Río, a rural region west of Havana known for its coffee and tobacco production. There, I met a local coffee grower. We spoke about the hardships farmers faced—lack of resources, outdated equipment, and no access to international markets due to the U.S. embargo.

Cuban coffee, once world-renowned, had been nearly forgotten. The grower spoke with quiet frustration and deep pride. Their struggle mirrored the country's larger one—resilience in the face of isolation.

Pinar del Rio, Cuba

Every day in Cuba taught me something new. I learned about the dual-currency system—the Cuban Peso for locals, and the Convertible Peso for tourists. I met professionals, like doctors, earning meagre salaries, yet still carrying themselves with dignity. Public buses were packed, cars were a luxury, and people did what they could to survive.

Many relied on support from relatives abroad, especially from the Cuban diaspora in Florida.

But despite all the difficulties, what struck me most was the spirit of the Cuban people. They were warm, resourceful, proud of their culture, and unwavering in their sense of identity. The embargo had put them through decades of hardship, but they never let go of their pride. They reminded me of what it means to resist, to adapt, and to preserve a sense of self against the odds. That resilience left a lasting mark on me.

Cuban Coffee Farmer. Pinar del Rio

Cuba gave me more than just a travel experience—it gave me perspective. When I left, I felt I had seen not just a country, but a living story of endurance. I knew I would return one day.

From there, my journey continued. A new season was beginning, and I returned to Martha's Vineyard. Life resumed—familiar faces, familiar routines at the coffee shop, the rhythm of summer work followed by winter travel. That seasonal cycle became my lifestyle: working in the

U.S. doing what I loved, and then traveling the world, learning through experience.

Those travels became my education—an open university, teaching me firsthand about cultures, histories, and lives outside the American lens. And while I was waiting to apply for U.S. citizenship, this combination of two passions—coffee and travel—gave me purpose. It gave structure to my years of waiting.

Being on the Vineyard and working in a café gave me a sense of control over my life. I didn't have to answer to anyone. I could do what I loved, connect with people from all walks of life, and continue to grow. My identity took root in those years. I wasn't just a barista. I was a traveler, a student of the world, a man searching for belonging.

Eventually, I found that sense of home—renting a room in the same house year after year. And in that house, I met someone who would become part of my story: Ann McKenzie, the woman who owned the home.

Ann McKenzie came into my life at a time when I was still navigating the uncertainties of statelessness, moving from one place to another, searching not just for a roof over my head, but for a sense of grounding. I met her through a local customer who went by the name OB in Edgartown, while I was looking for a long-term room to rent on Martha's Vineyard. The house was a modest but warm place tucked away in a quiet neighborhood, not far from the bustling center of the island during the summer, yet peaceful enough to retreat to when the season faded and the tourists disappeared.

Ann was an older woman, in her sixties at the time we met, and she carried with her the kind of calm that comes from having seen much of life. Her eyes were sharp, filled with curiosity, and her voice had a kindness to it that put me at ease. She had lived on the island her whole life, and over time, she became more than just a landlord—she became a steady presence, a witness to my in-between life.

Ann McKenzie

At first, we kept to our own routines. I would leave early in the morning to open the café, returning in the evenings to a quiet house. She would often be in her garden, tending to her flowers or sitting on the porch with a cup of coffee, reading. Over time, our conversations began to stretch beyond polite greetings. She would ask about my day, about the people I met, the places I'd been. And I found myself sharing more and more stories about my travels, my experiences in Cuba and Rwanda, my dreams of finally becoming an American citizen.

She listened without judgment, sometimes nodding quietly, sometimes asking thoughtful questions that made me reflect even deeper. She told me stories of the Vineyard as it used to be—before the summer crowds and the real estate boom, when it was still a sleepy place full of fishing families, artists, and those who simply wanted a slower pace of life. She spoke of how the seasons shaped her life more than the calendar ever could.

What stood out most about Ann was her dignity—how she lived alone, unbothered by solitude, content with her books, her garden, and the rhythm of island life. And in her quiet way, she gave me something I hadn't felt in years: stability. I knew I had a place to return to after my travels. I had someone who would ask me how my trip was and genuinely want to hear about it. I had someone who reminded me that home isn't always a country—it can be a room at the back of an old house, where someone leaves the porch light on for you.

As the years passed and I continued my seasonal work, traveling during the winters and returning each spring, Ann and I developed an unspoken bond. She never pried, but she always cared. When I finally became eligible to apply for U.S. citizenship, she was the first person I told. And when I received the letter confirming my naturalization ceremony date, she hugged me with tears in her eyes and said, "It's about time."

That moment will always stay with me. It wasn't just about gaining a passport. It was about being seen, being recognized, and finally being able to say—I belong.

The longer I stayed with Ann, the more I began to understand her character. Anne was a tough, no-nonsense kind of woman. She knew how to stand her ground. She didn't care much about what people thought of her, and she certainly didn't seek their approval. She lived with a quiet resilience, surrounded by a few close friends she occasionally socialized with, but most of her time was spent at home, in her own world, in her own rhythm.

Ann and Quadri celebrating our first wedding anniversary

Ann and I were different in many ways. She was conservative, molded by a lifetime of values reinforced by the television she watched, primarily Fox News, which shaped many of her views about the country and the world. I, on the other hand, had a more liberal mindset—open to change, grounded in acceptance and diversity, and shaped by my own journey as a stateless immigrant. Our perspectives often stood in contrast: hers leaning toward preservation, mine toward transformation.

And yet, we never clashed. Sure, we disagreed—sometimes passionately. We debated politics, immigration, and the future of the United States. She believed the country needed to return to its core conservative values, while I believed it had to evolve, to adapt, to reflect the richness of its immigrant identity. But even in the heat of disagreement, we managed to maintain mutual respect. We could agree to disagree, then move on to the next conversation over dinner.

For me, the United States has always been—and will always be—a country built by immigrants. You cannot erase that truth. From the earliest settlers who arrived from England seeking freedom to the diverse waves of newcomers that followed, the American identity is a tapestry of global roots. The only true native inhabitants of this land are the Indigenous people, whose homes and heritage were taken long before the idea of the United States existed. Everyone else—no matter how long ago their ancestors arrived—came from somewhere else. And I always believed that understanding this was essential to understanding America.

Anne didn't necessarily see things the same way. But she respected my perspective, just as I respected hers. She had her own truth, shaped by her upbringing and life experience. She had built a personal boundary around her beliefs, and no one could cross it. "This is how I see the world," she seemed to say, "and I'm not here to be persuaded otherwise." That, in a way, was what made her strong. She was a tough cookie, as people might say.

She had spent most of her adult life alone. She'd had a boyfriend in the past, but for many years she lived independently. Originally from Cincinnati, Ohio, Ann's roots on Martha's Vineyard began with her parents, who used to vacation there. Eventually, she left Ohio for good and made the island her permanent home. Her house—her "chateau," or "fortress" as I came to think of it—was her sanctuary, fiercely protected, quietly lived in, and deeply loved.

Despite our differences, we shared many quiet moments. Conversations about life on the Vineyard, about her travels— particularly a trip she'd taken to France in her youth. I would cook and sometimes bring home meals from the café to share with her. Our dinners became little rituals of connection. Over time, she became more than just a landlord. She became a companion. A friend. Perhaps not quite a mother figure, but someone close, someone I could talk to, someone who listened.

Ann was also deeply engaged with the island's life. She read the Vineyard Gazette religiously, keeping up with every local development. She was curious about my past, too. We spoke often about my life, my upbringing in the former Soviet Union, and the winding road that eventually brought me to the United States. She listened carefully, trying to understand a world far removed from her own. And as the months turned into years, our mutual understanding grew. We got to know one another in a way that transcended political views or cultural backgrounds.

Living with Ann was eye-opening. She was the first American woman I had lived with. Before that, most of my friends and acquaintances in the U.S. were either immigrants like me or first-generation Americans—people whose parents came from somewhere else. The only other true American I had lived with was my ex-boyfriend from East Texas. Ann offered a new window into American life—one that was rooted in its traditions, its small-town culture, and its sense of belonging to a land that, for her, had always been home.

The more time I spent with Ann, the more I came to understand a defining part of her nature—Anne loved to talk. Conversation, for her, was essential. It wasn't just small talk or idle chatter; it was how she connected, how she affirmed her presence, how she processed her world. Often, after long days when all I wanted was some solitude to retreat into my own thoughts, I'd find myself pulled into her stories. Ann needed an audience, and I was there, seated across from her, nodding, listening—or at least appearing to.

But Ann was different. She came from a world where honesty didn't need a soft cushion. If she didn't like what I was saying, she wouldn't hesitate to interrupt. "I don't care," she'd say bluntly. "I don't want to hear that." And then she'd disappear into her room, leaving me mid-sentence, stunned. Her emotional boundaries were clear and immediate—if something didn't suit her, she cut it off, no apology necessary.

That was Ann—unfiltered, direct, and unapologetically herself. There was no malice in it, just a kind of raw honesty that I wasn't used to. And though it could sometimes be frustrating, it was also oddly grounding. It showed me a side of American individualism I had rarely encountered so up close. In our own way, we had carved out an understanding. She talked, and I listened. And when I talked, she listened—until she didn't want to anymore.

Ann and Quadri

Even in those moments of quiet frustration or emotional mismatch, there was something deeply human in our dynamic. Two people from completely different worlds, sharing a roof, navigating the edges of each other's habits, boundaries, and expectations—trying, in our imperfect ways, to coexist and understand.

That was the unspoken rhythm of our life together.

And through her, I gained a deeper, more complex understanding of this country I was trying so hard to belong to. We were two very different people, brought together by circumstance, but bonded by something more subtle—respect, patience, and the quiet willingness to listen.

A Home Between Departures

My seasons on Martha's Vineyard became a rhythm—a steady cycle I returned to, year after year. From 2015 through 2020, the island welcomed me back each spring like a long-lost friend. I'd arrive in April, throw myself into the coffee shop work, and pour my energy into six intense months of labor. Each year, I knew exactly what I was doing it for: not just for survival, but for the freedom to travel, to grow, and eventually, to close the long chapter of statelessness behind me by applying for U.S. citizenship.

But there was always a clock ticking in the background.

As a permanent resident, I had to be cautious not to spend too long outside the United States. Any absence over six months risked being interpreted as abandonment of my residency. Anything over a year required official permission—otherwise, I risked losing everything I had built. My freedom, my green card, my chance at citizenship. I never crossed that line. I measured my time carefully, like a monk counting beads.

So, each year, I negotiated to keep the coffee shop open beyond its typical closing date. Normally, Behind the Bookstore would shut its doors in October. But I stayed through November, sometimes until Christmas, stretching the season as far as I could before my winter migrations. This arrangement gave me just enough time to travel—and to return without jeopardizing my residency.

And what journeys those winters became.

Moroni. Comoros

I visited Brazil several times, standing among coffee plants on sun-drenched farms, learning their cultivation from the source. I danced in the chaos and color of Carnival, mesmerized by the vibrancy of life. My path twisted through Thailand, Nepal, Bhutan, and Tibet—each place a spiritual thread in the tapestry I was slowly weaving for myself. Africa called to me most of all. I returned to the continent again and again, unable to resist its pull.

There was something about Africa—the spirit of it, the raw beauty, the warmth of its people—that felt like home. I traveled through Kenya, South Africa, Namibia, Mozambique, Cape Verde, São Tomé and Príncipe, Ghana, Benin, Togo, Uganda, Burundi, Madagascar, Comoros. Each name, a new story. Each border, a new lesson.

In those places, I discovered a different kind of wealth. Not the material kind, but the wealth of simplicity, of human connection. These were cultures that valued community, friendship, and family above all else. It reminded me of something I'd lost, or perhaps something I'd never fully had before—a grounding, a deeper understanding of what it means to belong.

Comoros

By then, I had stopped caring about material things. After everything I had lost—after detention in Texas, exile in American Samoa—I had learned how fragile possessions could be. I wore the same clothes for years. I didn't need anything fancy. I needed experience. I needed expansion. I saved every dollar I could, not to buy things, but to buy freedom—the freedom to see the world, to learn, to heal, to grow.

Travel became my university—the one I never finished when I came to America. Every country was a course. Every journey a thesis. With each continent, I earned a new kind of degree: not on paper, but in wisdom, perspective, and understanding. I was writing my own curriculum, collecting knowledge not from classrooms, but from crowded markets in Lagos, sunrises in the Himalayas, and roadside conversations in Lusaka.

And it was all possible because of one man: Jeffrey.

Jeffrey gave me the opportunity to work at Martha's Vineyard. He didn't just offer me a job—he offered me stability, a safe harbor after years of drifting. Because of him, I was no longer the lost, struggling barista in Los Angeles. I was someone who was finally able to live a dream I had carried since childhood: to see the world, to live freely, to connect deeply.

That job gave me more than income. It gave me security, identity, and purpose. It gave me the means to turn pain into perspective. And perhaps most importantly, it gave me the chance to finally imagine a future beyond statelessness.

That, I will always carry with me.

I Traveled Alone, But Never Empty

Every time the season came to an end on Martha's Vineyard, as we swept the floors and locked the doors of the coffee shop for the winter, my pulse would quicken—not from exhaustion, but from anticipation. The closing of one chapter meant the beginning of another: a new journey, a new country, a new self-discovery. It was like shedding an old skin. With my bags packed, documents in hand, and plans barely finalized, I would board a plane and watch the familiar recede below me, trusting that something meaningful awaited on the other side.

I always traveled alone. Not because I was lonely, but because solitude was essential to how I understood the world—and myself. Traveling alone gave me the space to be fully present, to feel, to make decisions without compromise. I didn't need to negotiate itineraries or justify my detours. If I got lost, I was free to wander; if I felt drawn to a quiet corner of a city or a remote village on the edge of a continent, I stayed. There was a certain purity in that freedom. It wasn't a rejection of companionship—it was an embrace of agency.

Planning these trips required precision. With my refugee travel document, each destination brought its own set of bureaucratic hurdles. Many countries—especially in Africa and Asia—demanded visas in advance, and the process was often long and uncertain. I became my own travel agent, researcher, and logistical planner. I remember sitting at the coffee shop on my day off with my laptop open, immersed in maps and airline websites, comparing routes, checking visa requirements, calculating costs. Every trip was a puzzle I learned to solve.

One summer, while talking to a waiter at Atria, a restaurant on the island, he mentioned Bhutan—a small Himalayan Kingdom I had only vaguely heard about. His description intrigued me. I was already planning a trip through Southeast Asia, and something about Bhutan pulled at me. Nestled between China and India, it seemed untouched by the noise of modern tourism. But then came the challenge: Bhutan didn't accept my refugee travel document. I couldn't get a visa on arrival, nor could I obtain one in advance.

And yet, at the bottom of my bag, I had the World Passport—a symbolic document issued by the World Service Authority, which once served as my only form of identification. I had long considered it more of a souvenir than a functional document, especially after the complications it caused during my exile in American Samoa. But something told me to try. To my astonishment, Bhutan accepted it. They issued a visa, no questions asked. I entered Bhutan not as a U.S. permanent resident, but as a "world citizen."

Bhutan was a revelation. It was unlike any place I had ever been. The landscape felt sacred—its rolling hills and monasteries radiating peace. The people wore traditional clothing with pride, and there was a stillness to their presence, a deep-rooted spirituality that could be felt in the air. Their national sport, archery, was more than just a game—it was a cultural ritual. Visiting Tiger's Nest Monastery, clinging impossibly to the cliffs, I felt something shift inside me. There was a simplicity in Bhutan's philosophy, a reverence for life, for happiness, for balance. They had consciously limited the number of tourists to preserve their culture. It was not a country that sought the world's approval—it was a country that guarded its soul.

From Bhutan, I journeyed to Nepal. The contrast was stark. Kathmandu felt chaotic and overwhelmed. The aftermath of a devastating earthquake still lingered in the crumbled streets and open holes in the ground. Pollution choked the air. While the country held a deep history and spiritual significance, especially in the shadow of the Himalayas, I couldn't ignore the heavy toll tourism and poverty had taken.

Tibet

Then came Tibet. There was something hauntingly beautiful about Tibet. Lhasa, with its temples and mountain air, offered a calm I hadn't expected. I visited the Potala Palace, once home to the Dalai Lama, and stood in its shadows reflecting on exile—his and mine. I admired the resilience in the Tibetan people—the way they smiled, the way they practiced their faith quietly under the watchful eye of Chinese surveillance. Their lives were restricted, their movement tightly controlled. They didn't hold passports, only internal identification cards that permitted them to move within certain parts of China. I saw echoes of my own experience in their silent endurance.

Tibet

It was in these quiet, sacred places that I often thought about the deeper meaning of identity. What does it mean to belong? To be recognized? To be free? My journeys were more than just travels. They were pilgrimages through the geography of the self. Each country, each challenge, was a mirror. Some showed me my strength; others showed me my fragility.

And always, I carried with me more than just a suitcase. I carried a memory. I carried hope. I carried the invisible weight of a past shaped by borders, politics, loss, and longing. I traveled alone, yes—but I was never truly empty.

Stranded Between Borders: A Lesson in Bureaucracy and Belonging

Nima Sherpa

Traveling was never simply about visiting new places—it was about navigating the strange and often hostile terrain of global bureaucracy. Every trip was a test of patience, endurance, and faith in the journey itself. And my time in Nepal, followed by a failed attempt to enter Laos, proved to be one of the most vivid examples of how precarious life can be when your documents don't fit into the world's bureaucratic boxes.

Nepal started with promise. I was curious about its emerging specialty coffee scene, and after doing some research, I came across Lekali Coffee Estate, owned by Nima Tenzing Sherpa—a bright, passionate entrepreneur deeply invested in changing Nepal's relationship with coffee. Nima had spent five years studying business in the United States and returned to Kathmandu with a vision to bring high-quality, sustainably grown coffee to both domestic and international markets. Most people in Nepal were still drinking instant coffee, he told me. But those who had lived abroad-those who had tasted something better—were slowly planting seeds of change.

Kathmandu, Nepal

We spoke for hours about harvesting techniques, fermentation processes, and how climate and altitude shaped flavor profiles. Nima's excitement was infectious. I admired his determination to create something world-class in a place where the infrastructure and market support were still catching up.

Through Nima, I was also introduced to his family's mountaintop retreat Chhahari Lodge, perched above the city. It became my refuge during what turned out to be an unexpectedly long stay.

Originally, I had planned to spend just a week in Nepal. From there, I was set to travel to Tibet, then fly on to Laos. I had mapped everything out—carefully calculating dates, airline routes, and visa requirements, as I always did. But what I couldn't prepare for was the rigid and sometimes irrational logic of immigration policy.

Kathmandu, Nepal

The issue began when I arrived in Vientiane, the capital of Laos. I had flown there from Kathmandu via Bangkok on Thai Airways. At check-in in Nepal, my refugee travel document had been examined, my visa was in place, and no one said a word about any problems. But upon landing in Laos, everything fell apart.

Immigration officers pulled me aside, explaining that my travel document was valid for only five more months, and Laos required a minimum of more than six months' validity for entry. I pleaded with them. I showed my return ticket, explained I was only staying for a week. I offered them my itinerary, my plans. But their answer was absolute: no six months, no entry.

In that moment, my fate was no longer mine to decide. They informed me I would be deported—sent back to the country from which I had last departed. That meant Nepal.

Luckily, when I applied for my Nepal visa, I had opted for a multiple-entry visa. That decision, which I made almost on a whim, saved me from being stranded. But I was not free yet.

Because my return flight to Kathmandu had already departed for the day, Thai immigration took custody of me upon my arrival in Bangkok. They escorted me to a detention area inside the airport—a cold, sterile space filled with others who had also been denied entry to various destinations. I sat there with no access to my travel document, which had been handed over to the airline's cabin supervisor for safekeeping, to be delivered directly to immigration upon arrival at my final destination. I felt helpless. I was not a criminal. I was simply someone who fell through the cracks of a system that has no place for exceptions.

Kathmandu, Nepal

What made it worse was the attitude of the immigration officer in Laos. When I tried to explain the absurdity of the situation, he looked at me and said, "Thank Donald Trump." He wasn't joking. He was pointing to the U.S. administration's policies at the time, particularly the travel bans on certain countries, and using that as justification. "If your country can deport people like that, why can't we?" he added.

It was a bitter moment. For someone like me—stateless for years, now a permanent resident of the United States, but still without a passport—the layers of exclusion kept multiplying. I wasn't enough of a citizen anywhere to be protected from this kind of treatment.

The next morning, Thai authorities gave me an ultimatum: buy your own ticket back to Kathmandu or remain detained indefinitely. I protested. Thai Airways had checked my documents and allowed me to board—they should be responsible for returning me. But no one listened. Faced with the possibility of prolonged detention and missing the rest of my planned journey, I relented and purchased the ticket.

Kathmandu, Nepal

Back in Kathmandu, I was emotionally drained and financially dented. I contacted Nima, who welcomed me back with open arms. He took me once again to Chhahari Lodge, where his father greeted me like family. What was meant to be a weeklong stay in Nepal became a month.

That month, however, turned out to be a gift. I spent my days helping at the coffee farm, learning more about the intricacies of roasting, and connecting deeply with the land and people. It reminded me that travel isn't always about ticking off destinations—it's about the unpredictable detours that force you to slow down and really see where you are.

Kathmandu, Nepal

And more importantly, it was a reminder of how fragile mobility is. When your existence depends on the validity of a piece of paper—one that the world sees as less than a passport—you're constantly at the mercy of systems that don't care about your humanity, only your documentation.

But even then, I found community. I found meaning. I found a place—if only temporarily—where I could belong.

Sanctuary Above the City: Reflections from Chhahari

Chhahari became my shelter in the storm.

Perched high on the Shivapuri hills, this boutique eco-lodge was unlike anywhere I'd stayed before. Architecturally, it echoed the traditional Nepali home—a celebration of craftsmanship, earthy textures, and handcrafted timber, all infused with the kind of quiet elegance that made you instinctively lower your voice. It was as though the space itself asked you to be still.

Chhahari Lodge

The lodge was nestled at the edge of Shivapuri National Park, where the city of Kathmandu melted away into a rolling canvas of green. No traffic. No horns.

No blinking screens. Just the wind brushing through the trees, the occasional call of a distant bird, and the stillness of fog weaving between branches at dawn. It was a world apart, where time unraveled slowly and the burdens of the outside world loosened their grip.

I didn't plan to stay long in Nepal. Just a brief stop—originally a week—before moving on to Tibet and Laos. But when Laos deported me for arriving with a refugee travel document valid for only five more months, I found myself back in Kathmandu with nowhere else to go. I had no home to return to, no status that guaranteed me safety or welcome. Statelessness is never just a legal term—it's a feeling, an ever-present vulnerability.

And yet, Chhahari opened its doors.

Chhahari Lodge

Nima Tenzing Sherpa, a young coffee producer I'd befriended through our mutual passion for specialty coffee, invited me to stay at his family's lodge without asking for anything in return. His kindness was overwhelming. He not only gave me a room, but also provided meals and space to breathe, without ever making me feel like a guest overstaying his welcome. In return, I gave what I could: sharing my experience in coffee, experimenting with processing in Puerto Rico, assisting him with the farm and roastery as he worked to elevate Nepalese coffee on the world stage.

It was an unspoken exchange built on mutual respect and genuine care—something rare and deeply human.

Chhahari Lodge

For a month, Chhahari was my refuge. An organic retreat powered by solar energy, it offered more than a roof—it offered a way of living. Panoramic views of the valley framed each morning. Meals were made from locally grown ingredients, rich in flavor and simplicity. There were

327

no phones ringing, no televisions humming. Just breath, breeze, and thought.

I began to slow down. I'd walk the trails alone, inhaling the crisp air of the northern hills, letting the forest speak where people could not. I listened to the wind press through the trees like water against stone, and with each day, I began to feel the weight of recent events settle into something more digestible. I thought about the deportation, about the disorientation of being denied entry, not just by a country, but by a system that didn't quite know where to place someone like me.

I was learning international borders not as lines on a map, but as layered barriers—dense with policy, politics, and interpretation. A document might be valid in one place, but meaningless in the next. Sometimes, a visa wasn't enough. Sometimes, the rules changed mid-journey. I was discovering the fine print of a system not built for the stateless, and I was having to navigate it blind.

Chhahari Lodge

Around this time, the U.S. had begun enforcing President Trump's new travel ban, and the United Nations High Commissioner for Refugees reached out to me with concern. Even some U.S. permanent residents were being denied reentry. They urged me to return early, fearing that my refugee travel document might not be honored if I arrived later in the season.

But I couldn't simply reroute. It was February—off-season on Martha's Vineyard, where I worked seasonally, and my return job wouldn't begin for another month and a half. I had already booked and paid for onward travel, most of which was nonrefundable. Flying to the U.S. early meant spending money I didn't have, returning to an island shut down for winter, jobless and isolated. And for what? A hypothetical risk?

As I sat on the porch of Chhahari, sipping hot milk tea and watching the fog lift from the valley below, I asked myself the difficult question: was I really safer turning back?

I wasn't from any of the countries listed in the ban. Technically, I wasn't from any country at all. My place of birth was in the former Soviet Union, and none of the nation's I'd lived in after its collapse were on the blacklist. What would they even classify me as? I had no citizenship, no allegiance on paper. If the rules were drawn based on nationality, then what box would I fit into?

I decided to take the risk and continue.

Through Mandalay and Onward

My next stop was Myanmar, a country steeped in tradition and shadowed by complex politics. I entered on a visa attached to my World Passport—Myanmar didn't recognize my U.S.-issued refugee travel document the same way as Bhutan, but for reasons I still don't fully understand, they accepted the World Passport.

I was skeptical at first. But they let me in.

Yangon buzzed with life—colonial facades crumbling under tropical sun, golden pagodas catching the light like fire. Mandalay was quieter, more poised, and in some ways more beautiful. A remnant of British Burma, it had pockets of botanical serenity that transported you to another era entirely. I visited coffee farms tucked into the highlands, met growers navigating the same global markets that Nima had back in Nepal hoped to reach.

There was a warmth to the people, a quiet resilience in the way they carried themselves amid a country led by a military junta. You could feel both hope and caution hanging in the air.

And then came Vietnam.

Vietnam was meant to be my next step—a continuation of my journey through Southeast Asia before eventually traveling to Bulgaria and the countries of former Yugoslavia. I had arranged everything in advance: accommodation, internal flights, even a plan to visit the highlands where Arabica was being cultivated in the Central Highlands. It was supposed to be a soft landing after Myanmar's intensity, a place where I could rest, observe, and explore.

But instead, it became another painful reminder that my statelessness was never far behind me.

I had applied for a visa to Vietnam in the US using my U.S. refugee travel document. It was processed and approved, at first without issue. But days before departure, the agency handling my visa reached out in a panic. They said Vietnam might not accept my refugee travel document after all. The language was vague, the certainty evaporating. I asked them what options I had. Their answer? Try a different passport. Perhaps the World Passport instead.

So, I applied again—this time with the World Passport, the only other document I had. They issued a second visa. I took a deep breath and moved forward.

I boarded an Emirates flight from Yangon to Hanoi, clinging to a fragile hope that everything would be fine. I had arrived in many countries under similarly grey circumstances—sometimes with extra questions, sometimes with side-eyes or confusion—but ultimately, I had been allowed to enter.

This time was different.

At immigration in Hanoi, the moment the officer saw my World Passport, his face hardened. He conferred with a colleague, then another. Within minutes, I was escorted to a side room. No explanation. No translator. Just a sense of foreboding that tightened in my chest like a vice.

They told me flatly: This is not a valid passport. Vietnam does not recognize it.

I tried to show them the US-issued refugee travel document instead, to explain the situation, the confusion with the agency, the two visas issued under different documents. But it didn't matter. That document wasn't accepted either.

Within the hour, they handcuffed me.

I wasn't a threat. I wasn't carrying anything illegal. I had a visa. I had a ticket. I had my documents. But none of that mattered because the very foundation of my identity—the right to enter a place—was under question. Again. And this time, there was no room for negotiation.

I pleaded with them not to send me back to Myanmar. My visa there was a single-entry. I had already used it. If they returned me, I would be arriving illegally, back in a country that had barely accepted me to begin with. But they were unmoved. They escorted me to the next available flight to Yangon and put me on board.

I was deported without ever leaving the airport.

The brief detention at Hanoi International Airport felt like a surreal, slow-motion nightmare. I wasn't handcuffed at the beginning, but I was confined—placed in a special room that served as a holding cell for people who had become paperless in the eyes of a bureaucracy that refuses to see nuance.

They gave me water. They allowed me access to Wi-Fi. But the uncertainty was paralyzing. I didn't know what they considered me—threat, mistake, ghost?

A Vietnamese security guard was stationed outside the door. He was kind. He tried to make sense of my situation. In broken English, he told me that since I had a visa, they should just let me in, especially with a U.S. refugee travel document. "You can go," he said softly. "You have the visa." But then he added, "Not my decision."

And it wasn't. The final word came from a frantic, argumentative Emirates Airlines representative—a Vietnamese woman who spoke with such intensity and sharpness that I couldn't tell if she was shouting or just speaking in her usual tone. Every sentence she barked at me felt like an accusation. I tried to explain: "I cannot go back to Myanmar. My visa was a single-entry and was already used. I will be illegal there."

Her response was chilling in its casual cruelty: "Then we deport you to the United States."

I told her I didn't want to go back to the U.S.—not yet. My itinerary was carefully crafted, my tickets non-refundable, and my season of work on Martha's Vineyard hadn't yet begun. I asked her to send me back to Nepal, where I had found brief refuge before. "We don't fly to Nepal," she said bluntly.

I explained I had a valid Turkish Airlines ticket to Bulgaria. She dismissed me again. "Turkish counter is closed. No representative. You have to go now."

I begged to stay in the airport overnight. According to international law, the airport is a transit zone. I hadn't technically entered Vietnam. I pleaded: "Let me stay one night. I'll go to the Turkish Airlines counter first thing in the morning and change my ticket."

But she wouldn't listen.

When I refused deportation to Myanmar, she escalated it—called security. Six uniformed officers arrived and surrounded me like I was a criminal. I was marched toward the Emirates gate, where a flight was about to depart back to Dubai via Yangon. The pilot was summoned. He asked me if I would be cooperative. I understood the weight of that question. Would I fight? Would I resist?

I told him, "No, I won't cooperate. I am being deported to a country I cannot legally enter. My visa is expired."

The pilot tried to reason with the ground staff, explaining that he couldn't allow a passenger onboard if he refused to cooperate. But then came the threat that shattered me: "If you refuse this flight, we will detain you and send you to jail in Vietnam."

That word—jail—brought back every memory of U.S. detention centers. The sterile walls, the endless waiting, the feeling of being less than human. I knew what that meant. I gave up.

"I'll cooperate," I whispered. "I'll go."

They forced me onto the flight. My passport was confiscated again. I was seated in silence as the aircraft taxied toward the runway. I stared at the seat back in front of me, numb, disconnected.

But I wasn't finished yet.

I pulled out my laptop—my ever-present companion, my tool for survival. The Emirates Wi-Fi is connected. I bought myself a ticket from Yangon to Boston via Dubai, on the exact same flight I was on. If I was going to be forced back, I would do it on my terms. I wasn't going to be "deported" anymore—I would be a passenger.

I showed the flight crew my new ticket I purchased online with Emirates Airlines. The message was relayed to the pilot. Minutes later, my passport was returned to me. I clutched it like a lifeline.

When we landed in Yangon, two immigration officers were waiting. They had been informed of my deportation. The flight crew assured them: "He's continuing on with us to Dubai and then to the United States." But the officers stayed close, hovering, following me through the terminal, trailing me even to the bathroom, making sure I didn't vanish into Myanmar's chaotic maze.

Eventually, my bag was taken off the plane and checked back in. I re-boarded the flight, holding my travel document tightly, silently promising myself: this is the last forced movement I'll endure on this journey.

We took off again, bound for Dubai, and then finally to Boston. I didn't know what awaited me. But for the first time in days, I could breathe.

Boarders That Bleed

After everything that had happened in Vietnam, the last thing I wanted was to go to the United States. I hadn't planned to return—not then, not under those circumstances. My next destination was supposed to be Bulgaria. I had a ticket from Hanoi to Istanbul and then onward to Sofia, a route I had carefully arranged. But after being denied entry to Vietnam and effectively forced onto an Emirates flight to Yangon, the only way I could retrieve my confiscated refugee travel document was by purchasing a new ticket. However, the problem was that Dubai— my transit point—did not recognize the U.S. refugee travel document as valid for entry. The only workaround was to purchase a ticket with a final destination in the United States, specifically Boston. This was not because I had any real intention to go there, but because such a booking would allow me to satisfy Emirates' requirements and reclaim my passport. I played along, out of necessity.

Once aboard the flight and enroute to Dubai, I quickly connected to the Wi-Fi and purchased the new ticket. That digital transaction, though done under pressure, became my lifeline. It was my ticket not to Boston, but to survival.

When the flight attendant saw the itinerary, she confirmed with the captain, and my passport was returned to me. It was a small, temporary victory.

Arriving in Dubai, I knew I had to act quickly. I approached the Emirates desk and asked to retrieve my luggage, which had been checked through to Boston. I explained the entire ordeal to the agent—a Vietnamese woman working for Emirates—and told her I never intended to continue to Boston. My true destination was Bulgaria. She listened patiently and told me that if I wanted my luggage back, I needed to show her a new ticket to Bulgaria. Again, I complied. I bought a new set of tickets: Dubai to Istanbul, and from there to Sofia, Bulgaria.

It felt like a mad chess game: every move calculated, every step forward contingent on sidestepping arbitrary rules and manufactured barriers. I collected my luggage and boarded the flight to Istanbul, my heart pounding—not with excitement, but with exhaustion. At every turn, I had to manipulate systems that weren't made for people like me, for stateless traveler who fall outside the neat categories of global mobility.

Sofia, Bulgaria

Arriving in Sofia, Bulgaria, I believed my troubles were finally behind me. Months earlier, I had communicated directly with the Bulgarian Embassy in Washington, D.C. I had explained my situation, submitted documentation, and in return, I received a written assurance: no visa was required for entry into Bulgaria as long as I carried a U.S. refugee travel document issued in accordance with the United Nations Convention relating to the Status of Refugees. I had that letter printed and folded neatly in my bag—a talisman of protection, or so I thought.

When I approached the immigration officer at the border, a woman with a stern face that seemed frozen in time, her presence triggered something in me. Her expression carried the cold, unyielding gaze of a former Soviet-era enforcer.

Without a word, she took my travel document and gestured for me to follow her to a small immigration booth, where two other officers, also women, equally expressionless, joined her. They examined the document in silence, their faces devoid of empathy.

Sofia, Bulgaria

When they finally spoke, they informed me that I needed a visa. I calmly responded that, according to the Bulgarian Embassy in

Washington, no visa was required for entry with my travel document. I even handed them the printed letter. They glanced at it and scoffed. One of them said bluntly, "The Embassy doesn't know immigration rules. We decide here."

It was a slap in the face. My months of planning, the paper trail, the assurances—all meaningless now. They stamped my passport with "Entry Denied," confiscated it, and told me to wait. It was already dark. My friend had come to meet me outside the airport. I managed to connect to the Wi-Fi and explain what had happened. She was outraged and told me to forward the email from the embassy to her immediately. She promised to contact someone she knew in Bulgaria's Ministry of Foreign Affairs.

Meanwhile, the officers handed me a document in Bulgarian. I refused to sign anything I couldn't understand. One officer tried to verbally interpret it, claiming it stated I would be deported to the United States at my own expense. I firmly said no. I was not going to be deported. I had not broken any laws. I had documentation proving my right to enter Bulgaria. This was not just a bureaucratic mishap; it was a violation of my human rights.

I was left to wander the empty airport overnight, trying to rest on benches, hungry and anxious. The shops were all closed. The terminal was nearly abandoned. I felt like a ghost—unwelcome, invisible, in limbo once again.

Sometime in the early morning, my friend's persistence paid off. She had reached someone at the Ministry. That official had reviewed the embassy's letter, the refugee convention laws, and confirmed that I was indeed allowed to enter. A young officer came to find me. His demeanor was different—calmer, more respectful.

"We are sorry," he said, lowering his voice. "There was a mistake. You are allowed to enter Bulgaria. Your travel document meets the requirements."

But then, a quiet request: "Please, if possible, don't report this mistake to anyone. It could cost us our jobs."

It was a surreal moment—an apology delivered with a plea for silence. I had no energy left to argue or retaliate. I just wanted my passport and my freedom. "I won't write anything," I said. "Just give me my document."

Sofia, Bulgaria

And so, after more than twelve hours of uncertainty, humiliation, and fear, I was finally stamped into Bulgaria. I stepped out into the cool air of Sofia, feeling both relief and a strange numbness. Freedom never came easily. For people like me, it was always borrowed, always conditional, always one mistake away from being revoked.

But I was in. I had made it. For now, at least, I was free.

I spent an entire month in Bulgaria, though not confined to Sofia alone. From the capital, I explored the hills and villages beyond, weaving through the soul of the country, feeling the shadow of its Soviet past and the grit of its cultural resilience. During this time, I even managed to fly to Berlin and return to Bulgaria again before continuing on. But the way my Bulgarian chapter began was far from ordinary.

Initially, I had planned to stay at a hotel. However, through social media, I had connected with someone who ran a small specialty coffee shop and roastery in Sofia. He was deeply interested in improving the quality of coffee in Bulgaria, eager to elevate the scene, and passionate about connecting with others who shared that same vision. Though we had never met in person, we had exchanged messages over time. When I told him I'd be visiting Bulgaria, he offered me a place to stay—an apartment he shared with his girlfriend. She picked me up from the airport.

The first few days passed smoothly. He was gracious, even taking the time to show me around Sofia. I visited his coffee shop, watched him roast, and offered some insights from my own experiences in the specialty coffee world. It felt like a small but promising collaboration between two people with a shared love for the craft.

But slowly, the atmosphere shifted. Something changed. He began to retreat, locking himself away in his room. Conversation with him dwindled to almost nothing, and the easy exchange of ideas dried up. At first, I couldn't understand why. I had done nothing inappropriate—never mentioned anything personal, never crossed any lines, never even hinted at my sexuality. That part of me I kept private, especially around people I didn't know well or trust yet. I had learned, over the years, how dangerous it could be to reveal that I was gay.

But somehow, something in me-my mannerisms, my presence—must have triggered something in him. I saw it in the way he began to avoid me, in the quiet discomfort that replaced our earlier warmth. I could feel the walls closing in, not just around his behavior, but in the apartment itself.

Eventually, his girlfriend and I had a quiet conversation. I told her that I felt unwelcome and would be moving out. She acted surprised, even confused, and asked if I had any idea why her boyfriend was acting that way. Of course, I knew. I didn't say it out loud, but I knew. And she probably did too. The unspoken hung heavy in the room.

The truth was simple: he had figured out I was gay, or at least suspected it. That alone was enough for him to withdraw and reject me, not because of anything I had said or done, but simply because I existed in a way that made him uncomfortable. There had been no flirtation, no impropriety—only assumptions and fear, fueled by deep-rooted cultural stigmas.

Eastern Europe, like many post-Soviet regions, still bore the scars of its authoritarian past. For decades, homosexuality was not only taboo but criminalized. People had been imprisoned, blacklisted, and erased for simply being themselves. That fear didn't vanish overnight with the fall of the Berlin Wall. It lingered in minds, in laws, and in the uneasy silences of rooms like the one I found myself in.

Rather than escalate the situation, I quietly packed my things and moved to a hotel, reclaiming the privacy and dignity I had always intended for this trip. I never spoke to them again.

The rest of my stay in Bulgaria I spent alone—wandering Sofia, soaking in the architecture, the melancholy of its boulevards, the warm clatter of its cafés. My steps took me beyond the capital, through ancient towns and old ruins, and eventually, onward.

From Bulgaria, I began what felt like a pilgrimage through the former Yugoslavia and beyond—Albania, Montenegro, Croatia, Romania. Each place, a fragment of a world that once stood divided behind the Iron Curtain. Albania, in particular, fascinated me. It had long been a closed nation, fiercely isolated even from other communist countries. During the Cold War, only citizens of China and the Soviet Union were permitted to enter. For everyone else, Albania was a sealed mystery—an enclave of secrecy and authoritarianism.

Tirana, Albania

When the walls finally fell and democracy began to trickle in, Albania slowly opened its gates. I had studied it as a child in the Soviet Union, and now, years later, I walked its streets with the weight of memory and curiosity. I wanted to see for myself what had become of this once-closed society.

Though my desire to explore Europe had dimmed over time, particularly after years of traveling through Africa, Asia, and Latin America, something still pulled me through the Balkans. Perhaps it was closure I sought, or the chance to confront the ghosts of a past that had shaped so much of my understanding of borders, belonging, and identity.

Tirana, Albania

And yet, even as I moved from one Eastern European country to the next, I felt a stronger pull elsewhere. The African continent called to me again, not just as a traveler, but as someone who had come to feel more seen, more free, and more understood in places often forgotten by the rest of the world. My journey through Eastern Europe was necessary, but I knew in my heart it was not where I would stay. Africa was calling me home.

A Wild Mirror

So, my life continued—full, as it had always been, with the shifting rhythms of travel, the stories gathered across continents, and the seasonal cycles of work on Martha's Vineyard. Yet even amid that gentle routine, I felt something pulling me again. Africa was calling.

Ostrich farm. South Africa

I couldn't fully explain the draw. It wasn't one place or one promise—it was something more elemental. A quiet urgency, a longing I couldn't ignore. I'd been to the continent before, but now I was called back with greater intention. I wanted to feel the land more deeply, to see its soul not just through the eyes of history or struggle, but through its raw, living heartbeat.

Kruger National Park. South Africa

That's when I decided to take a safari through South Africa—a three-week journey by overland truck, starting in Cape Town and ending in Johannesburg, crossing the borders of Lesotho and Swaziland along the way. It was the kind of trip I had once only seen in documentaries or read about in books. But I wanted more than stories—I wanted to witness it myself. I wanted to stand in the vast silence of the bush and come face-to-face with the wild.

We traveled through dusty roads, winding mountains, and wide plains. And then, we entered Kruger National Park.

Kruger National Park. South Africa

The moment we crossed the gates, something shifted inside me. It was as though I had stepped into another world—one older, more primal, untouched by the noise of cities or the clockwork of modern life. Here, everything was governed by instinct, strength, and the rhythm of survival.

Kruger taught me a quiet truth about the vulnerability of life. There, everything lived with one eye open. The antelopes, impalas, wildebeests, and waterbucks moved with tension in their steps, mothers constantly scanning the horizon for predators as they shielded their young. The tall, elegant giraffes paused with every movement, their height an advantage but never a guarantee. Even the monkeys—clever, mischievous—knew when to run.

And then, there were the predators. Lions, cheetahs, leopards, hyenas. They, too, were mothers. They, too, were hungry. Their survival depended on the kill, just as their cubs depended on them. Watching a pride of lions stalk a herd or a cheetah explode into a sprint wasn't simply a spectacle of nature—it was a lesson. Every move had weight. Every decision carried the cost of life or death. There was no waste, no indulgence. Only necessity.

It shook me.

Because in their fight for survival, I saw something of myself.

Kruger National Park. South Africa

I thought of my own journey—arriving alone in the United States with no safety net, no familiar faces, no financial security. A stateless soul drifting through a system that did not recognize me. My struggle wasn't in the savannah, but it was a struggle all the same: for recognition, for stability, for safety. For the basic right to exist without fear.

Kruger National Park. South Africa

While the impalas ran from lions, I navigated a bureaucratic labyrinth, trying to prove my humanity to those who saw only paper and borders. While lionesses hunted to feed their young, I moved from city to city, job to job, trying to survive without a legal identity. My predators didn't have claws, but they held power over my movement, my future, my very presence. The weight of being unwanted, unprotected, invisible—it mirrored the tension I saw in those animals.

Yet, what struck me most wasn't just the danger. It was the care. The deep, fierce protectiveness that ran through the animal kingdom. Mothers are guarding their young with their lives. Herds work together to shield the weakest. Even predators—those so often portrayed as ruthless—moved with purpose. They didn't kill for cruelty. They killed to live.

It reminded me how precious life is. How fragile. One moment you are here, the next you are gone. In the wild, that truth is not hidden— it is the backdrop of every breath. And I began to understand: that same law governs us all, whether we live behind walls or beneath open skies.

In that awareness, something inside me softened. I began to see my own life not only as a battle, but as part of something greater. A shared instinct. A shared hunger—not just for food, but for belonging. Safety. Continuity. I, too, was trying to protect the little life I had built. I, too, wanted to feed the parts of me that had long been starved—dignity, peace, recognition.

And maybe that was what I had come to Africa for—not just the adventure, not just the landscapes—but to remember who I was. To reconnect with something older and deeper than identity papers or immigration status. To see in the eyes of a lioness or the stillness of a gazelle a reflection of myself.

South Africa

347

Zambia

That journey—through Kruger and beyond—stayed with me long after the dust settled. It reminded me that survival, in all its forms, is sacred. That invisibility is not the same as insignificance. And that, whether in the wild or in the world of men, the fight to exist is universal—and deeply human.

But Africa was never just about the landscapes or the wildlife. It was a feeling—a presence. Something that seeped into my bones, slow and certain, like heat settling in the earth at midday. It wasn't always beautiful in the conventional sense. It wasn't polished or easy or gentle. But it was honest. And for someone who had spent so much of life in-between—between homes, between statuses, between identities—that honesty meant everything.

Africa didn't ask me who I was on paper. It didn't demand a visa number or question my worth. It didn't care where I was born or why I had no country. It simply let me be. The same way it let the lion roam, the same way it let the rains fall—indiscriminately, unapologetically.

There was a kind of belonging in that.

Even as a visitor, even as a drifter passing through, I felt grounded. The air felt heavier but more real, as if every breath carried memory. Every step I took seemed to echo those who had walked this land before me—centuries of lives etched into the soil, long before borders carved up the map.

Father and son. Malawi

And still, there was something else. A sense of resilience. Of people carrying on in the face of so much—colonialism, apartheid, exploitation, abandonment, and yet still dancing, still creating, still resisting erasure. I saw it in the townships, in the markets, in the quiet pride of those who told their stories not with bitterness, but with truth.

There was music in the streets and laughter in the struggle. Not a naive joy, but something far deeper—a celebration of survival itself.

Cotonou. Benin

Not always gracefully. Not without pain. But I endured.

Africa became for me a mirror—not only of my past, but of my strength. It reminded me that survival is not just about getting by. It's about holding on to your essence when the world tries to strip it from you. It's about finding ways to laugh, to build, to love, even when nothing around you feels certain.

350

And perhaps most of all, it showed me that even in the wildest, harshest conditions, life insists. It insists on growing, on blooming, on being seen.

That insistence was something I carried with me when I left. Even when I returned to the cold indifference of immigration lines and seasonal jobs and cities that didn't know my name, I carried Africa in me, not as an escape, but as an anchor.

Because if the wild can survive, so can I.

Whispers from a Continent

It was late October 2018, just before we closed the coffee shop for the season on Martha's Vineyard. The winds had shifted, the island had begun to empty out, and I found myself once again at the edge of something new. Africa was calling me again—whispers of red earth, ancestral echoes, unknown faces and places I hadn't yet touched. I had been reading, researching, tracing routes on maps, and planning a new journey across the continent. Ethiopia. The Democratic Republic of Congo. Zimbabwe. Zambia. Togo. The list kept growing like a constellation of places I felt drawn to, even if I didn't fully understand why.

But alongside the excitement of the unknown, something else had begun to stir within me—a longing I hadn't allowed myself to fully feel for a long time. I wanted love. Not the fleeting connections I had brushed against during my travels. Not the transactional offers masked as romance. But something real. A genuine partner. A person who would see me not as an opportunity, not as a ticket out, not as a walking wallet, but as someone to love, to understand, to build something lasting with.

It had been years since my relationship with Michael in Texas. Years since I let anyone close enough to break through the walls I'd built out of necessity and survival. And I knew I wasn't easy to love—I carried history with me like a second skin. But I was ready. I didn't want to travel the rest of my life alone, even if solitude had become my default.

Tea plantation. Burundi

Africa offered connections in many forms. I met men along the way—some charming, some sweet, some curious. But too often, there was a shadow behind their smiles. A calculation. In many parts of the continent, homosexuality was taboo, whispered about behind closed doors, never acknowledged in public.

Even affection had to be hidden. And so the connections were often secretive, fleeting, or steeped in expectation. I quickly learned that being from the U.S.—even as someone who had arrived there stateless, undocumented, and broke—marked me in their eyes as "wealthy." As a gateway. As someone who could change their lives.

But I wasn't looking to rescue anyone. I wasn't looking to be used. And I couldn't pretend to be someone I wasn't—nor could I ignore how much that narrative hurt. I tried, wherever I went, to explain to people that being American didn't mean being rich. Most people who travel have saved for years, sacrificing comforts, working jobs they don't love, drowning in credit card debt or student loans or mortgages. That not all foreigners are walking banks, and that relationships built on money or escape never last.

I met some who understood. And others who didn't.

Lake Kivu. Rwanda

But it was the children who really got to me.

Everywhere I went, I saw children on the streets—some begging, some selling, some offering trinkets or fruit. Many of them were sent by their parents, not out of cruelty, but out of necessity. Still, it never sat right with me. A child's place is in school, in play, in laughter—not in the harsh business of survival. I knew that firsthand. And every time I saw a child thrust into labor, I saw a little piece of myself—those early years when I had to grow up fast, to fend for myself, to figure things out alone.

There was one boy I'll never forget. I think it was in Zambia or Zimbabwe—I can't remember exactly. He had a small tray of bananas balanced on his head and approached my table at a Mediterranean restaurant, hoping to sell me some. But instead of brushing him off or handing him a few coins, I stopped. I talked to him. I asked about his life.

Zanzibar. Tanzania

He didn't ask me for anything. He told me his truth plainly: that his mother was hustling, trying to feed their family, that he didn't go to school because he needed to help her earn money. That he didn't know what his future would be, but he wanted to be someone. Someone big. Someone important.

That moment cracked something open in me. He reminded me of a younger version of myself—dreaming of something beyond the present, even when the present felt like a cage. I bought him food and sat with him a while. I told him he mattered. That he had worth. That one day he would look back and see how far he had come. I don't know if he believed me. But I hope he felt, even for a moment, seen.

Traveling through Africa gave me many things: awe, frustration, revelation, and heartbreak. But perhaps most of all, it gave me mirrors. Reflections of myself in strangers. In their struggles, their resilience, their hope. And it reminded me that while survival is the first battle, dignity must follow. That we all deserve more than just to get by—we deserve to be loved, to be respected, to be valued.

And maybe, just maybe, to no longer be alone.

An Island Apart

Madagascar had long fascinated me—an island seemingly adrift from both the African continent and the rest of the world. When I finally decided to go, there was an outbreak of plague being reported in the news, and some of my coffee shop customers tried to talk me out of the trip. But I was determined. The flights hadn't been canceled. The country was still open. And something deeper was pulling me there.

Antananarivo. Madagascar

From the moment I landed in Antananarivo, I felt like I'd entered a world both haunting and beautiful. The capital was a chaotic sprawl of hills, colonial architecture, and crowded streets. French influences still lingered—in the crumbling balconies, in the occasional patisserie—but the soul of the city belonged to the Malagasy people.

Antananarivo. Madagascar

Driving from the airport into the city center, poverty confronted me immediately. It was everywhere. Even the lake in the heart of Antananarivo—originally gifted to the people by the French—had transformed into something between a swamp and a public washbasin. People were doing laundry there, bathing, even urinating. What once may have been a symbol of generosity now reflected the harshness of life for many residents.

And yet, Madagascar pulsed with a quiet resilience.

Lemurs leapt through the trees in protected sanctuaries. Chameleons changed color before my eyes. The people, though struggling, were resourceful, dignified, and endlessly curious about the foreigners who wandered through their country. I quickly learned that while Madagascar is geographically part of Africa, its people tell a more complex story. Most locals didn't look like the African populations I encountered in other countries. There was something distinctly Southeast Asian in their features—Malagasy ancestry tracing back to Indonesia and Malaysia. It was a reminder of migration, of the endless paths people have taken across oceans and centuries.

Madagascar

French was still spoken, but mostly by those who worked in hotels or had access to private education. Malagasy was the language of the street. English, rarely. Communication was a dance of hand gestures, smiles, and patience.

I came to Madagascar more than once. It became a quiet retreat, a place of reflection. I explored beyond Antananarivo—to the majestic Avenue of the Baobabs, where these towering trees stood like silent guardians of the land. I learned that baobabs store water in their thick trunks, allowing them to survive long dry seasons. Their fruit—slightly sour, slightly sweet—tasted of endurance.

Sainte-Marie island. Madagascar

On another trip, I went to Île Sainte-Marie (Sainte-Marie Island), a peaceful place nestled along the Indian Ocean. There, time slowed. Wooden bungalows stretched into turquoise waters, and the days drifted by with the tide. Some came here to relax. I came to think, to observe, to write in silence.

And in the most unexpected corners of the island, I encountered coffee—Zebu coffee, grown and roasted by hands who were trying to redefine Madagascar's place in the specialty coffee world. It was a thread tying me back to Martha's Vineyard, to the shop I'd helped close for the season, to the conversations over espresso and pour-overs that led me here in the first place.

But Madagascar wasn't just about beauty. It forced me to confront hard truths—about inequality, about post-colonial realities, about how children were being raised in hardship, sometimes taught to beg from foreigners.

Discovering Madagascar's Hidden Coffee Treasure

Madagascar is perhaps most famous for its vanilla, considered the best in the world, and its exceptional cacao beans. But did you know that it also has the perfect conditions for growing Arabica coffee? Few people in the specialty coffee world know about this hidden gem, and I was determined to uncover its secrets.

My journey into Madagascar coffee began unexpectedly. While searching for exotic, lesser-known coffees from regions off the beaten path, I stumbled upon Sea Island Coffee, a small roastery in the UK. They focused on coffees from rare and hard-to-access places like St. Helena and Madagascar. Their mission was to offer beans that reflected the unique combination of soil, climate, and elevation that makes great coffee. After reading about their offerings, I knew I had to visit Madagascar to see for myself.

By January 2018, I had secured my flight from Accra, Ghana, with Kenya Airways, excited to explore the island's potential beyond its spices and tropical crops. I had just visited coffee plantations in São Tomé and Príncipe, and Madagascar seemed like a natural next stop. If this island could produce world-class vanilla and cacao, surely its coffee had untapped potential.

Madagascar

I landed in Antananarivo on January 11, 2018, the capital of Madagascar. The island, sitting in the Indian Ocean off the southeast coast of Africa, is vast and diverse. The country is a tapestry of African, Asian, and European influences, reflected in its people, culture, and architecture. Yet, despite its beauty, Madagascar is one of the poorest nations, burdened by corruption and an unreliable government. It has incredible potential, though, if given the right support.

Haja and Njaka

The story behind Zebu Coffee intrigued me. Danny Skutelis, a Latvian living between London and Dubai, first visited Madagascar in 2013 for his honeymoon. He fell in love with the island and, recognizing its coffee-growing potential, returned six months later. Partnering with local entrepreneurs Haja Rasambainarivo and Njaka Ramandimbiarison, they founded Zebu Coffee to help develop the industry and create jobs for the local community.

The opportunity to meet the people behind this project was too good to pass up. On January 12, I was picked up at my hotel, La Pavillon de l'Emyrne, by Haja and Njaka. We began our journey to the coffee farm, leaving early to avoid Antananarivo's notorious traffic. The roads leading out of the city were lined with green rice fields, rolling hills, and small villages where people traveled long distances to sell their goods in the capital. With a national unemployment rate hovering around 2.4%, the country faced significant challenges. There was a palpable sense of struggle, but also resilience.

Stuck in the mud. Madagascar

After a three-hour journey, we encountered a minor setback when our car got stuck in the mud. Fortunately, the local villagers came to our aid, and we were soon back on our way. Finally, we arrived at Zebu Coffee's farm, a new project that was still growing and developing, just like the coffee industry in Madagascar itself.

I was eager to learn more about the vision behind Zebu Coffee. Haja shared his and Njaka's story—how they both left Madagascar for higher education abroad. Haja studied computer science in Madagascar and later earned a degree in e- business from HEC Montréal, Canada. He then worked as an IT engineer for a non-profit organization in Washington, DC. Njaka, on the other hand, studied administration and finance in Madagascar before pursuing an MBA in marketing at the University of Moncton in Canada. He worked in the skincare industry and later in IT in South Africa. Both Haja and Njaka had returned to Madagascar with a shared goal: to create jobs and contribute to their country's future through the specialty coffee industry.

It was inspiring to meet people who had not only followed their entrepreneurial dreams but were also deeply committed to making a difference in their community. Zebu Coffee, born in 2014, was already proving the potential of Madagascar's coffee farms. With the right blend of passion and vision, it was clear that this country could become a rising star in the coffee world.

Coffee tree. Zebu farm. Madagascar

Madagascar

As we toured the farm, I marveled at the lush, fertile land that stretched out before us. The combination of altitude, soil, and climate made it the perfect environment for growing Arabica beans. Madagascar's rich history, from its colonial past to its struggles with poverty, seemed to inform every corner of the island. And in that moment, I realized that Madagascar's coffee had a story to tell—one that needed to be shared with the world.

Every country I visited had its own challenges and triumphs, but Madagascar stood out as a place of potential, waiting for the right people to invest in its future. As I tasted the coffee that day, I felt a deep sense of excitement.

Madagascar's coffee might not yet be widely known, but it had everything it needed to join the ranks of the world's great coffee producers.

A Journey to Benin and Finding Love

In October 2018, as I prepared for my next journey through Africa, I had no clear idea where it might lead. My annual trips to Rwanda had become a tradition, and I felt drawn to its rich history, vibrant culture, and the beauty that seemed to surround every corner of the country. Rwanda had become a safe haven for me—politically stable, economically steady, and, most importantly, a place where I felt completely at ease. I could wander around the streets at any time of day or night without worrying about safety. It was a relief, especially after years of navigating the uncertain world of statelessness.

Lake Ganvie. Benin

Since my first trip to Rwanda in 2015, I had promised myself I would return every year. In 2019, I booked a full month's stay, excited to immerse myself in the country once again. But as the trip approached, a thought crossed my mind: perhaps I could explore a new destination while in Africa. Maybe four or five days in another country—one I'd never visited before.

At that time, I was still holding my refugee travel document and permanent resident card. Navigating the visa process was always a challenge. I was tired of sending my passport to various embassies, waiting for approval, and dealing with the costs of shipping and application fees. So, I began searching for African countries with electronic visa systems—places where I could apply online without the hassle of sending my passport away.

That's when I stumbled upon the Republic of Benin. I hadn't planned to visit Benin, but I was intrigued. I had initially intended to travel to Togo because one of our co-workers, Sam, who had worked with me at the coffee shop, was originally from there. Togo was a Western African country I'd never been to, and I thought it would make an interesting addition to my itinerary. What I didn't realize was that Benin bordered Togo. As I looked up visa information for Benin, I discovered that the country offered an e-visa system, which allowed me to apply online.

I was skeptical at first, but I decided to give it a try. To my surprise, within 20 minutes, my electronic visa was approved, and I learned that Benin accepted the United States refugee travel document. So, I booked a flight to Benin from Rwanda, planning to spend four days there before returning to Rwanda. At the same time, I found myself hoping that this trip would bring me something I had longed for: connection, companionship, and love.

Traveling in Africa had shown me how family-oriented and welcoming the people were. I had always felt a deep spiritual and emotional connection to Africa, and I wanted to find someone from the continent to share my life with—someone I could build a meaningful relationship with. I prayed fervently, asking God to guide me on my journey, to help me find the right person, someone kind, intelligent, and most importantly, someone from Africa, the land I felt so connected to.

My tour guides in Benin

As I made my way from Rwanda to Benin, I couldn't help but feel a sense of anticipation. I had booked a flight with Rwanda Air, not knowing exactly what would unfold in Benin. But during my stay, as I immersed myself in the culture and history of the Republic of Benin, something unexpected happened.

One evening, while staying at a hotel in Cotonou, I decided to reach out online to see if I could connect with someone in my community. That's when I met Quadri. He started asking me questions about my travels and what I was doing in Benin. We decided to meet in person before I left for Rwanda.

Quadri and Mikhail

When the day arrived for him to visit, I had no idea how it would feel, but as soon as I opened the door to meet him, my heart skipped a beat. His presence was electrifying. His smile, his charm, the way his eyes seemed to penetrate into me—it was as if everything fell into place. I knew instantly that this was the person I had been searching for.

The connection between us was undeniable. As we spent time together, I felt a whirlwind of emotions—my heart racing, my mind in a daze. I couldn't stop thinking to myself, this is the person I want to spend the rest of my life with.

When I first met Quadri, everything in my life seemed to fall into place in a way I hadn't expected. Up until that point, my travels had been driven by curiosity, a desire for new experiences, and a longing for connection, but nothing could have prepared me for the overwhelming pull I felt when I first laid eyes on him. I truly understood the meaning of fate. Quadri's presence was magnetic. His calm demeanor, warm smile, and those striking, soulful eyes made me feel like I had found something I didn't even know I was looking for.

He was a man of few words at first, but his energy spoke volumes. It wasn't just his appearance that captivated me; it was the way he carried himself with such grace and authenticity. I had met many people during my travels, but there was something about him that stood out—a quiet strength, a wisdom that seemed to transcend the usual small talk and pleasantries.

Quadri and Mikhail

As we spent time together during my last days in Benin, I found myself opening up in ways I hadn't done in a long time. We talked about everything—from our personal histories to our dreams for the future. Quadri shared his journey with me, and I learned that he had grown up in Nigeria but had spent some time in Benin, graduating from the University with Bachelor Degree in Diplomacy and International Relations, volunteered for NGO AIESEC, gaining a perspective that was both global and deeply rooted in his culture. He spoke with pride about his heritage, his family, and his connection to the land.

Portrait of Quadri

What struck me most was his deep respect for people. He listened with intent, and when he spoke, it was always thoughtful, always kind.

It was clear that he valued authenticity in relationships, something I had come to cherish in my own journey.

I found myself reflecting on what had brought me to this moment. As a traveler, I had spent years seeking a place to belong, to find my roots in a world that often felt too big and too complicated to navigate. But in Quadri, I felt a sense of belonging that I hadn't anticipated. He was someone who understood what it meant to connect—not just with someone's story, but with their soul.

We spent our time together in the hotel, getting to know each other, laughing, talking, and simply being in the moment. His presence felt like home. It was effortless, like we had known each other for much longer than just a few days. I couldn't help but wonder how it was possible that someone like him had crossed my path in such an unexpected way.

Cotonou, Benin

I realized how much I admired him, not just for his outward qualities, but for the person he was at his core. His intelligence, his compassion, his sense of humor—it all came together in a way that made him someone I could see myself building a future with. I didn't know where this journey with Quadri would lead, but in that moment, I knew one thing for sure: my life had already changed, and I was willing to take the leap to see where it would go.

I couldn't explain it then, but I knew that Quadri was the one. The person who would walk beside me, sharing in the joys and challenges that lay ahead.

And so, in the heart of Benin, amidst the beauty of the land and the depth of its history, I found more than just a connection—I found love.

That night, as he slept beside me, I couldn't help but look at his face and silently thank God. It was as if my prayers had been answered. I knew that I had found someone special, someone who had crossed my path in the most unexpected of places. Now, I just needed the courage to keep him in my life and build the future I had always dreamed of.

In that moment, everything felt right. My journey had brought me to a place of peace, of connection, and most importantly, to the love I had been yearning for. What started as a simple trip to explore the history and culture of Benin turned into a life-changing experience—one that I would carry with me forever.

Cotonou. Benin

Cotonou. Benin

Ouidah. Benin

Lake Ganvie. Benin

National dish of Benin

Cotonou. Benin

A Promise in Ouidah, A Dream in Kinshasa

Gate of No Return, Ouidah, Benin

The Republic of Benin was unlike any place I had ever been—fascinating, complex, and steeped in a history that continues to echo through its red-dusted streets and coastal winds. A small country on the western curve of Africa, nestled between Togo and Nigeria, Benin offered more than just landscapes and culture. It offered a confrontation with history, with colonialism, and with the ghosts of a past the world still struggles to acknowledge.

During my journey across Africa, I became increasingly aware of how vital it is to learn history not just from books or museums, but from the soil itself—from the places where pain was planted and has never truly been uprooted. In Benin, that place was Ouidah.

Ouidah is a quiet town by the coast, but its silence holds a thunderous weight. It was one of the principal ports in the transatlantic slave trade. Standing at the "Door of No Return," I could feel the anguish of countless lives lost to greed and empire. Families torn apart, entire communities shattered, people reduced to commodities and shipped across oceans to build the wealth of others. Much of that wealth fueled the grandeur of Europe and the Americas, built on stolen bodies and stolen land. Ghana, Benin, and so many others paid the price in blood and history.

Ouidah. Benin

Visiting Ouidah wasn't a tourist excursion. It was a reckoning. I felt a personal responsibility to witness the remnants of this horror, to feel its lingering presence, and to carry its story with me. It was heartbreaking—impossible to ignore or compartmentalize. As I stood before monuments and memorials, I found myself filled with sorrow and rage. European colonial powers didn't just steal lives; they stole futures, culture, resources, and then had the audacity to claim progress while Africa was left bleeding.

Ouidah. Benin

We must never forget. We must keep remembering, so that nothing like this ever happens again.

As my time in Benin came to an end, it wasn't just the memory of Ouidah that I carried with me—I also carried the beginning of something deeply personal and unexpected: love.

His name was Quadri. We met in Cotonou, and from the first conversation, there was something unspoken between us, something gentle and magnetic. Quadri had graduated from university and was volunteering with a nonprofit organization called AIESEC, which promotes youth leadership and diplomacy. He was thoughtful, intelligent, and full of vision—a quiet determination in his eyes.

Quadri and I in Nigeria

We spent our short time getting to know each other, and the bond between us deepened quickly, sincerely. As I prepared to leave Benin, I asked him if he might consider visiting me in Togo when I passed through in March. At first, he was hesitant. Understandably so. But eventually, he agreed. We exchanged contact details and made a promise to reunite. When he saw me off at the airport, our goodbye was tender but unfinished. In my heart, I hoped it was just the beginning. I was in love, and I knew I didn't want distance or borders to separate us.

As I flew out of Benin, my next destination was Kinshasa, in the Democratic Republic of the Congo—a place I had long dreamed of visiting.

Congo is not just a country; it's a vast and complex nation, roughly the size of Western Europe and rich in natural resources—diamonds, cobalt, rubber, and gold. But that wealth has long been both a blessing and a curse. Under Belgian colonial rule, Congo became a theatre of unspeakable atrocities. The regime of King Leopold II, driven by insatiable greed, subjected the Congolese people to horrific violence. Those who didn't meet rubber quotas often paid with their lives—or with the lives of their children. It was a reign of terror masked by the illusion of civilization.

Kinshasa. DRC

Kinshasa. DRC

Despite its turbulent history, I was drawn to Congo not only by its pain but also by its heroes. Chief among them was Patrice Lumumba.

Lumumba was a visionary—a man who believed that Congo could be united, prosperous, and free from foreign domination. He fought for independence and tried to steer the country toward self-determination. But his dream was short-lived. Caught in the crosshairs of Cold War politics, and betrayed by those who feared his growing influence, he was murdered in 1961, with the complicity of the Belgian government, and the silent endorsement of others, including the United States.

Standing in Kinshasa, I thought about the weight Lumumba must have carried. He was not just a politician—he was a martyr for the soul of Africa. Even after Congo gained formal independence, Belgium and other powers continued to manipulate its internal affairs, installing leaders like Mobutu Sese Seko who were more interested in pleasing their Western backers than uplifting their own people.

Kinshasa. DRC

Congo today is still marked by instability, poverty, and exploitation. But it also brims with potential—untapped, resilient, and waiting for a new chapter to be written. I left Kinshasa with a deepened admiration for Lumumba's legacy and a quiet hope that his vision might still be realized someday.

Kinshasa. DRC

And through it all, through the grief of Ouidah, through the memory of Lumumba—there was Quadri, threading his way through my thoughts. Our story wasn't over. We had made a promise in Benin, and I was determined to keep it. In my heart, I carried the hope that love could bloom even in the shadow of history—and that perhaps, together, we could build something that transcended the borders that had tried so hard to keep people apart.

Reunited in Lomé

Lome. Togo

After visiting the Democratic Republic of the Congo and Ethiopia, March finally arrived—the month I had been quietly waiting for with a mix of nerves and hope. I was headed to Lomé, the capital of the West African nation of Togo, and more than the country itself, I was going for someone: Quadri. The man I had met in Benin. The one who had surprised me by entering my life so unexpectedly and yet so perfectly. The one I had fallen in love with.

Before my departure, we spoke on the phone, and he promised he would meet me there. I was giddy with anticipation—not just to see him again, but to spend uninterrupted time together, to explore whether what we shared was real and lasting. I had booked a comfortable accommodation in Lomé with a swimming pool—somewhere peaceful, where we could be ourselves, away from curious eyes. I asked Quadri if he could arrive early, so he could settle in and make the place feel like home before I got there. He said yes.

Lome. Togo

When my plane touched down in Lomé and I stepped out of the airport, the hot, humid air wrapped around me like a blanket. But I barely noticed the weather.

There, sitting calmly outside the terminal, was Quadri.

He wore a traditional Nigerian outfit—beautifully handcrafted, regal in its elegance. The colors were vibrant, mostly turquoise with hints of gold and maybe red or yellow. The outfit was completed by a matching hat that resembled a turban, sitting proudly atop his head. He looked radiant. Dignified. And mine.

I wanted to run to him, to throw my arms around him and kiss him right there, but I held back. This was West Africa, where public displays of affection between same-sex partners were taboo, sometimes dangerous. I forced myself to restrain the excitement bubbling in my chest. Still, I couldn't stop smiling as I walked up to him and wrapped him in a long, tight hug. His scent, the texture of his fabric, the warmth of his body—I had missed it all.

Lome. Togo

We made our way to the guesthouse. For five days, we shared that space—swimming, walking the streets of Lomé, talking about everything and nothing. Quadri had been to Togo before, but it was all new to me. Every corner held curiosity. We visited bustling markets, tasted local dishes, and strolled through dusty streets with French colonial echoes still lingering in the architecture. One afternoon, I invited him to join a guided tour I had organized, and we explored different neighborhoods together, discovering small alleyways, local artisan stalls, and coastline views where the Atlantic seemed to stretch forever.

At night, we lie beside each other, talking about our families, our fears, our dreams. That was when Quadri opened up.

He admitted something I hadn't expected. In Benin, when we first met, he hadn't believed that my feelings were real. He assumed it was just a fleeting attraction, maybe the result of a one-night encounter like many others he had heard about. In fact, he told me something deeply unsettling—that there was a rumor, a belief passed around among some gay men in Benin, that American men came to Africa, seduced African men, and brought them to the United States only to control them, sometimes even hold them captive as sex slaves.

I was stunned.

I had never heard of anything like that, let alone imagined it. It horrified me that this was what he feared—that I, someone who had felt nothing but sincerity toward him, might be seen through that lens. I reassured him gently but firmly. I told him that my love for him was real. That it wasn't about sex or power or control. It wasn't a transaction. It wasn't a fantasy. It was love.

And slowly, he believed me.

He saw that I wasn't bluffing. That I wasn't one of the men he'd heard about. He realized that what I wanted was a true relationship, a partnership built on mutual respect, affection, and honesty. I told him I was thankful to God every day for bringing me to Benin. I had never even planned to visit—it wasn't originally on my itinerary. But something had pulled me there. A whisper from the universe, maybe. And if I hadn't gone, I never would have met Quadri. It felt fated.

Togo

We spent those days in Lomé opening up to each other, learning about one another's pasts. I told him about my own difficult journey—coming to the United States when I was twenty-two, facing immigration chaos, statelessness, and endless bureaucracy. I laid bare my traumas and uncertainties.

And Quadri opened up, too.

He told me about his childhood in Nigeria. His father had once been a known actor in Nollywood, but he was absent—more interested in chasing women than raising a child. Quadri's mother had been very young when she got pregnant, and she, too, hadn't been ready. So his grandmother raised him. She was his world—his protector and his moral compass. When she passed away, it left a wound he still carried quietly. His bond with her had shaped who he was: thoughtful, gentle, responsible.

Listening to him, I saw his soul more clearly than ever. He wasn't just a man I had fallen in love with. He was a survivor. A dreamer. A kind, introspective soul who deserved every bit of love and safety the world could offer.

When I finally left Lomé, it felt like leaving home. But this time, the goodbye was different. It wasn't an ending. It was a promise—to stay in touch, to meet again, to keep building what we had started.

Love, I had learned, sometimes finds you when you're lost. It doesn't always arrive with fireworks or fanfare. Sometimes it comes quietly, dressed in turquoise, waiting outside an airport in a place you never expected to be. And when it does, you hold on tight—even if the world tells you not to.

Across the River, Tethered to Fear

One incident in the Democratic Republic of the Congo unsettled me more deeply than I anticipated. I had planned two excursions in Kinshasa—first, a visit to a bonobo sanctuary to witness these extraordinary primates in their protected habitat, and then a scenic boat ride along the Congo River. I was fascinated by the geographical and symbolic nature of this river—a fluid line dividing two nations with nearly identical names. Kinshasa, where I stood, belonged to the DRC; directly across the water lay Brazzaville, the capital of the Republic of Congo. Two countries, two histories, one powerful river separating them like a mirrored rift.

Congo River

I imagined a peaceful, tourist-friendly boat ride. But when I arrived at the embarkation point, my heart sank. Instead of a proper tour boat, I was met with a small, rickety fishing vessel—barely stable, visibly worn, and clearly unfit for a comfortable cruise. I hesitated. The boat bobbed like a cradle caught in a storm, and the idea of tumbling into the Congo River haunted me.

The guide, however, was persistent. He dragged a plastic chair onto the deck as if that would somehow provide the balance and safety I craved. Against my better judgment, I climbed aboard. Every step I took made the boat tremble. I gripped the edges like lifelines and quietly prayed for the tour to end before it even began.

The guide paddled us past riverside villages. I watched people going about their day—fishing, washing clothes, and unloading goods. I filmed snippets with my phone, marveling at the resilience and rhythm of daily life along the river. At one point, the guide took us farther out, edging closer to Brazzaville. That's when I heard the sirens.

A police boat approached fast, cutting across the water like a blade. Officers shouted in a local dialect, then in French. One climbed aboard, his face stern and unyielding. A heated exchange erupted between him and my guide. I couldn't understand much, but it was clear something was wrong. When I asked what was happening, the officer turned to me and demanded to know why I was filming and why I was approaching Brazzaville.

I was stunned. I hadn't realized we'd come so close to the border. I tried to explain I was just a tourist on a river tour, taking harmless videos with my phone, not a professional camera, no documentary crew, just a solo traveler fascinated by the river.

But the officer didn't want explanations. He demanded to see my footage. I showed him my phone, flipping through photos and short clips—fishermen casting nets, women laughing as they washed clothes, sunlit ripples on the water. Nothing provocative. Nothing secret. But still, the suspicion lingered.

Village by Congo river

Then the guide handed him a wad of cash—about $30. A bribe, no doubt. Yet even after pocketing the money, the officer ordered us back to shore. Our boat was tied up, and I was escorted to a dim, cramped room barely large enough to fit three people. No windows. No electricity. Just shadows and questions.

Congo River

They began interrogating me—asking where I was from, what I was filming, and what I planned to do with the footage. I asked for a translator before signing anything. Eventually, someone arrived to interpret the French report they'd written on my behalf. I refused to sign until I understood every word.

Things escalated when they tried to confiscate my phone. I stood my ground.

"This is mine," I said. "You can't just take it from me."

I showed them again what I had filmed and tried to make them see: I wasn't portraying the Congo as a place of war or fear. Quite the opposite.

"People outside the Congo," I told the officer, "know nothing of your country beyond war, rebels, and violence. What I'm trying to show is beauty, life, simplicity, and humanity. But after this experience, how can I tell others the DRC is safe?"

Eventually, they let me go. But the tension still clung to my skin like sweat.

THE WHITE HOUSE
WASHINGTON

Dear Fellow American:

On behalf of the people of the United States, congratulations on becoming a citizen of this magnificent land. No matter where you come from, or what faith you practice, you are now an American citizen, and you share the sacred rights, responsibilities, and duties that unite us as one people.

Our Nation has always welcomed newcomers who embrace our values, assimilate into our society, and pledge allegiance to our country. In turn, America embraces you and ushers you into a fraternity defined by mutual kinship and affection. Our patriotism is the bond that holds us all tightly together.

Although you and your fellow naturalized citizens hail from many places and come from many backgrounds, as Americans, you all now bear the torch of American history—inheriting a legacy of common heroes, values, and traditions that stretches back through the centuries. This American legacy is now your legacy. This history is now your history. Our traditions are now your traditions. You now share the duty to pass the legacy of liberty, history, and tradition to the next generation of Americans.

The United States is now your homeland, and all Americans are now your brothers and sisters. You have pledged your heart to America. And when you give your love and loyalty to America, she returns her love and loyalty to you.

We celebrate this special day. We welcome you into our national family. We applaud your devotion to America. And we embrace the wonderful future we will have together.

Congratulations and welcome. May God bless you and may God continue to bless America.

Sincerely,

The next day, as I boarded my flight out of Kinshasa, I thought the ordeal was behind me. But then the plane sat on the tarmac for thirty long minutes. Engines off. Doors closed. No explanation. My heart pounded with anxiety. I imagined being pulled off the plane, detained again, or worse. I kept glancing out the window, praying.

When a flight attendant finally told us there was just a minor technical issue, and we'd be departing soon, I nodded, but I didn't breathe freely until the wheels lifted off and the ground shrank below us.

Looking out the window at the vanishing skyline of Kinshasa, I whispered, "Thank you, God."

I loved the Congo's soul—the music, the people, the energy—but its systems had left me feeling vulnerable. I came seeking stories of beauty, and I found them—but I also brushed the sharp edge of fear, something that would stay with me long after the river disappeared from view.

The Day I Belonged

So the year 2020 came, and with it, something I had waited for nearly my entire life in America—the chance to apply for U.S. citizenship. After twenty-five years in the United States, since first arriving in 1995, the moment had finally come.

I had grown up on this land. I had worked hard, lived independently, and survived through sheer will. I had built a life out of fragments, out of uncertainty, out of resilience. I paid taxes. I followed the law. I avoided trouble. I contributed. I did everything I was supposed to do. But for all those years, I still lived in the shadows—unseen, unrecognized, unnamed. I had no country. I was stateless.

But now, I was finally at the threshold. The possibility of calling myself an American—not just in spirit, but in law—was within reach. It meant the world to me, not just for the paper or the passport, but for what it symbolized: protection, dignity, belonging. If something happened to me somewhere in the world, I would now have someone to call. I would no longer be alone.

I gathered every document I needed, carefully assembled the pieces of my life into the paperwork that would finally define me. I filed the application. And then I waited.

When the day of the citizenship interview came, it was August. I remember sitting in the waiting room of the immigration office, nervous but focused. I watched as immigration officers called out names. My mind began to pray—not for an easy test, not even for immediate success—but for the person who would interview me. I prayed it would be someone who understood hardship. I hoped for someone either African American or Latino, not out of bias, but because I had witnessed time and again that officers from these communities often carried a deeper sense of empathy. They understood the weight of displacement. They treated you like a person.

White immigration officers, in my experience, especially from the time I spent reporting to ICE in Houston, or fingerprinting for my refugee travel documents, often seemed colder, harsher. There was an edge of superiority in their tone, a way of making you feel small. I wasn't imagining it. I had lived it.

And then my name was called. My prayer was answered: the officer who would interview me was African American. I smiled inside.

The interview went smoothly. I was asked questions about U.S. history and government: What is the longest river in the United States? Who was the president who abolished slavery? What is the highest court in the country? I had studied all 100 possible questions beforehand. You're only asked 10, but you need to get at least six correct. I got them all right.

Then came the English language test—written and verbal. I passed that too.

When it was over, I asked the officer, "Did I pass?"

He looked at me with calm professionalism and said, "You'll receive a notification by mail."

I looked at him again and said, "I've been waiting for this moment for so many years. You have no idea what I've gone through just to get to this room, to take this test. Please. I just need to know."

He paused and then said, "Yes. You passed."

I was elated. I left the building with tears in my eyes, joy bursting from my chest.

A few weeks later, I received the notice: I was to return to Boston for the oath ceremony. The date was set—October 2020.

It was snowing that morning as I made my way to the ceremony. I arrived, holding the little American flag they handed me. I surrendered my permanent resident card and stood with others from all over the world. We raised our right hands and took the oath of allegiance to the United States. We pledged to support and defend the Constitution. We became Americans.

And just like that, after decades of uncertainty, I was handed my certificate of naturalization. I was, officially, a citizen of the United States of America.

I wept. I thanked God. I thought of everything that had led to this moment—fleeing Azerbaijan, surviving Turkmenistan where I suffered for my sexuality, the long and uncertain life in the U.S., my time in detention, the looming threat of deportation, the agonizing years on an order of supervision, and even the surreal exile in American Samoa. I thought of all the people who had helped me—advocates, friends, strangers, the Congressman from American Samoa, the United Nations High Commissioner for Refugees, my immigration lawyer, David Baluarte. I thought of the pain, the loneliness, the hope, the prayers.

And now, here I was. Standing in the snow. Holding my certificate. Crying tears of joy. No longer invisible. No longer a shadow.

I belonged.

One Passport, One Planet

The moment I held my United States passport in my hands, it felt surreal. After years of waiting, of wandering, of existing without a nation to claim me, I was finally recognized. I was no longer stateless. I was a citizen. A real passport—my first true passport. Not a refugee travel document. Not a strange, misunderstood World Passport that invited suspicion at borders and rejection from immigration officers. No. This time, it was a passport that carried weight. One that meant protection, belonging, recognition. It was the passport of the United States of America.

I was ecstatic. I felt proud. I felt safe.

But somewhere deep in my heart, I still carried a quiet, enduring hope—Gary Davis' dream. His belief is that one day we could all be citizens of the world. Those borders wouldn't divide us. That we could all hold one passport, not as citizens of separate, unequal nations, but as fellow human beings on one shared planet.

Because Earth did not create borders—we did. This planet belongs to all of us. The rivers, the skies, the deserts, the forests—they never asked for lines to be drawn through them. They belong to humanity, not to bureaucracy. And I believe deeply that we, as people, must learn to see one another through that lens. Not by color, not by creed, not by language or sexuality, but as members of a single human family.

I had left statelessness behind—but I hadn't forgotten it.

Because statelessness, in truth, is a crime against humanity. No one should be born into limbo. No one should grow up unrecognized, invisible, unprotected. I wouldn't wish my experience on anyone. The feeling of being refused, of being unwanted, of having no legal identity—it's deeply dehumanizing. It strips you of dignity.

Every person on this earth deserves to belong. Every person deserves a nationality.

Governments—elected by the people—must understand this. It is not just a political issue; it is a moral one. No one should be deprived of citizenship because of who they are. Because they were born into a minority group.

Because they love differently. Because they speak a different language, or practice a different religion, or come from a family on the margins. These are not crimes. They are simply part of what makes us human.

I didn't choose how I was born. None of us does. But I am proud of who I am. I am proud of every part of me—my past, my pain, my resilience. I am proud of the scars, the survival, the silence I broke. I'm proud of the strength it took to stand tall through every detention, every rejection, every moment of fear and exile.

I'm thankful to God for protecting me, guiding me, and never letting me go. Surrounding me with angels, visible and invisible, human and divine. For showing me the way when there was no road in sight.

And I have no regrets. Not for the past. Not for the system that failed me. Not for the heartbreak or the years lost. Because I made it through. I stood my ground. I survived.

But statelessness must end.

It must be abolished globally. Every country should commit to fighting this silent injustice. Citizenship laws must evolve. Immigration systems must recognize the human cost of leaving people in limbo. And nations must create pathways for those who, through no fault of their own, find themselves without a place to belong.

We have a responsibility to ensure that no child, no person, ever again has to wonder where they belong, or whether they matter.

Because every human being deserves that one word:

Home.

A Love Letter in Transit

Just before the world was thrown into chaos by the pandemic, I had returned to the United States, preparing to resume my seasonal job at Behind the Bookstore Café on Martha's Vineyard. But my heart was still very much elsewhere—in West Africa, with my charming, kind, and inspiring boyfriend, Quadri, who remained in Benin.

Tallinn. Estonia

At the time, Quadri was volunteering with AIESEC Benin, an NGO that connects young people to leadership opportunities and international work placements. Each year, AIESEC opens positions around the world, allowing volunteers to apply for one-year assignments in different countries. That year, there were openings in Estonia, Seychelles, and a few other locations. I hoped Quadri would consider staying in Benin or applying to Seychelles—both options would have made it easier for me to visit him during my usual winter travels to Africa.

But Quadri had a different dream: Europe.

He had never been to Europe, and the idea of Estonia—quiet, northern, and far from familiar landscapes—appealed to his sense of adventure. He prepared his application with care, submitting a demo video, a written statement of interest, and interviews highlighting his goals, experience, and commitment. The process was long and competitive, but he made it through. Quadri was selected to represent AIESEC in Estonia.

That's when the real challenge began.

Tallinn. Estonia

To take up the position, he needed a visa for Estonia. But Estonia didn't have an embassy in Benin. The usual procedure for Beninese applicants was to apply through the Estonian embassy in Cairo, Egypt. But to get to Cairo, Quadri, who holds a Nigerian passport, needed an Egyptian visa first. That process dragged on endlessly. I contacted the

Egyptian embassy in Benin myself, trying to understand the holdup. They told me they were waiting on approval from Cairo, which made little sense considering Quadri only needed transit access, not long-term residency.

Meanwhile, AIESEC Estonia began pressuring him. If he didn't secure a visa soon, they would have to offer the position to another candidate.

That's when I encouraged Quadri to take another route—one that bypassed Egypt altogether. Estonia was represented by the French Embassy in Benin, and we hoped it might be possible to obtain a short-term Schengen tourist visa through France, and then regularize his status in Estonia after arrival. He submitted his documents to the French embassy, and to our immense relief, the visa was granted within three days.

He packed his bags immediately. That same day, he boarded a flight from Cotonou to Tallinn, transiting through Istanbul. Just like that, my boyfriend was on his way to a year-long assignment in a country neither of us had ever seen.

Estonia—so far north, so cold, so different from the heat and pulse of West Africa.

And I realized, my plans had to change, too.

I had never imagined myself traveling to the Baltic, especially not in the winter. Even during the Soviet era, when I lived in that part of the world, I'd never ventured to the Baltic states. Estonia wasn't part of my travel dreams—it was cold, snow-covered, and the opposite of the African warmth I usually sought out during my winter breaks.

But love changes plans.

So, I began mapping my route: I would spend one full month in Tallinn with Quadri. From there, I would continue to Rwanda and Madagascar—my traditional winter African destinations—and then return to Estonia in March to celebrate Quadri's birthday. After that, I would head to Cape Verde, a place I had long wanted to explore.

Tallinn. Estonia

There was one problem: at the time, I was still a U.S. permanent resident and traveled on a refugee travel document. Estonia, like many Schengen countries, did not grant visa-free access to travelers with such documents. I needed a Schengen visa.

So, I made a stop in New Bedford, Massachusetts, and applied through the Portuguese consulate. Portugal approved my visa, and my route was set. First Lisbon, then Brussels, with a quick side trip to Luxembourg, and finally onward to Tallinn.

And just like that, a love story born in Benin was pulling me into the frostbitten charm of the Baltic winter. It wasn't the plan I imagined— but it was the one my heart chose.

Between Forteresses and Snowfall

After a brief stop in Lisbon and a few days in Brussels, I boarded an Air Baltic flight bound for Tallinn. I wasn't headed there because Estonia had never been on my travel bucket list. I was going because my heart was there. My boyfriend, Quadri, had recently moved to Estonia for a one-year assignment with AIESEC, and it had been eight long months since we last saw each other. I could hardly contain my excitement—I was about to hold him again, feel him beside me, and share the same space after all the distance, all the waiting. My joy bubbled over. As the plane ascended, I felt like I was flying toward warmth, even if I was headed into Baltic winter.

Narva. Estonia

Tallinn greeted me with a slate-grey sky. It was cold and intermittently snowing or raining, the kind of weather that makes you question all your choices—except this one. I had rented a small apartment in the city, and Quadri moved in with me for the month. He still had to report to the AIESEC office each morning, so I spent my days wandering the cobblestone streets of Old Town Tallinn, trying to make sense of the place that once stood as the "Western Europe" of the Soviet Union.

During Soviet times, the Baltic states—Estonia, Latvia, and Lithuania—were seen as the most European, the most modern, the closest to something beyond the Iron Curtain. Walking through Tallinn, I began to understand why. The architecture was steeped in medieval charm, and the culture felt subtly distinct from the rest of the post-Soviet world I'd known. Estonia looked east and west at once, but it didn't feel like it belonged entirely to either.

Narva. Estonia

One weekend, I suggested we take a day trip to Narva, a border city that fascinated me. I had read about the twin fortresses—one on the Estonian side, the other directly across the river in Russia—connected by a bridge that spanned both time and territory. The symbolism was too compelling to resist. We took a train to Narva, not realizing that we were about to walk into another unexpected chapter of our journey.

The town felt immediately different from Tallinn. Most of the people we encountered spoke Russian, and nearly every sign and storefront bore Cyrillic script. Narva was in Estonia geographically, but culturally it felt like Russia. As we neared the bridge that separated the two countries, we were stopped by Estonian police. They asked for our documents.

I was caught off guard. We weren't crossing the border—we were just sightseeing—but the officers insisted that anyone entering Narva needed to carry valid identification due to its proximity to the Russian frontier. Our passports were back in Tallinn. I tried to explain, calmly, in English. Another officer arrived, then a third. To my dismay, a Russian border official joined the group. The presence of the Russian officer made everything feel heavier, more official, more dangerous.

I didn't want to switch to Russian, despite being fluent. Something in me resisted returning to that language in a moment of vulnerability. But Quadri, visibly anxious and unfamiliar with the language, pleaded with me to speak Russian—anything to help them understand we weren't a threat, that we were just visitors caught in a misunderstanding.

Quadri in Narva. Estonia

I relented and began speaking Russian. I explained that I was visiting from the United States, and Quadri had legal residency in Estonia through his AIESEC assignment. We hadn't known about the document requirement, and we certainly had no intention of crossing into Russia. After an hour of questioning, phone calls, and visible tension, they finally let us go, with a warning. If we returned to Narva, we'd need to carry our passports.

We nodded politely. But as we walked away, I turned to Quadri and said, "There won't be a next time." He agreed, still shaken. I could see he just wanted to get back to the train and return to the safety of Tallinn.

Still, we had five hours until our return train. I urged him to stay, to make the most of the day we had. Slowly, he softened. We visited the fortress and walked along the riverside, marveling at the eerie symmetry of the two ancient stone castles facing one another across a thin strip of water.

Narva. Estonia

411

It was also the kind of place where we stood out, especially Quadri. In that predominantly Russian-speaking town, he was the only Black person we saw all day. Wherever we went—cafés, corner shops, restaurants—people greeted us with curiosity. Locals addressed him in Russian, not realizing he didn't understand, and I became his translator. At one point, a shirtless man emerged from a hole in the icy river— doing a traditional cold-water plunge—and approached us. He was so struck by Quadri's presence that he asked for a photo with him. We obliged, partly out of politeness, partly out of fascination with the strangeness of the moment.

After our five hours in Narva, we returned to Tallinn, both relieved and a little wiser.

In the days that followed, Quadri went back to his routine at the office, and I kept exploring Estonia. I made a solo trip to Tartu, Estonia's renowned university town, once celebrated in Soviet times as a hub for higher education. It was quaint and charming in its own way, though not quite what I had expected. Still, I appreciated seeing a different side of the country.

Estonia had never been on my list. And yet, life had brought me there through love. Even the snow and border patrols couldn't change that.

Now it was time to continue my journey—from Tallinn to Rwanda, Madagascar, and eventually back to Estonia in March for Quadri's birthday. Then onward to Cape Verde. But that's another chapter.

Grounded in Cape Verde

Cabo Verde

Just like that, the months flew by.

I returned to Rwanda in January 2020, my heart still restless, always moving, always seeking. Rwanda had become a familiar place—its gentle hills, its measured pace, the quiet comfort it offered me. But soon, I was on the move again, this time to Madagascar, another destination I had put in my travel plan. It was wild, lush, unfiltered. I wandered through rainforests and coastal towns, letting the rhythm of the island wash over me.

At the end of February, I boarded an Ethiopian Airlines flight that would take me from Madagascar to Addis Ababa, then onward to Paris, and finally back to Tallinn to surprise Quadri for his birthday. I was aware of murmurs in the news—something about a virus spreading— but I hadn't paid much attention. It felt distant, abstract, like something that belonged to a different part of the world.

On the flight from Addis Ababa to Paris, I began to notice things that didn't add up. All the flight attendants wore face masks. Every single one of them. Yet none of the passengers—except for a small group of Asian tourists—were wearing masks. I remember thinking it was odd. Maybe someone was sick.

Maybe it was just a precaution. The idea of a looming global pandemic hadn't yet crossed my mind. Not really.

I landed in Paris with a seven-hour layover and met up with a friend. We walked along the Seine, admired the Eiffel Tower and the Arc de Triomphe. Paris was magnificent, even in the brief hours I had. As a child, I used to dream of living in France. But this wasn't the time for nostalgia. The clock was ticking. I promised myself I'd return one day— really return, not just pass through.

From Paris, I flew to Tallinn, just in time to celebrate Quadri's birthday. We rented an Airbnb, cozy and quiet. On March 8th, we went to the top of the Tallinn TV Tower for dinner. It was packed with couples, most of them celebrating International Women's Day. We were probably the only ones there for a birthday. I remember looking around, realizing how special it felt to be sharing that space with him— two men, in a high-rise restaurant, surrounded by candlelit tables and cishet traditions.

Cabo Verde

After a few days together, I left for Cape Verde. I had mapped out a meticulous route: from Tallinn to Brussels, then on Royal Air Maroc to Casablanca, and finally to Praia, the capital. It was just a short stop, four or five days. After Cape Verde, I planned to visit Tunisia, then return to Estonia, and from there, Quadri and I were going to explore Finland, Austria, and a few other countries before I returned to the U.S.

When the Sky Closed

Cape Verde was everything I imagined—sunlit coasts, volcanic terrain, the smell of salt and smoke in the air. I visited Fogo Island and São Vicente, spending days drifting between landscapes. But while I was in Praia, the world shifted.

Cabo Verde

The first sign came in the form of a text message from Royal Air Maroc. My return flight had been canceled, just like that. I called them, and they told me it had been rescheduled for the next day. A minor inconvenience, I thought. I'd gain an extra day in paradise.

Then Quadri called.

His voice trembled slightly. "This thing is getting out of control," he said.

"What thing?"

"Haven't you seen the news?"

I hadn't. I'd been too absorbed in my travels to pay attention. When I finally checked, the headlines hit like a tidal wave: COVID-19 cases surging, international borders closing, airports shutting down. Lockdowns were being announced across Europe. People were panicking. Flights were grounded. The world was grinding to a halt.

Another message came through. My newly rescheduled flight was canceled again. I called Royal Air Maroc, desperate for clarity, only to be told that Cape Verde had closed its airspace. All flights were suspended indefinitely.

I was stranded.

Fogo island. Cabo Verde

Panic began to set in. I scrambled to find alternatives. Air Portugal was still operating—or so I thought. I bought a ticket for the next available flight. Within two hours, I received another message: canceled. My refund was processed, but no options remained. Every route out was closing.

I tried contacting the U.S. Embassy. It was closed to the public. Phone lines were jammed. No one had answers. The Airbnb I was staying in had emptied out—most of the tourists had fled in time. I was the last one left. The woman managing the property told me I had to leave. She was renting the entire building from someone else and couldn't afford to keep the place empty any longer. She needed to shut it all down.

I had nowhere to go.

Cape Verde had become the latest in a string of islands I hadn't meant to be stuck on. I contacted my local tour guide in a moment of desperation. I explained everything—how I was stranded, how my flights were canceled, how I had nowhere to stay.

He came through. He introduced me to a man from Portugal who lived in Praia and owned several apartments. With tourism ground to a halt, the units were empty. The man agreed to rent me a one-bedroom apartment at a reduced rate. It wasn't luxurious, but it was safe. It gave me time to figure out what would come next.

Each day, I checked the news, waited for updates, and scrolled through rumors of repatriation flights and rescue missions. But nothing was certain. My entire itinerary was wrecked. Tunisia was no longer possible. Estonia seemed impossibly far. And the United States—well, even that felt like a distant dream.

I had been everywhere. But now I was stuck, grounded by an invisible force that no visa, no passport, no amount of planning could overcome.

And so, in Cape Verde, as the world shut down, I waited—paranoid, restless, unsure of what came next.

The Island of Empty Streets

Cabo Verde

I arrived in Cape Verde expecting to stay only four or five days. It was meant to be a short pause, a quick detour in my journey. But the world was beginning to unravel. COVID-19 cases were exploding, fear and confusion spreading faster than the virus itself. Borders were closing. Countries were locking down. And just like that, Cape Verde became a place I couldn't leave.

As the situation worsened, the government declared a full lockdown. Cape Verdeans, deeply religious and community-oriented, were urged to stay inside. But the message wasn't just a government advisory—it was broadcast like a sermon. Trucks rolled through neighborhoods with massive speakers mounted on the back, blaring messages about the dangers of the virus, the death toll rising around the world, and the urgent need to stay home. It was haunting, like a scene from a dystopian film. The streets emptied, shops shuttered, and the island transformed into a ghost town overnight.

Cabo Verde

But as a foreigner, I noticed something strange. While locals were strictly policed—ordered to remain indoors unless shopping for essentials—foreigners like me were mostly left alone. I could walk to the beach, even without a mask, and nobody stopped me. It was as if the police had quietly decided that the rules applied only to their own. A strange, silent privilege in a place I had no roots in.

My apartment was large enough to be bearable. I had a TV, some news, some movies. There was a tiny grocery store on the corner, one of the only places still open, and I walked there occasionally, just to feel the air on my skin. Taxis still ran now and then, so I would take one to the city center to wander through silent, lifeless streets. Once-bustling cafés and markets stood dark and abandoned. It was eerie—like walking through the memory of a place rather than the place itself.

Life on the island, though uncertain, began to fall into a strange rhythm. My days were filled with quiet rituals—little things that helped me preserve some sense of normalcy while the world unraveled outside. I started every morning by checking the news, watching the numbers rise, borders close, and restrictions tighten. Sometimes, I made silly videos—goofy attempts to laugh at the absurdity of it all. Humor became a small act of rebellion against isolation.

Cooking became my grounding ritual. I'd walk to the corner store, carefully choosing ingredients, then return to the apartment and prepare my meals—breakfast, lunch, dinner—every bite infused with patience and purpose. It wasn't just about food; it was about creating order in chaos. I kept the apartment spotless, just as my mother had taught me growing up. Whether it was a hotel room or a long-term rental, I always made sure the space around me reflected care and respect. I didn't want to be seen—or feel—as someone careless or messy. Cleanliness, for me, was a way of maintaining dignity in uncertain times.

Friends I had made in Cape Verde began visiting me more often. We'd sit together, watch movies, talk about life, about what this pandemic might mean for the world. We shared food, stories, silence. In many ways, those moments made the days bearable. Cape Verde wasn't just a place I got stuck—it became a place where I connected, listened, and learned.

Cabo Verde

And yet, beneath all the calm routines and temporary friendships, there was an ache I couldn't soothe.

I missed my boyfriend.

Estonia had sealed its borders, and I knew there was no chance I'd be allowed back to reunite with him. I had to return to the U.S. instead. All the travel plans we'd made together were canceled—one by one, email after email confirming the obvious. Refunds were issued, but they didn't matter. What I wanted couldn't be refunded. What I needed was presence—his presence.

So, I stayed in Cape Verde and waited. I tried to stay strong, to enjoy the slow life and the warm sun. But in the back of my mind, I was always calculating:

How long will this lockdown last? When will airports reopen? When will we be together again?

There were no answers. Just time. Waiting. And the quiet hope that soon, somehow, I'd be holding the person I loved again.

As the lockdown intensified, tourists—mostly Europeans—grew anxious. Many had been stranded just like me. The European Union swiftly organized repatriation flights for their citizens. Germany, France, Switzerland, the Netherlands—they all sent planes and offered one-way tickets back home for about 400 euros. I watched them leave one by one.

I wasn't so lucky.

The United States had no clear plan for its citizens, let alone green cardholders like me. When I contacted the U.S. Embassy, I was told that repatriation flights, when they came, would be reserved for citizens first. Permanent residents would be considered only if there were empty seats. That infuriated me. I paid taxes like any citizen. I built my life in the United States. Yet here I was, denied a seat on the very plane sent by the country I called home.

Cabo Verde

The first U.S.-affiliated repatriation flight came in mid-March. It was too early—I still had hope things would change, that borders would reopen. I skipped it. Another came in early April. I passed again, reassured that more flights were coming. Then came a final announcement: there would be one last flight on May 28. After that, no more.

I immediately requested a seat. Days passed. Then weeks. Nothing. Finally, the embassy told me the flight was fully booked. I panicked. If I missed this flight, I'd be stranded indefinitely. There were no ferries, no other islands to escape to. Cape Verde was beautiful, yes—but it was also a cage with clear blue skies.

Worse, as a green card holder, I couldn't remain outside the U.S. for more than six months without jeopardizing my immigration status. I needed to return in 2020 to be eligible for citizenship. When I reached out to immigration authorities, I was told that due to the pandemic, exceptions would be made. But uncertainty still haunted me. Bureaucracy rarely made room for grace.

I pressed the embassy again. Pleaded. Explained that this wasn't by choice, that I had a job to return to, a life, responsibilities. Finally, they relented. A seat opened up.

The flight would be operated by Icelandair, part of an agreement with the U.S. government. It flew all the way from Iceland to Praia just to pick us up and return to Boston. But it wasn't a free ride. We were required to sign a debt agreement: $1,600 for a one-way ticket, repayable within three months. If we defaulted, our passports wouldn't be renewed. In contrast, the EU had charged their citizens only 400 euros. The U.S. turned a humanitarian evacuation into a billable service.

I signed.

By the time I boarded that plane on May 28, I had spent three months in Cape Verde. What was meant to be a short visit had stretched into a long, surreal chapter of waiting, uncertainty, and suspended life. In that time, I got to know the island more intimately than I ever expected. My tour guide, who had once shown me around as a client, became a friend. He visited often. We talked about life, about politics, about the strange situation the world was in.

When the plane finally lifted off, I felt relief, but not joy. It was the end of an ordeal, but also a reminder of how easily one can be forgotten in the cracks of systems designed for citizens, not people like me.

Wedding flowers from the customers at Behind The Bookstore

A Wedding Without Borders

Quadri's assignment in Estonia was nearing its end. His time with AIESEC in Tallinn had been a transformative experience—he had grown, led, and inspired—but like all chapters, this one, too, was closing. The question now was: what next?

There were two clear paths ahead—return to Benin, or continue the AIESEC journey in another country. As it turned out, several new assignments had opened up across Europe. The shortlist included Moldova, Latvia, and Finland. Each came with its own set of promises and unknowns.

His colleagues encouraged him to apply for Moldova. But I was hesitant. Moldova, despite its charm and cultural depth, wasn't part of the European Union, which added layers of uncertainty. Beyond that, the ongoing tensions surrounding the breakaway territory of Transnistria—where a large Russian-speaking population had long desired closer alignment with Russia—made me uneasy. I didn't want Quadri navigating that kind of political ambiguity. Not when there were safer, more stable alternatives.

So I gently, but firmly, nudged him toward the Baltic region—Latvia or Finland. Both EU member states, both known for strong institutions, safety, and modern infrastructure. They also shared cultural proximity to Estonia, which meant the transition might feel less abrupt.

Quadri chose Latvia.

It made sense. Riga, the capital, was just hours from Tallinn. Another Baltic gem, with cobblestone streets and a river running through it. It would be a new chapter, but not a disorienting one. He submitted his application, sat through virtual interviews, and, after what felt like an agonizing wait, he was accepted. Quadri had won his next opportunity—a leadership role with AIESEC Latvia.

I remember how proud I felt. Proud of him. Proud of us.

His transition to Latvia was seamless. New apartment. New team to assemble. New city. But the same radiant energy that made him such a magnet wherever he went. Quadri was made for this kind of work—recruiting, leading, and networking. He had a gift. He could walk into a room full of strangers and leave it full of friends. People gravitated toward him, pulled by something deep, genuine, and warm.

He thrived in human resources, not because it was a job, but because it aligned with his spirit. He loved helping others discover their own potential. He loved bringing people together. AIESEC wasn't just a position for him—it was a calling.

Meanwhile, I remained in the United States. The distance was still real. I spent that time preparing. Reflecting. Planning the next move. Whatever it would take, I was ready. We had already crossed so many borders. What was one more?

When I finally arrived back on Martha's Vineyard after my unexpected repatriation, life shifted into fast-forward. There was little time to process what I had just been through in Cape Verde—the months of waiting, uncertainty, longing. The island, though still reeling from the shock of a global pandemic, was slowly awakening to the rhythm of another summer season. And we had a coffee shop to open.

Preparations began immediately. But this wasn't going to be a typical summer. A health inspection was required before we could serve a single cup. The inspector's list was precise and non-negotiable: we needed plexiglass at the counter, social distancing signage, mandatory face coverings for both staff and customers, and a proper number of tables spaced on the patio. COVID had reshaped everything.

Still, we were bracing for a quiet season. We assumed tourists would stay away. Instead, to our surprise, the island was packed. With international borders closed and Europe turning Americans away, people sought refuge in local getaways. Martha's Vineyard, with its salty breeze and sense of seclusion, became a haven.

Business boomed. Yet we didn't let our guard down. Every day, we sanitized. We masked up. We made sure each of our guests and team members felt safe. We weren't just trying to serve coffee—we were trying to survive, in every sense of the word. COVID cases were surging across the country, and the weight of that reality pressed on us daily. But we made it. We pulled through.

As the season neared its end and the summer air began to cool, I started thinking about what came next. My future. My heart.

I thought of Quadri.

We had been apart for months. The borders between us felt impossibly wide—wider than oceans. He was in Estonia, I was in Massachusetts, and the pandemic showed no signs of loosening its grip. There were no guarantees, no promises that we'd see each other again anytime soon. The world was changing in ways no one could predict.

And yet, in the middle of all that uncertainty, I picked up the phone.

"Baby," I said, "we are together no matter what. Not even COVID, not borders, not distance can separate us. I love you—and I know you love me."

I didn't hesitate.

"What do you think if we got married?"

It wasn't an impulsive question. I had never been more certain of anything. I wasn't just looking for comfort in crisis—I was ready. Quadri wasn't just my boyfriend. He was my protector, my best friend, my mirror. With him, I felt safe. Whole. Home. I wanted to commit. Officially, fully, eternally.

He said yes.

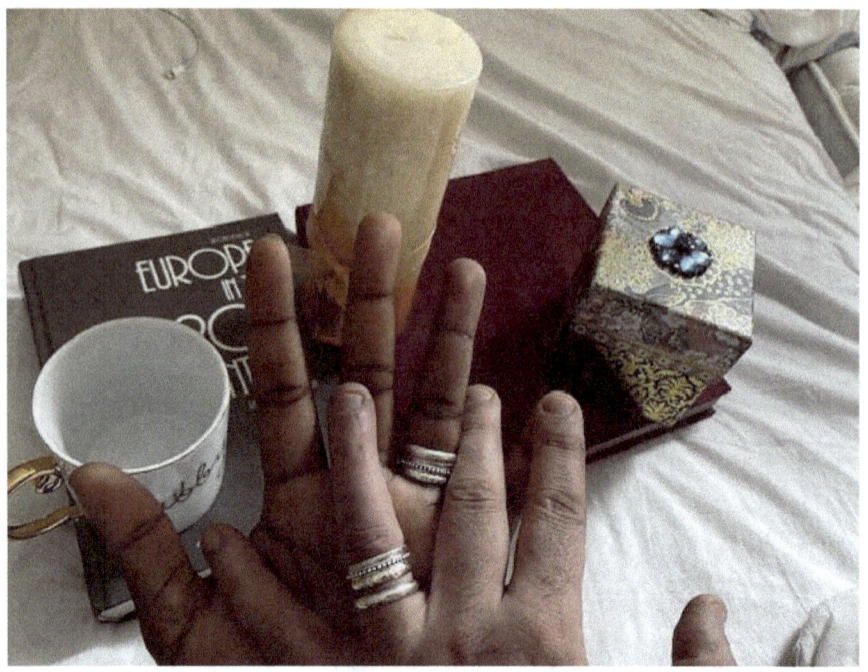

But love, of course, wasn't the only variable. Reality hit quickly: Americans weren't allowed to enter Europe, and Quadri didn't have a visa to come to the U.S. Worse, embassies weren't even processing new applications. It felt impossible—two people in love, ready to marry, unable to stand in the same room.

So, I began searching.

Late into the night, I scoured the internet for answers, for loopholes, for hope. And that's when I stumbled upon something unexpected: Utah. Of all places, it was Utah offering a lifeline to couples like us. The state had launched a virtual marriage program for those separated by COVID-19 one partner needed to be in the U.S., but the other could be anywhere in the world.

We moved quickly.

We gathered documents. Coordinated time zones. Arranged witnesses—he had his, I had mine. And finally, the date was set: July 15, 2020.

Wedding Day

It was a beautiful, sunny day on the Vineyard. I dressed in a traditional Nigerian outfit in honor of Quadri's culture. The coffee shop buzzed with quiet celebration—customers brought me flowers, congratulated me, and smiled behind their masks. A few of them had become friends over the summer, and now, they were part of this chapter of my life.

I stood in front of a screen.

He stood on the other side of the world. And we said our oaths.

VINEYARD GAZETTE

Quadri Okunuga and Misha Sebastian.

Mikhail (Misha) Sebastian Weds Quadri Okunuga

Thursday, August 13, 2020 - 12:55pm

Mikhail (Misha) Sebastian married Quadri Okunuga in a Zoom ceremony on July 15. The virtual wedding took place at Behind the Bookstore Cafe in Edgartown and Riga, Latvia.

The couple met in 2019 in the Republic of Benin. Misha is the manager of the Behind the Bookstore Cafe, and Quadri is president of the nonprofit youth organization AIESEC.

YOU CAN HELP SUPPORT LOCAL NEWS

Subscribe (http://vineyardgazettestore.com) or become a Friend of the Vineyard Gazette (https://www.vineyardgazettestore.com/product/6/view) and receive our free newsletters and free and discounted tickets to Gazette events along with our award-winning news and

We promised to love and cherish each other, in sickness and in health, in wealth and in struggle. We promised to protect one another. To stay strong, no matter what evil or hardship crossed our path. This wasn't a performative gesture. This was sacred. This was real.

We were married.

I rushed across the street to the Claudia Jewelry store and bought matching rings—one for me, one for him. I sent his by FedEx. A small token, yes, but something physical to remind us both that this was more than just a screen, more than a workaround. This was love made official.

The marriage license arrived soon after, stamped by the State of Utah. We were husbands. Two men joined in love, defying distance, defying a pandemic. It wasn't the wedding we had dreamed of. But it was the one we needed. And it was perfect.

כי תבואו אל הארץ ונטעתם (ויקרא י"ט:כ"ג)
"When you shall come to the land you shall plant trees." – Leviticus 19:23

A Tree Has Been Planted
In Celebration Of Your Wedding
Mikhail & Quadri
Mazel Tov!
Planted With Love
By
Jeffrey & Joyce Sudikoff

Even now, I can't fully describe what it felt like. That moment—two souls uniting across continents, against all odds—is still etched into my heart.

Marriage changed something in me. It deepened the love I already felt, rooted it. And even now, years later, I carry that vow with me. It wasn't just a promise we made. It was a truth we live.

Travel During Pandemic

On my way to Latvia via Iceland

And just like that, after the wedding was over, and season was over, it was time to leave Martha's Vineyard and fly across the ocean—to Latvia, where my husband, my love, my everything, was waiting. Quadri was there continuing his volunteer work with AIESEC and pursuing his master's degree in Business Administration at Baltic International Academy. He was building a future, and I was ready—more than ready—to join him.

But this was still the world of COVID. Borders were sealed shut. Americans couldn't simply enter the European Union. Only under rare, essential circumstances—like a family reunion—could one even dream of traveling.

So I began the long process. I contacted the Latvian Embassy in Washington, D.C., and asked them for special permission. I told them everything: that I was married, that my husband was waiting for me, that this wasn't just a trip—it was a return to the person I loved. They asked for documents: our marriage license, our passports, his residence permit, and a letter from his university. I sent everything. And then, I waited.

Finally, the green light came.

I was approved to travel.

Flights were scarce. The world was still on pause. The only airline flying out of Boston was Icelandair, bound for Reykjavik. So that became my path—through the icy edge of the world to get to the warmth of the one I loved. I booked the flight, took the COVID test, had my vaccination card in hand, and gathered all the letters and documents. My heart beat faster with each step closer.

Boston Logan airport. Icelandair

At Boston Logan, the Icelandair staff asked to see the embassy letter before they handed me a boarding pass. When they finally printed it, I clutched it like it was made of gold.

Reykjavik was snow-covered, grey, and strangely quiet. When I landed, the border guard eyed me carefully. "How long will you be in Iceland?" she asked.

"Five days," I said.

She frowned. "You're only allowed to stay 24 to 48 hours. This is during the pandemic."

I looked her in the eyes, and I told her the truth: "If there were daily flights to Latvia, I would be on the first one tomorrow. But there's only one flight a week. I have no choice but to wait."

She softened. Told me to isolate. Stay in my hotel. Limit contact. I already had a negative test and the vaccine, so I declined a second test.

And then, for five days, I wandered the ghostly streets of Reykjavik. It felt like the end of the world, and yet oddly safe. Cafés and restaurants were still open. People dined indoors. The world outside seemed locked in fear, but here, there was a whisper of normal life. I walked through the cold, tucked into corners of the city, visited the Harpa Concert Hall, and the site of that historic summit between Reagan and Gorbachev—two leaders meeting at the edge of the world to talk peace.

The Reykjavik Summit took place on October 11–12, 1986, at Höfði House in Reykjavik, Iceland. This summit brought together U.S. President Ronald Reagan and Soviet General Secretary Mikhail Gorbachev in what began as an informal, exploratory meeting—but ended up being one of the most remarkable turning points in Cold War diplomacy.

By 1986, the Cold War had dragged on for decades. The nuclear arms race between the U.S. and the Soviet Union had reached terrifying heights. Both countries possessed vast arsenals of nuclear weapons, and tensions were high. But change was in the air: Gorbachev had recently come to power and was introducing reforms in the Soviet Union—

glasnost (openness) and perestroika (restructuring). He wanted to improve relations with the West and reduce the risk of nuclear war.

House, a quiet white villa by the waterfront in Reykjavik, became the stage for one of the most intense and unexpected diplomatic showdowns in modern history. No one expected much from this meeting—it wasn't even supposed to be a full summit, just a preparatory talk ahead of the formal arms negotiations planned for Washington.

But then... something unexpected happened.

Reagan and Gorbachev began to talk—really talk. They found that they shared a common horror of nuclear war, and both wanted to find a way to drastically reduce their nations' stockpiles. They made stunning progress, and within hours, they were discussing the elimination of all nuclear weapons.

But it fell apart.

The deal-breaker came when Reagan refused to give up his Strategic Defense Initiative (SDI)—often called "Star Wars"—a missile defense system that the Soviets believed would upset the nuclear balance. Gorbachev wanted it restricted to the lab; Reagan refused. The talks collapsed.

Reykjavik was quiet and strange and beautiful. It felt like a waiting room between one chapter of life and the next. I knew I wouldn't forget it.

Reykjavik in winter is a world of contrasts—harsh yet gentle, dark yet glowing, quiet yet full of secrets. It's a city that hums beneath the snow, where the cold feels personal, but never cruel, and where every gust of wind carries with it the breath of something ancient and untamed.

Reykjavik in winter feels like a village wearing a city's coat. Its colorful buildings stand out against the snow and grey skies, cheerful and resilient. Hallgrímskirkja, the iconic church rising over the city, looks even more striking in the wintertime—its stark architecture mirrored in the frozen world around it.

Then, finally, it was time.

Riga, Latvia

I contacted Air Baltic, who asked again for my documents, my letter from the embassy, proof that I wasn't just a tourist. I sent it all. They approved me to fly.

When I arrived in Riga, the airport was nearly empty. I had made it. I was told to quarantine, but Quadri and I were staying in the same apartment, and I had tested negative. So we simply stayed close, tucked in together, wrapped in the safety of each other.

And when I saw him—really saw him—at the airport, I couldn't hold back. I ran to him. I threw my arms around him and held on for dear life. We were no longer just partners or boyfriends. We were husbands. We were family. And we were finally, finally in the same place again.

That winter in Riga was pure magic.

We walked through frozen parks, hand in hand, as snowflakes kissed our skin. We discovered quiet streets and tucked-away cafés, little pieces of Latvia we hadn't known before. Through lockdowns and curfews, we had each other—and that was everything.

Quadri introduced me to his friend Roberto Meloni, an Italian singer and celebrity who had represented Latvia at Eurovision. He had a cooking show on Latvian TV and a larger-than-life personality. With Roberto, we explored hidden gems of the country, places still open to us despite the restrictions. I especially fell in love with Jūrmala—a quiet, frozen beach town on the Baltic Sea. Even in the dead of winter, its beauty was undeniable.

Quadri, Roberto and Mikhail

But more than the snow or the sea or the stillness of lockdown, what I remember most is the feeling: peace.

For the first time in so long, I felt whole. I had my love. I had my home. Not a place, but a person. And wrapped in his arms, I didn't feel lost anymore. I felt found.

That winter in Latvia changed everything.

The Old Town of Riga, known as Vecrīga, is a beautifully preserved medieval heart of Latvia's capital, where every cobblestone seems to whisper centuries of stories.

Walking through the Old Town feels like stepping into a living fairy tale. Narrow, winding streets open onto cozy squares, lined with colorful facades

Riga, Latvia

Dominating the skyline are the spires of St. Peter's Church, Riga Cathedral, and St. John's Church. These Gothic and Baroque masterpieces stand as reminders of the city's deeply layered religious and architectural history. The House of the Blackheads, with its ornate façade and dramatic sculptures, is perhaps the crown jewel of Vecrīga—an emblem of Riga's proud mercantile past.

Cafés tucked into centuries-old buildings offer shelter from the cold, serving strong Latvian coffee and warm pastries. Antique shops, small galleries, and artisan stores are hidden behind wooden doors, inviting the curious to explore.

While staying in Riga, Latvia, as the snow gently coated the rooftops and the world remained hushed under the weight of the pandemic, we often found ourselves gazing at flight radars, hoping for a sign. A sign that one day soon, the airport would reopen for regular commercial travel. A sign that we could escape the grey cold and return to the warmth of the African continent—to the Republic of Benin, the place where Quadri and I first met, where everything had begun.

Quadri enjoying snow in Latvia

Turkish Airlines appeared to be one of the few carriers still weaving its way through the skies, its flights flickering like distant stars on the map. It gave us hope. We tried—more than once—to book tickets, only to have them cancelled, rebooked, and cancelled again. Each time, our hearts sank a little deeper. The uncertainty of the world at that time made every plan feel fragile, every departure a gamble. Eventually, we looked at each other, took a breath, and decided: we wouldn't risk it anymore. We would stay in Latvia through the winter and wait for a better, safer time. Africa would wait for us, and so would Benin.

But Benin was never just a destination. It had become a symbol—our place, our beginning. The land that brought us together, that opened my heart after years of wandering, of not knowing where I truly belonged. It was in Benin that I discovered not just Quadri, but love itself. Real, unconditional, life-altering love.

And though we couldn't return right away, we knew we would go back. We knew that one day, we would walk again through the streets of Cotonou, but this time as a married couple. And we eventually did. Because some places aren't just part of your journey—they become home, no matter how far you go.

Rwanda: A Love Story

Rwanda captured my heart in a way no other place had. It became a part of me, a part of my soul, and eventually, the country I truly call home. I remember my first visit to Rwanda as if it were yesterday, and I promised myself that I would return. And return I did.

Rwanda, in so many ways, is the epitome of what Africa can be. It is one of the most politically stable, safe, and prosperous countries on the continent. In the heart of East Africa, Rwanda stands tall—a beacon of hope, especially after the horrors of the 1994 genocide, where an estimated 800,000 people were killed. The brutal slaughter of the Tutsi population left deep scars—scarred hearts, lost families, orphaned children, and survivors still haunted by the trauma.

As an Armenian, the pain of Rwanda resonated deeply within me. My own history carries the scars of genocide, inflicted by the Ottoman Empire in 1915, where 1.5 million Armenians were massacred. The echoes of those atrocities, the grief of a nation decimated, the deep wound that remains in the collective memory, are experiences I shared with the people of Rwanda. Their pain was my pain, and their healing became my mission.

Rwanda is small, nestled between Uganda, Tanzania, the Democratic Republic of the Congo, and Burundi. It is a land of breathtaking beauty, with mountains, lakes, and lush greenery stretching as far as the eye can see. The climate is temperate, and the air is fresh, something rare in many African nations. The country's natural beauty is simply mesmerizing, and the warmth of the people is unmatched.

The country's journey post-independence, from being a Belgian colony to adopting English as a primary language for business and education in 2008, speaks volumes about its resilience. Under President Paul Kagame, Rwanda transitioned into a globally competitive nation, with English opening doors to international trade and fostering opportunities for the younger generation.

Rwanda stands as one of the cleanest nations in Africa, largely due to a nationwide initiative called "Umuganda," a community cleanup day that happens on the last Saturday of every month. It's not a mere volunteer project; it is a law, with police ensuring that everyone participates. This initiative has become a symbol of the country's commitment to preserving its environment and fostering a sense of communal responsibility.

Lake Kivu. Rwanda

In 2008, Rwanda also became the first country in the world to ban plastic bags. The law was a turning point, not just in environmental policy but in the way the country embraced sustainable development. It was a powerful statement that Rwanda was not just recovering from its painful past but building a future with a vision for the planet.

What I loved most about Rwanda was the people. There is a genuine kindness that permeates the air. I never once felt unsafe, unlike many places I had visited. There was no begging on the streets, no sense of fear when walking alone. The government's commitment to security and stability is felt everywhere. It's one of the safest countries in Africa—a sanctuary for peace.

Lake Kivu. Rwanda

Same-sex relationships are legal here, and while marriage equality has not yet been achieved, there is an openness from some government officials toward the LGBT community, which was incredibly encouraging to me. Rwanda's health system is another marvel, considered one of the best in Africa, offering universal healthcare that's accessible to most of its citizens.

The country also boasts a thriving tea and coffee industry, with its high-altitude plantations producing some of the finest beans in the world. The coffee, especially, has captured my heart. Rich, full-bodied, and sweet, the Rwandan coffee is a metaphor for the country itself—nurtured, strong, and with a deep, lasting impact.

Rwanda's transformation since the genocide is nothing short of miraculous. From the ashes of pain, the country has risen to become a leader in Africa, a model of progress, unity, and hope. And it is a place that feels like home. Every time I return, I feel embraced by the land and its people, a place where I can truly be myself—open, free, and alive.

Children of Rwanda

The children of Rwanda, with their laughter, their joy, and their boundless energy, are a constant reminder of the future that is possible. Every time I visit, I bring donations of school supplies, not just to help, but to give back a little of the warmth and love they've shared with me. The spirit of the Rwandan people is one of strength, hope, and love for the future.

Rwanda wasn't the last country I would visit on my African journey, but it was the first to make me fall in love with the continent. Each place offered its own unique experience, but none captured my heart like Rwanda did. There are places you visit where you don't feel at home, where you're unsure if you'll ever return. But Rwanda? Rwanda is the place that calls you back, that feels like a part of you. It is my second home, the place that will forever live in my heart.

Musanze, Northern Province, Rwanda

As I reflect on my travels, I know Africa has a bright future ahead of it. The continent is rich with resources, culture, and potential, but it must rise above corruption and mismanagement to truly flourish. Rwanda has shown me that, with the right leadership, Africa can be a self-sustaining, prosperous force in the world.

And so, as I continue my journey, Rwanda will always be the place that captured my soul, the place that made me fall in love with Africa— and the place I will always call home.

Africa: The Heartbeat of Humanity

Mother with child. São Tomé and Príncipe

As I continued my journey across Africa, I was once again astounded by the continent's power to surprise, inspire, and teach. From the most unexpected places to the most breathtaking landscapes, Africa remains a continent brimming with potential, still waiting to be fully discovered.

Africa is an extraordinary place, unique in every sense. It is rich not only in natural beauty but also in cultural heritage, with a diversity that is unlike any other region of the world. The continent's wealth of natural resources is matched only by the wealth of its spirit and resilience. Africa is the most centrally located continent on Earth, the cradle of civilization where human history first began.

Visiting school in South Luangwa, Zambia

When I took a DNA test through National Geographic, I was humbled to learn that 2% of my ancestry can be traced back to Africa. As National Geographic noted, "The origin of our species lies in Africa: It's where humans first evolved, and where our species has spent the majority of its time on Earth. We have since migrated to every corner of the globe, a journey that is written in our DNA." My maternal and paternal roots, based on this DNA, trace back to East Africa.

From there, my ancestors spread in many directions—some staying in Africa, others moving northward, and eventually leaving the continent. This journey is part of what makes us who we are today, and it reminded me that Africa is the beginning of all our stories.

I love Africa with all my heart. It is a place of unparalleled warmth and hospitality. The people, no matter their circumstances, are always ready to welcome you with open arms, a smile, and a generosity of spirit that is unmatched. Even in the face of adversity—be it poverty, war, illness, or water shortages where people walk an average of 3.7 miles daily to collect water—Africans remain resilient, hopeful, and joyful. Their ability to smile, share, and find happiness, despite the harshest of conditions, is a testament to the strength of the human spirit.

Akagera National Park, Rwanda

Africa, in its beauty and its hardships, has taught me the most important lesson: survival. It is a place where instincts sharpen, where every challenge is an opportunity for growth. As one traveler aptly put it, "Despite the harsh conditions, I have rarely come across anything but warm and friendly people, willing, perhaps wanting to tell you their story. They don't have many of the trappings of modern life that we take for granted in the 'developed' world, but they seem to be content with their lot. Of course, it could and should be better."

Africa will forever be in my heart. It has shown me the essence of living—of understanding existence in its simplest, rawest form. I have the deepest respect for this continent and its people, whose resilience and warmth make Africa an incredible place on Earth.

Reuniting with my friend Siphokazi in Johannesburg, South Africa

During the All-African Peoples' Conference in Accra, Ghana, in 1958, Kwame Nkrumah, the leader who guided Ghana to independence, shared his bold vision for the future of Africa: the formation of a united continent. I believe that vision is still as vital today as it was then. In my heart, I hope that African leaders, now and in the future, will embrace the strength of a united African Union—one that thrives without the influence of foreign powers, that achieves self-sustainability, eliminates corruption, and builds systems of strong education and healthcare. If Africa can harness its incredible resources and spirit, it will inevitably lead the world toward a brighter future.

Africa is not just a continent, I fell in love with for its people, its culture, and its landscapes. Africa gave me a gift—a gift I never expected, but one I will forever cherish. It found the love I had been searching for all those years, the love I thought was lost.

For so long, my heart had been closed, guarded by years of pain and sorrow. But Africa, in all its vastness and beauty, gave me a chance to open that heart again. To fall in love, to be loved, and to be in love once more. Africa offered me not just a place, but a space for healing and connection.

It was here that I learned that love, the kind that heals and fills your life with warmth, was still possible for me. I could open my heart without fear and embrace the possibility of finding love again. And through that love, I would have someone by my side who would remind me of Africa every day, someone who would carry the warmth of the continent within him. And that person is Quadri.

The End

As I reflect on my journey, I see how every step, every encounter, every obstacle, and every triumph have shaped me into the person I am today. My story is not just my own; it is a story of resilience, of overcoming the odds, and of finding hope even in the most uncertain of circumstances.

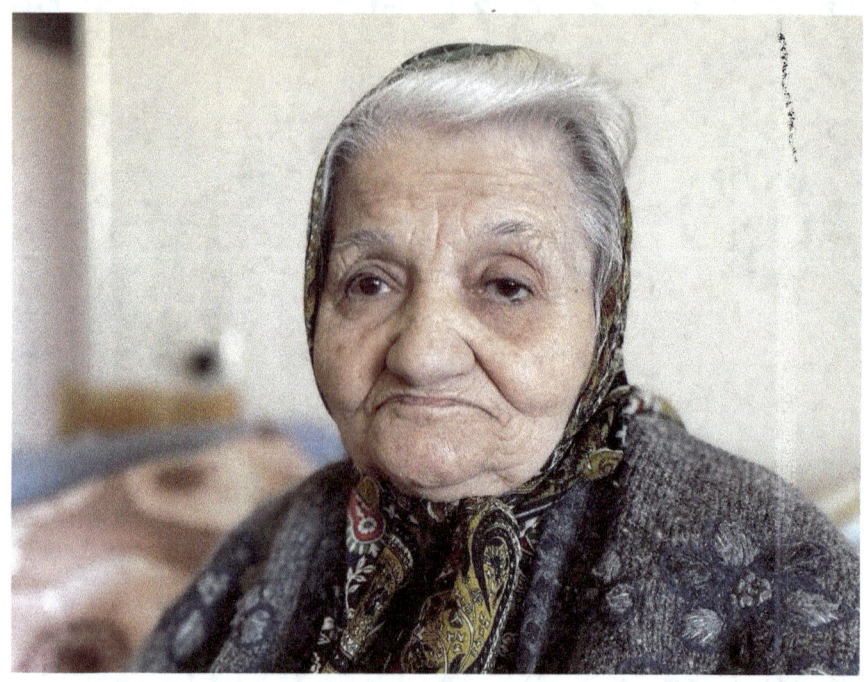

I love you, mom

My late mother, the cornerstone of my strength, taught me the value of perseverance, the importance of kindness, and the significance of family. She showed me what it means to love without limits and to keep pushing forward, no matter how hard the road may seem. Her spirit continues to guide me, and her lessons will live on forever in my heart.

Jeffrey, my mentor and friend, believed in me when I struggled to believe in myself. He saw something in me that I couldn't always see in myself, and his unwavering support has been a beacon in my life. He has shown me that even when doors close, others will open if you have the courage to walk through them. His kindness, generosity, and wisdom have had a profound impact on me, and for that, I will always be grateful.

My love

And then there is Quadri, the love of my life, my soulmate, and my unwavering partner. He is the person who brought light back into my world, who showed me that love is still possible even after all the pain. Through him, I found a love I never thought I would experience again. His unwavering presence in my life has given me the strength to embrace the future with open arms, knowing that no matter what challenges lie ahead, we will face them together.

These three people—my mother, Jeffrey, and Quadri—have been my pillars of strength. Each of them has played a vital role in my journey, and without them, my story would not be what it is today. This memoir is a testament to their love, support, and the profound impact they have had on my life.

As I continue to write this story, I know that I am not alone. I am surrounded by people who love and believe in me, and I carry their lessons and their love with me every day. And as I share this story with the world, I hope it will inspire others—whether they are stateless, struggling, or simply searching for their place in the world—to never give up. There is always hope, always a way forward, and always a chance for a new beginning.

STATELESS

The world's most invisible people?

Up to 15 million people have no nationality. They live in limbo, denied the basic rights most of us take for granted.

Statelessness is a crime. No one should endure being stateless. No one should be born stateless, and no one should be deprived of their citizenship just because a state collapsed, a country broke apart, or because someone refuses to recognize you as part of their community because of your religion, your sexual orientation, or simply because they don't want to recognize you.

Statelessness should be punishable. Governments that encourage statelessness should be held accountable for their crime.

Quadri and Mikhail. Kilimanjaro, Tanzania

Quadri and Mikhail. Machu Picchu. Peru

Mikhail Sebastian Okunuga holds an Associate Degree in Foreign Languages (English, Russian) from Turkmen State University. Completed Certificate Programs: Harvard University Certificate in Religion, Conflict and Peace. London University Certificate in Global Diplomacy (Diplomacy in the Modern World). Kyoto University Certificate in Origin of the Human Mind. University of Geneva Certificate in International Organizations Management. Studied online courses on Human Rights and International Humanitarian Law at the Peace Operations Training Institute. Studied at the International Academy of Specialty Coffee and Specialty Coffee Association. Studied Multicultural Awareness at the University for Peace.

www.ingramcontent.com/pod-product-compliance
Lightning Source LLC
Chambersburg PA
CBHW061131120626
46546CB00005B/1737